D0929985

Royal Mysteries of the Anglo-Saxons and Early Britain

Royal Mysteries of the Anglo-Saxons and Early Britain

Timothy Venning

PEN & SWORD
HISTORY

First published in Great Britain in 2021 by
Pen & Sword History
An imprint of
Pen & Sword Books Ltd
Yorkshire – Philadelphia

Copyright © Timothy Venning 2021

ISBN 978 1 52678 356 1

The right of Timothy Venning to be identified as Author of this work
has been asserted by him in accordance with the Copyright, Designs
and Patents Act 1988.

A CIP catalogue record for this book is
available from the British Library.

All rights reserved. No part of this book may be reproduced or
transmitted in any form or by any means, electronic or mechanical
including photocopying, recording or by any information storage and
retrieval system, without permission from the Publisher in writing.

Typeset by Mac Style
Printed and bound in the UK by CPI Group (UK) Ltd,
Croydon, CR0 4YY.

Pen & Sword Books Limited incorporates the imprints of Atlas,
Archaeology, Aviation, Discovery, Family History, Fiction, History,
Maritime, Military, Military Classics, Politics, Select, Transport,
True Crime, Air World, Frontline Publishing, Leo Cooper, Remember
When, Seaforth Publishing, The Praetorian Press, Wharncliffe
Local History, Wharncliffe Transport, Wharncliffe True Crime
and White Owl.

For a complete list of Pen & Sword titles please contact

PEN & SWORD BOOKS LIMITED
47 Church Street, Barnsley, South Yorkshire, S70 2AS, England
E-mail: enquiries@pen-and-sword.co.uk
Website: www.pen-and-sword.co.uk

Or

PEN AND SWORD BOOKS
1950 Lawrence Rd, Havertown, PA 19083, USA
E-mail: Uspen-and-sword@casematepublishers.com
Website: www.penandswordbooks.com

Contents

Introduction

This book will give an account of some of the more famous and less well-known mysteries involving British royalty of the post-Roman era, the centuries from around AD 400 to 1066 which used to be referred to as the 'Dark Ages' – largely on account of the lack of reliable written evidence compared to later periods. Our sources are sketchy for much of this period, and those that survive often turn out to have mixed motives for their 'narratives', writing as much what would now be called political propaganda as objective 'history'. Archaeology can fill in many of the basic gaps and tell us more about the lives of ordinary people in an era where the written narratives dealt mainly with the elite, their dynastic history and feuds, and major political and military developments – but it can turn out to be at variance with the established literary/'historical' picture (e.g. on the presumed 'invasions' of or migration to Britain by the Anglo-Saxons between c. 450 and 650).

All of this makes what used to be accepted as genuine history seem to be on shakier grounds than when nineteenth-century and early-mid-twentieth-century 'determinist' histories and school textbooks were being written about the evolution of the post-Roman Anglo-Saxon kingdoms, the imagined 'Heptarchy' of seven neatly-arranged regional states, into one 'English' monarchy which evolved after the Scandinavian 'Viking' invasions and was then taken over by Duke William of Normandy at the battle of Hastings in 1066. This picture also left out the questions of the surviving British kingdoms of the post-Roman era, now known as 'Welsh' (the Anglo-Saxon word for 'foreigner'), in upland western Britain and the British or Gaelic kingdoms in the north of the main island of Britain in what became 'Scotland', not to mention the survival of 'Britons' and their society and culture in lowland 'England' 'under the radar' of what was now assumed to be a 'Germanic' society made up of incomers from north-west Europe speaking a Germanic language. The plethora of new evidence for and perspectives on post-Roman Britain to 1066 and re-examination of the reliability of long-accepted 'hard evidence' had made for general acceptance that much we assumed to be certain about this period is not so, although most of the basic narrative remains – with new emphases and new uncertainties – and it is the period from c.400 to 650 where even the surviving written chronological framework for events (mostly written much later if based on earlier lost documents) is now often treated as dubious. This has duly affected our interpretation of how early English society and its neighbours in Wales and Scotland developed – and, crucially, how they interacted – with the 'devolution' of mainstream historical studies from one linear Anglocentric narrative to consider the rest of Britain reflecting an era of political devolution and new uncertainties about British unity. This fluidity in studies and interpretation has also affected the many mysteries that surround these early kingdoms – both the 'proto-states' themselves, their history, their social makeup and cultural orientation, and their interaction and the lives and motives of their rulers. Many of the latter are no more than names about whom a few basic details survive, the latter reliant on not always reliable sources – and as with the most famous of the early British rulers, 'King Arthur', it is not even certain that some of them were genuine men as opposed to the creations of later literary myths.

This book tackles the question of some of these 'founders' of the early kingdoms, such as Hengest of Kent and Cerdic of Wessex, plus some of their British (or Brittonic) contemporaries in lowland, western and northern Britain. In the case of the first two, their very existence as well as their 'dodgy' genealogies are in question – and questions arise of how 'Germanic' as opposed to British Cerdic was. Then there follows some of the mysteries surrounding the royal line of Wessex which under King Alfred and his successors came to re-mould an Anglo-Saxon world politically shattered by the Scandinavian invasions of the later ninth century, and finally the central mystery of the truth concerning the succession disputes of 1066 and the audacious 'power-grab' by the English kingdom's predatory neighbour William 'the Bastard', duke of Normandy. Did he have any genuine claim on the crown, was he promised it earlier as he alleged, and even if this did occur did it have any legal weight in English politics? Some of the mysteries, such as that of the succession in 1066, have been favourites for both historians and enthusiastic amateurs for centuries, with the remodelling of old and the creation of new modern theories about them. Others, such as the mysterious stabbing of England's teenage king Edward 'the Martyr' at Corfe Castle by his half-brother's supporters (and his stepmother?) in 978, are generally off the radar of most readers – though Edward is the only English king to have a church dedicated to him as a saint surviving. They involve a mixture of kings from the 'Dark Ages' who might or might not have existed, royal genealogies that may or may not have been fraudulent or the product of imaginative dynastic 'spin-doctors' centuries later, contradictory stories about the careers and motives of once famous warlords that may have been hijacked for propaganda, and the equally intriguing question of what crucial details seem to have 'dropped out of history' and if so why. In an era of minimal literacy and that usually restricted to clergy and monks (who had their own agendas when writing 'history'), the survival of stories might depend on either approving monastic chroniclers, important descendants keen to keep up the glorious history of their family, or celebratory bardic poets telling exaggerated versions of past deeds to a hall-full of appreciative lordly retainers and warriors. Those who lost out or whose families became extinct would have no literary or oral commemorators and could easily drop out of memory – and, as Donald Rumsfeld might have said, the 'known unknowns' and the 'unknown unknowns' are equally important as what we think we do know.

Chapter One

British/Welsh Kings

More Real than Arthur or Uther Pendragon? Ambrosius and Other Over-Kings of Britain

The background

As with so much of early Britain, there are basic questions to answer about how accurate is the traditional picture of the islands' rulers after the end of Roman rule. The alleged dynasty that ruled a state of 'Britain' (i.e. the former Roman lands South of Hadrian's Wall) after the 'Roman withdrawal' of AD 410 were first described in detail in literature by the Anglo-Norman/Welsh writer Geoffrey of Monmouth, writing in the 1130s in his largely fictional *History of the Kings of Britain*. This was seen as defining the post-Roman 'British' governance of Britain in one over-kingdom, as superseded around the early seventh century by Germanic 'incomers', the (Anglo-) Saxons. There was a sharp break in continuity and in culture at this point, defined by 'alien' conquest – a 'given' which was duly incorporated into the narrative of Britain's history thereafter. But at the time of Geoffrey 'historians', in the sense of writers of literary epics set in the past rather than chroniclers noting events by date, were not what would nowadays be seen as objective analysts. Rather they were writing for their audience among the literate upper classes, and often for contemporary 'political' objectives too – which has raised serious doubts in recent decades about their reliability. Did they care about 'accuracy', or even see it as their business to use reliable sources verbatim and not invent missing details? This is especially true of Geoffrey, the first great publiciser in England of the legends of 'King Arthur' and 'Merlin' (both known to earlier writers and oral poets in Wales, where the post-Roman Brittanic kingdoms had survived). He was also our only known source of much material about other rulers of ancient Britain – the historically dubious pre-Roman 'kings of Britain' in particular, though that concept was present in Welsh myth by the ninth century. His concept of an over-kingdom and 'empire' of the British Isles owed a lot to the contemporary claims and military successes of his patron earl Robert of Gloucester's father, King Henry I (d. 1135), and he used contemporary terminology and titles for his characters not plausibly 'ancient' ones. He did not however invent the notion that there was a distinct dynasty that ruled over the ex-Roman regions of Britain in the fifth century, though his accuracy concerning the survival and national roles of pre-Roman tribal kingdoms' dynasties under Roman rule (for example the enigmatic AD 60s king 'Arviragus', allegedly Emperor Claudius' son-in-law) is more doubtful.

Geoffrey's is the first full literary account of the post-Roman era to survive, though some of his names occur in earlier Welsh literature. The end of the production of coinage with the end of Roman rule means that no coins of any of his fifth-century 'kings' (which would prove their reality) have survived, and what information we do have on the period is mostly from archaeology – which as we shall see casts doubt on the notion of widespread and genocidal 'Germanic' settlement. Indeed, as there are no surviving contemporary accounts of Britain and the historians operating within the shrinking Western Roman Empire after 410 did not mention British events it is a complete blank as to who ruled the region or what form (or number) their states took. This is in sharp contrast to the lands remaining within the Empire at the same time, and shows an 'atomisation' of society and a sharp drop in literacy or written as opposed to oral memory – at the same time as the end of Roman institutions. The physical structure of Roman towns (in steep decline during this time but not all abandoned) and the multitude of ordinary rural farms survived across Britain through the earlier fifth century, but the structure of governance and its records did not and Continental historians within the Empire (e.g. Orosius) did not bother about British events. Did any or all of the senior administrators – civil governors, 'praeses', and military governors, 'duces' – of the five late Roman provinces take over command as Roman troops left? Or did the governors and their administrators back their bags and leave too, or retreat to rural estates? And what of the personnel of the Roman Catholic Church in lowland Britain, which was presumably run by bishops based in the principal towns as elsewhere in the Empire? (Three bishops had attended the Empire-wide Church Council in 359.) The elite were probably all nominally Christian by this date, as seen by the Christian mosaics in great rural villas (e.g. Lullingstone and Hinton St Mary) and the Christian faith of the former commander in Britain who became Emperor in 383, Magnus Maximus. It is unclear, indeed, if all the troops stationed in Britain left – though it is probable that when rebel Emperor Constantine III took the army off to Gaul to fight invading Germanic tribes in 407 most troops went with him and did not return on his overthrow and capture by the legitimate government in 411.

Emperor Magnus Maximus, aka 'Macsen Wledig'.

Notably, as far as the 540s 'historian' (more accurately polemicist) Gildas, probably a monk given his ultra-Biblical tone of writing and our only surviving near-contemporary British source, was concerned the last Roman leader to rule in Britain had been Maximus, who was also the man who took the last Roman troops there off to the Continent. Gildas and our next source, the early ninth-century Gwynedd cleric 'Nennius' in his *Historia Brittonum*, both give this role to Maximus not to the actual rebel Western Roman ruler who took the final local army off to Gaul, Constantine III. Neither of them mentions his existence or his expedition, and Maximus' expedition two decades earlier becomes the 'cut-off point' for Roman rule instead. It is Maximus, as 'Macsen Wledig' (the latter Welsh term probably meaning 'over-ruler' or a sort of 'High King'), who is played up in later Welsh literature as the final Roman ruler in Britain and the ancestor of many of its post-410 British dynasties. He also starred in the collection of early medieval Welsh stories of the 'Mabinogi' ('Young Men'?) which has been known in recent times as the *Mabinogion* from the title chosen for its early Victorian translation by Lady Charlotte Guest, a cultural revivalist married into a major Gwent ironworks dynasty. This presents us with an opening 'Royal Mystery' for the post-Roman era – why it was Maximus not Constantine who was the 'last of the Romans' and the leader of the final Roman military expedition to the Continent in Welsh historical memory? Why was this ruler so important and chosen as the subject for myths? And why choose Maximus for the alleged ancestor of later dynasties, as with Morgannwg/Glamorgan and Dumnonia/Devon and Cornwall? In fact we have no proof that the latter claim was accurate, as the Roman sources (contemporary histories plus the writings of Gallic bishop St Martin of Tours who tangled with him in Gaul post-383) only refer to one son of his, Victor, either a boy or a youth at the time, who was made Maximus' nominal co-emperor as his father took over the westernmost provinces of the Empire (Britain, Gaul, Spain and the Rhineland) in 383–8. When Maximus tried to take over Italy too in 387, his foe Emperor Valentinian II, teenage half-brother of the Emperor he had overthrown and murdered in 383 (Gratian), fled to the East and enlisted the help of its emperor, Theodosius 'the Great'. Ironically, Theodosius was the son of Maximus' old commander in Britain, Count Theodosius. The Eastern Emperor then invaded Italy in 388, captured and executed Maximus, had Victor killed too, but spared Maximus' wife and younger children (who are not named in the sources). Maximus' wife was a pious and orthodox Christian on good terms with St Martin so she might well be the person named as his wife in Welsh legend, Helen 'of the Hosts', the alleged daughter of a Welsh ruler or nobleman called Eudaf/Octavius. Their younger children might have included the son named in medieval Welsh legend (and by Geoffrey of Monmouth) as the first major post-410 ruler of Britain, Constantine aka 'Custennin the Blessed'. But this is still unclear, and the various other descendants of Maximus named in medieval Welsh genealogies as ruling Welsh kingdoms are not mentioned in any other, more contemporary sources so many modern historians regard them as the inventions of medieval courtly 'spin-doctors' seeking to give their kings a famous lineage linked to a major Roman Emperor.

More mystery surrounds Helen, assuming her to have been Maximus' wife in reality as in legend. By medieval Welsh legend she was known as the woman who had commissioned a chain of Roman roads across Wales, some of which were known as 'Sarn Helen' ('The Road of Helen'), but as these seem in reality to have been built when the area was conquered by Rome in the first century how did this story come about? She was evidently seen in retrospective 'memory' – or bardic invention? – as a formidable woman linked to the military, but did this reflect reality? And was she mixed up with the identically-named mother of earlier fourth-century Emperor Constantine 'the Great' (ruled 306–37), St Helena the discoverer of the 'True Cross' from the Crucifixion, who was erroneously called a Briton?

The reasons for the literary choice of Maximus as the 'last Emperor ruling in Britain' and 'dynastic founder for much of Wales' are unclear. Arguably if he had a British wife, had led troops in Wales to defeat Irish pirates, and had commanded in Britain since the late 360s (as some suggest) he made more impact on Britain than the obscure Constantine III did. Maximus seems to have been a Spaniard by birth, and came to Britain with Count Theodosius, the Spanish-born commander of a Roman army sent to drive out a major raid or invasion by Saxons, Picts (i.e. the Brittonic peoples north of Hadrian's Wall), and Irish in 367–8. He is associated in Welsh legend with the major Roman fortress of Segontium, later site of King Edward I's Caernarfon Castle, where he may have commanded a garrison. In the *Mabinogion* story, he comes to Wales to marry a fair princess who he has seen in a dream at a location that turns out to be Caernarfon; however he is a Roman Emperor who comes to Wales and enlists his wife's kin's help to restore himself to Rome after a rebellion, not a British commander who goes to the Continent to overthrow a legitimate ruler. His role and Constantine's as challenger to the extant Western Emperor in a campaign in Gaul were identical, but only one of them made it into Welsh legend and dynastic propaganda. Both he and Constantine III ended up defeated and executed by the legitimate Western Roman government, Maximus in 388 and Constantine in 411–12, but Maximus ruled more lands for longer and had a definitive British/Welsh link via his wife so he may have had a better reputation. He was also said by Welsh and Breton legends to have taken a large force of British troops to the Continent and settled them in lands in Armorica, the new 'Brittany' (i.e. 'Little Britain'), which fits Roman military pratice and may well be accurate if exaggerated.

After 410: the reality.

The significance of '410' as 'the end of Roman rule' with a neat withdrawal of Roman troops and officials to shore up the crumbling Empire on the Continent was thus not remembered in post-fifth-century British/Welsh history and legend. For that matter, the only survival of Constantine III's story into the medieval period appears to be the fact that his son Constans left his Gallic monastery to aid his invasion in 407–8 and ended up executed too – in Geoffrey of Monmouth's garbled story his post-Roman ruler 'Constantine son of Emperor Maximus' is succeeded by his son Constans, an ex-monk, who is then murdered by his chief minister and brother-in-law 'Vortigern'. The actual 'break' in Roman political control in 410 was not a withdrawal as the British 'took back control' from a European super-state but an abandonment. The senior civic authorities in the leading British towns wrote to Constantine's foe Emperor Honorius (ruled 395–423), son and successor of Maximus' foe Theodosius, to resume allegiance to him and were told to look to their own defences.[1] With the rampaging Goths sacking Rome and roaming around Italy looting at will in 410 Honorius, a timid ruler hiding from the 'barbarians' in his new capital in the marshes of Ravenna, had other priorities – and once his general Constantius had defeated and captured Constantine III and forced a treaty on the Goths in 411–17 he did not bother to reclaim Britain either. Its rulers remain unknown, nor if the five extant Roman provinces temporarily survived as the basis for administration – possibly with a regional military command for the whole island, the 'Count of Britain', as listed in the ?410s administrative lists of the *Notitia Dignitatum*. All that is clear from archaeology is that production of coinage ceased – no coins have survived for any rulers of Britain after Honorius and Constantine III, so clearly the pre-410 mints gave up their role as they lacked either government orders or a supply of metals. As seen from the drop in the locations of widely-traded British goods (e.g. pottery) within Britain, trade soon declined steeply too and the economy reverted to a small-scale local interchange of goods, presumably based on barter. Whether the increased amounts of 'Germanic' goods and Germanic burial-practices in scattered settlements in eastern England (especially East Anglia and Kent) reflect the arrival of new Continental traders from outside the Empire, and/or existing settlers importing goods from their homeland and passing them on to Romano-Britons, is still debated. But it is clear that the main stimulus to the prosperous fourth-century British 'export economy', the Roman government and army, had collapsed.

The difficulties of timing over when and how residence in towns and the use of 'high-status' residential rural villas ended is similar to the lack of information about politics in post-Roman Britain. In fact the lurid stories in the account of Britain's 'fall' by the mid-sixth-century monk Gildas of invading Germans a generation or so after 410 sacking all the major towns and burning their way from sea to sea[2] are inaccurate as there is little archaeological evidence for fire except at a few places near the east coast. Even there, piles of bodies do not necessarily mean attacks by Saxons as opposed to internal political strife or brigands. Fourth-century Roman towns in the prosperous Fenland, e.g. Castor, do not appear to have been sacked, and nor do those contemporary farms which have been excavated (e.g. around Peterborough). As will be seen, the notion of Gildas (our only contemporary source) as a 'historian' in the modern sense of the word is problematic given his Old Testament-style polemics, and since the 1970s historians have reassessed his intentions in writing his book *De Excidio Britanniae/On the Ruin of Britain*. The only archaeological evidence of damage probably caused by violence (i.e. both fire and piles of bodies) comes from Colchester/'Camulodunum', the first Roman capital of Britain, and Caistor-by-Norwich/Venta Icenorum, both in East Anglia, and possibly Lincoln/Lindum. Fires in the sprawling residential houses, 'villas', on the great rural estates could well be due to accident not arson and are proof of nothing; modern experts reckon that most of these economic units were abandoned as the demand for their products (e.g. corn for the Roman army) collapsed around 400. Some major towns survived in the west albeit on a smaller scale, as at Wroxeter/'Viroconium' into the sixth century, with work in wood not stone and for small-scale local crafts and trade not for Romanised civic institutions. They may have survived in the east too, as former regional administrative capitals such as Venta Belgarum/Winchester, Noviomagus/Chichester, and Lindum/Lincoln re-emerged as the capitals of new 'Anglo-Saxon' kingdoms, though proof of continued occupation through the period is patchy. Significantly the major centre of Londinium/London seems to have had its main inhabited administrative/residential/trading zone within the walls moved by c.600 to a new Germanic settlement higher up the Thames at the 'old wick' i.e. 'old settlement' (the Aldwych), centred on traders' wharfs along the riverside.

Recent detailed investigation of how the post-410 'Romano-Britons' lived in rural areas even makes it unclear if all the fifth-century wooden farm buildings that were once attributed to incoming Anglo-Saxons from a different ethnicity and culture were indeed 'German'. Is the new longhouse-style 'grubenhaus' building exclusively 'Germanic'? The rural Britons' building-styles may have been identical to that of 'incomers' and largely based on wood rather than the elite urban and villa 'Roman' reliance on stone, and a distinct break in continuity between 'Romano-British' and 'Anglo-Saxon' residents at some well-studied estates (e.g. Mucking in Essex) is far from obvious.[3] The boundaries of some pre-'invasion' estates survived as if they were taken over seamlessly rather than being abandoned in an invasion and subsequently re-created, and there is no evidence in the record of local plant-life of the usual plants that grow up in abandoned fields suddenly replacing those of 'settled and regularly used' Roman farms before 'incomers' re-settled the land.[4] This does not rule out a transfer of ownership at some point, but it does rule out widespread chaos and abandonment of estates in one major disaster for the Britons. Indeed, it has even been suggested that the continuity in useage of land and evidence of increased pastoral farming as the 'corn-market' for Roman military purposes ended could imply a 'boom' in fifth-century British lowland farming – aided by the end of Roman taxes? (This would have been negated by insecurity from wars, but we have no evidence of the latter bar Gildas' generalisations on 410–11 and the 440s.) And was the change of burial-customs to 'Germanic' cremations attended by new 'Germanic' cultural artefacts in firstly south-east coastal Britain and then inland really a sign of total 'ethnic cleansing' by the newcomers? This and the 'DNA' evidence of the survival of over 50 per cent pre-'Anglo-Saxon' (and some pre-Roman 'Iron Age' and Neolithic) 'British' genetic material to a large extent in post-410 Britain has resulted in modern arguments over how extensive the so-called 'Anglo-Saxon takeover' of lowland Britain was. Expert archaeologists of the period such as Francis Pryor have doubts over the extent of 'invasions' with such little evidence of upheaval or a break in residential continuity. But the predominant language used certainly altered between c.400 and c.600 to a new one of Germanic cultural affiliation, with very few words surviving from Latin or the 'proto-Welsh' Brittonic tongues that would have been spoken in Roman Britain. There was certainly a transfer of power and 'identity' at an elite level, although the notion of a neat 'Germanic invasion' and total ethnic/cultural transformation as stated by the 540s British or Armorican historian Gildas has now been shown to be distinctly unlikely. The same applies to the notion long peddled by mainstream modern historians and generations of school textbooks that a steady flow of immigrant Germans migrated to the east coast from the Low Countries and then steadily west, driving out the Britons as they went. More recent historians, with

'DNA' and the notion of Germanic objects being spread west by trade not conquest, tend to argue that proportionally perhaps only 20–40,000 'Germans' arrived during this period, though they had a major cultural and social (and linguistic) impact. As we shall see, the idea of 'all Germans' being at war with 'all Celtic Britons' is also a simplification of what now looks like a rather more complex and messy process over two centuries. Do we have a case of an aggressive and culturally coherent incoming elite imposing their own fashions and language on the majority locals, as with the Normans after 1066? But this does not rule out the extant literary narratives of conflict, or the basic stories of major rulers of both cultures – though not all rulers at all times – at war with each other.

It can be assumed that the local sub-divisions of the Roman provinces, based on and named after former pre-Roman 'tribal' territories, were used as the basis for local authority after 410. Possibly the extant rural aristocracy, some of them descended from old pre-Roman 'Brittonic' dynasties (the word 'Celtic' for Britain was not used until the late seventeenth century), governed as local councils or their most determined and well-resourced leaders set up new regional kingships. In the 540s Gildas was to complain of the emergence of the abuses of power in post-Roman Britain by 'illegitimate' kings and 'tyrants', men who had seized power by violent means not inherited legal authority – which may mean self-created military leaders thrusting to power in a era of competition and war.[5] These men were often killed by the same men who had earlier raised them to power, implying instability – partly due to their lack of legal authority, though Gildas blamed the chaos and tyranny on the Britons' sloth and greed too in the manner of the Old Testament prophet Jeremiah attacking the sins of the Israelites. By implication, their wickedness caused God to abandon them to be conquered by pagans, as Israel had been conquered by Assyria and Judah by Babylon. The dynastic genealogies of those regional British kingships – mostly in the less 'Romanised' and more 'tribal' west and north of Britain – that survived into the subsequent history of medieval Wales cite obscure 'founders' and their 'sons' and 'grandsons' who seemingly ruled in the fifth century, but our extant information is from 600–800 years later and so may owe much to legend. Nowadays most historians assume that the Welsh 'royal genealogies' constructed in the tenth century was later 'back-dated' propaganda by rulers seeking an illustrious ancestry to boost their legitimacy. This is part of the question of Ambrosius' identity and role – one version of this dynastic 'history' made him a grandson of Maximus.

The 'states' that emerged in post-Roman Britain were all regional kingdoms, for example, of 'Dumnonia' (Devon and Cornwall) in SW England, 'Morgannwg'/Glamorgan and Gwent in south-east Wales, 'Dyfed' in south-west Wales, 'Powys' in central Wales, 'Gwynedd' in North Wales, and the subsequently overrun kingdoms of northern Britain from the Humber and Dee to the Firth of Forth. As some of these 'states' (e.g. of the Dumnonii) were centred in the same locations as and held similar names to the tribal kingdoms of the pre-Roman era it is logical to assume that they emerged from these regions' existing political and social geography and so were indeed set up in a political vacuum in this period. Following precedent in Gaul, the Romans presumably based their administrative sub-divisions of the province (later provinces) of occupied Britain on the local tribal 'states' that they found – and they used local tribal names for their new cities, for example, 'Venta Belgarum' (Venta of the Belgae) for their new administrative centre in the lands of the 'Belgae' in southern Hampshire (later Winchester) and 'Isca Dumnoniorum' for the one in the lands of the Dumnonii (later Exeter). In south-west Wales, the old tribal lands of the 'Demetae' became the centre of the new kingdom of 'Dyfed', based on Pembrokeshire and Carmarthenshire, though the archaeology shows some Irish settlement (e.g. from the use of Irish 'ogham' script in writing on stones). This fossilization of pre-conquest tribal regions in Britain by Rome has implications for the nature of the 'kingdoms' that a post-Roman ruler in fifth-century Britain such as Ambrosius would command. Other kingdoms had 'administrative' origins to their names, e.g. Powys (mid-Wales) as the land of the 'pagus', i.e. a rural district dependent on a major town – probably either Viroconium, old tribal capital of the Cornovii in modern Shropshire (which has extensive fifth-century wooden building) or Glevum aka Gloucester. The kingdom of 'Morgannwg' in south-east Wales was based in the old lands of the Silures tribe but was now called after an early ruler, Morgan (probably either late sixth century or mid-seventh century); the kingdom of North Wales, 'Venedotia' aka Gwynedd, occupied the lands of the pre-Roman Ordovices and Deceangli but used a new name.

British kingship and Anglo-Saxon invaders?

In terms of a national kingship or 'over-kingship' of all post-Roman Britain, held by the politico-military superior of these kings, there is even less evidence. There is no indication that the administrative leadership of the five Late Roman provinces of Britain survived the end of Roman authority in 410 or that the island's mobile central 'field army' ('comitatus') survived either, though the Britons co-operated enough to repel attacks by Germans, 'Picts' from north of Hadrian's Wall, and Irish pirates soon after 410. This is agreed by both Gildas and fifth-century Continental writers. But an obscure and often legend-influenced Welsh clerical 'historian' in the late 820s, 'Nennius' from Gwynedd (or whoever edited his original work in the eleventh century as David Dumville and others prefer to claim), as well as Gildas refers in the *Historia Brittonum* to the emergence of a national leader in southern Britain after the end of Roman rule. This was 'Vortigern', a word in fact meaning the 'over-king' and thus a title.[6] Gildas uses a nickname as usual, namely 'the proud tyrant' – 'superbus tyrannus' in Latin, probably an echo of the tyrannical last king of ancient Rome, Tarqinius Superbus. Supposedly linked to the Roman town of Gloucester according to later legend, he may have succeeded an even more obscure ruler called 'Constantine', who was later supposed to have been a connection of the late fourth-century Western Roman Emperor Magnus Maximus (killed 388) and/or an expatriate British dynasty founded by Maximus' wife's brother in Brittany/Armorica.[7] By the medieval Welsh Triads he was remembered as coming from overseas, i.e. the dynasty of Maximus wife's brother Gadeon in Armorica, not being Maximus' British son. Vortigern was named in a ninth-century Welsh dynastic memorial stone in Powys, the 'Pillar of Eliseg' (extant but now illegible) as the son-in-law of Maximus,[8] and by Geoffrey of Monmouth's time was presented as Constantine's brother-in-law and his son's alleged murderer.[9] Seizing the 'British throne' from Constantine's young sons but insecure as a usurper, he called in the first Germanic immigrants from the Continent, led by the shadowy 'Jutish' captain 'Hengest' (see Chapter Two), to serve in his army and fight off invading 'Picts' (from modern Scotland north of Hadrian's Wall) and 'Irish'. He was allegedly tricked by the cunning Hengest into hiring more of them to add to the original three shiploads, including the warlord's kinsmen Octha and Ebissa, and to send part of their force north to fight the Picts around Hadrian's Wall. Possibly this is connected to the archaeological finds of early Germanic settlements on the lower Humber in Yorkshire, close to the local Late Roman province's capital at York/'Eburacum'.

The ethnic identity of Hengest's settlers as 'Jutes' rather than Saxons was stated by the first English historian, the Tyneside monk the Venerable Bede, in the 730s and Kentish Germanic discoveries are indeed culturally different – and closer to Frankish ones – from those of the 'Saxon' peoples (as located by Bede) in Sussex, Wessex and Essex. Vortigern was eventually overthrown in the mercenaries' revolt when the immigrants, based in Kent, turned on him. The Continental *Gallic Chronicle* dates the German 'conquest of Britain' at AD 441/2, but may be inaccurate[10] as some of its other dates are questionable. Legendarily Vortigern's son Vortimer drove the invaders back in a campaign that included three or four major battles, for which 'Nennius' gives their locations first in 'Saxon' names and then in Welsh – from which some have deduced that he was using a local Kentish legend as a source as well as the old Welsh books which he claimed to have consulted. Vortimer expelled the invaders from their toehold at the Island of Thanet, but he soon died; according to the *Triads* Vortimer had his body buried on the seashore as a magical talisman to protect Britain and disaster followed when it was removed. The leaderless Britons now invited Vortigern back. The latter had earlier married Hengest's daughter, Ronwen or Rowea, and he recalled his father-in-law. Hengest then captured Vortigern and killed his councillors (300 of them according to 'Nennius') by a trick ambush at a peace-conference, the infamous 'Massacre of the Long Knives', and forced his captive to hand over Kent and possibly Essex too. The ruined Vortigern then fled to the 'left-handed part of' (i.e. North) Wales, where he is linked to the hillfort of Dinas Emrys in Arfon. He was later killed in a fire at a hillfort (possibly at Nant Gwerthyrn in the Lleyn peninsula or at Doward near Monmouth).[11] This story was famous by the time of 'Nennius' and clearly made a major impact on Welsh folklore, with Vortigern becoming a stock villain, and the Welsh writer first mentioned the legend of how Vortigern sought to sacrifice the young 'Merlin' to stop the magical collapse of the walls of his new fortress every time he built them and Merlin showed him the white and red dragons (i.e. the emblems of the Saxons and the British) fighting in a pool under the fortress.

Modern historians doubt the veracity of the story of a major and catastrophic war between Vortigern and Hengest's invaders, and in fact archaeology shows that there were already people using 'Germanic' artefacts living in south-east England soon after if not before 400 so the 'Jutish captain' was not the first of his ethnicity to be invited to Britain. The so-called 'Saxon Shore' in the south-east, which had its own military command under the Late Empire plus a network of coastal fortresses, was undoubtedly an area of military action to be the location of such activity, and was presumably the main site of the Saxon (i.e. north-west German) part of the multiple invasions mentioned for 367 by the contemporary Roman historian Ammianus. But the coast may have been settled by Roman-hired 'Saxons' as well as being invaded by them, and it has been pointed out that not all the chain of 'Saxon Shore' fortresses were built and manned at the same time. The earliest were early-mid third-century, before any literary evidence of Germanic raids. It has also been pointed out that no barracks have been found at these alleged military bases, and it is now suggested (as per Andrew Pearson) that they may have been collection-points for corn being shipped out of Britain to the Roman army on the Rhine and for other exports.[12] The use of Germanic mercenaries by late Roman leaders and their subsequent rebellions and seizures of land from their hosts was a common occurrence in the era and is not an implausible scenario for early-mid fifth-century Britain, but the 'stock' strorylines and characters of this narrative and lack of any literary fifth-century evidence for it cast doubt on its accuracy. The same applies to the concept of an 'overkingship of Britain', though some historians, e.g. Robin Collingwood in the 1930s, have considered it possible that the Late Roman military 'supreme command' of the army in Britain – the office of 'Count of Britain', recorded in the early fifth-century administrative list of the '*Notitia Dignitatum*' – could have been revived after 410 and held by the leaders of Britain's defence.[13] Arguably this scenario could fit the story in Geoffrey of Monmouth of the (unidentified) leadership of post-Roman Britain calling in the expatriate British-descended military commander 'Constantine', related to Emperor Maximus, to take command against the mixture of Germans, Picts and Irish who Gildas says attacked Britain around 410–11.[14] This command could then have been held by subsequent British leaders such as the elusive 'Vortigern' who preceded Ambrosius around the 430s-440s – and it thus feeds into the question of whether there was a real 'King Arthur' around 500. There is also the question of Constantine's even more mysterious kinsman Owen or Eugenius, son of Maximus and 'dux Gewissae' ('commander of the confederates'?) who was according to medieval Welsh legend called upon as a commander or chief councillor in Britain by its elite after 410.[15]

Ambrosius: the man

'Ambrosius Aurelianus' or 'Aurelius Ambrosius', as he was variously known, was usually regarded as 'the last of the Romans'. This follows the wording of the mid-sixth-century monkish writer Gildas (our only contemporary source for this period), probably writing in the 540s two generations after his time, who thus differentiates Ambrosius from other contemporary rulers. This follows the vague statement c. 480 of the Gallic biographer of the evangelising St Germanus, bishop of Auxerre in Gaul from 418 and a visitor to Britain on a misson to convert 'heretic' 'Pelagians' in or near 429, that Ambrosius was 'the great king who succeeded Vortigern'. Ambrosius was presented by Gildas as the successful leader of British resistance to the invading 'Anglo-Saxons', probably in the 460s to 480s as he started the successful war which led eventually to the victory of Mount Badon.[16] The modern raising of problems about the veracity of the notion of 'invasion' and major wars and conquest has an impact on the question of the reality behind the traditional story of Ambrosius and his fight against the Germanic invaders. Indeed, the archaeological evidence of the atomisation and localisation of society in post-Roman Britain makes it dubious if any large-scale military campaigns of 'invasion' – or large-scale resistance to 'incomers' – existed. But the archaeology shows us new burial practices and an influx of high-status goods (e.g. jewellery and valued weapon trimmings) that are far less likely to be totally indigenous than to have been brought by 'incomers' – though some recent historians see these as arriving via trade not warfare. The proto-'Welsh', Brittonic dialects and Latin that were presumably spoken in southern Britain around 410 were replaced over the next few centuries by a Germanic tongue that had very few borrowings from these languages – an obvious sign of at least a partially alien new 'elite' emerging. This is more important than the apparent continuity in the use of boundaries for pre-'conquest' Romano-British and post-'conquest' Germanic estates as far apart as the Fenland

and the Cotswolds – or the non-existence in the vegetation 'record' for these estates of those plants that would have grown up in fields that had reverted to the wild if the Romans' tilled land had been abandoned after c.410 due to the chaos of invasion and 'genocide'. It can be assumed that there was a substantial degree of conflict over land between 'Briton' and incoming 'Anglo-Saxon' in some lowland areas (though not all) in the shadowy decades of the middle fifth century. Probably there was conflict between indigenous rival British kingdoms too, given archaeological remains such as the Wansdyke in Wiltshire and Somerset. Some major hillforts in the south of Britain were refortified at this time, e.g. Cadbury Castle in southern Somerset, Cadbury-Congresbury in the North of the county, and Cissbury in southern Sussex – as secure bases for the embattled locals?

Certainly Ambrosius, agreed as the main British commander of the mid-late fifth century by both Gildas in the 540s and 'Nennius' (or his sources) in the 820s, must have made a major impact on his times to be remembered in later accounts when the names of most fifth-century rulers have been forgotten. The didactic and moralistic Gildas had reason to play up his role as the 'good', just, and Christian ruler who stood up to and defeated the incoming 'pagans' where Ambrosius' predecessor 'Vortigern' ('Over-King', implying that he had some sort of authority over a wide area) had failed. Given Gildas' learned monastic background – he wrote in educated late Roman scholarly Latin – and probable use of the Old Testament as a model as assessed recently by Nicholas Higham,[17] he would have seen the leader of the British 'fight-back' as a recent equivalent of the great generals of the 'Chosen People' of ancient Israel who God had rewarded for their virtue, such as 'Judges' like Gideon. Gildas may also have sought to play up Ambrosius' Roman heritage and background as implying that he was a legally-appointed ruler from the elite of the defunct Christian Empire of Rome, and thus better than the illegal, self-appointed, unjust warlords of his own day. Part of his polemic involved attacking the moral turpitude of the 'tyranni' of his own time, and hence Ambrosius was held up as a model in contrast to them. But Higham also argues that as Ambrosius was a 'Roman' rather than a Briton in cultural terms, by clear statements to that effect by Gildas, he was less politically useful to 'Nennius' in the ninth century than was 'Arthur' the Welsh hero, protagonist of contemporary myths. A 'British' warlord who was from the same background as Nennius' own sovereign and probable patron, King Merfyn 'the Freckled' of Gwynedd (ruled 825–44), was more use than an 'irrrelevant' Roman in presenting a picture of a hero whose example Merfyn could claim to be following in fighting the invading Anglo-Saxons from Mercia in the 820s.

Ambrosius was thus sidelined in the 'Nennian' creation of a politically useful story of a heroic British fight-back leading to the battle of Mount Badon, and a line of twelve victories over the Saxons – including Badon – was wrongly attributed to Arthur. Notably, the early Welsh stories of Arthur feature him and his warband fighting a mixture of (sometimes Otherworldly) foes, not just Saxons – was he only later turned into a 'national' anti-German leader, taking another man's actual role? By this reckoning Ambrosius might have presided over the entire war and won the battle of Badon himself, as is championed by other recent historians, and the unusual name of 'Arthur' – likeliest to be connected to 'Artu-wiros', i.e. 'Bear-Man' – could be a nickname for someone whose real name was something else. Was this Ambrosius?[18] But even if the similarity between the name 'Arthur' and the Brittonic for 'Bear' indicates that it was a nickname, it would seem unlikely that Ambrosius was the man in question as Gildas usually used nicknames for his historical figures (including 'Vortigern' and the shadowy 540s dynast Aurelius 'Caninus'/Conan) but used Ambrosius' authentically Latin 'real' name. Also, as the *Annales Cambriae* (written in the tenth century in Dyfed and mostly using Irish sources for sixth-century events) dates 'Badon' at '516' or '518' and does not make any obvious wildly inaccurate datings elsewhere, it would seem unlikely that the compilers were that far out in their dating of the battle. Would an Ambrosius who had been a boy in the 430s and a young ruler in the 460s really still be fighting in the 510s?

Ambrosius' rise to power in the literary story followed the end of the reign of the elusive 'Vortigern' who had called in the first Anglo-Saxon mercenaries to Britain. The date for the latter was set at AD 449–50, the consulship of emperors Marcian (East) and Valentinian III (West), by the Northumbrian historian Bede (writing in the early 730s) but placed around twenty years earlier by the 820s North Wales historian 'Nennius'.[19] The war between the digraced Vortigern's supplanting son Vortimer and Hengest plus the time after Vortimer's death before his father recalled Hengest was estimated at lasting at least five years by 'Nennius'. Date-wise, he does not provide any clues but a different version of the war appears in the later ninth century *Anglo-Saxon Chronicle* as occurring in the 450s, with the crucial Germanic victory at 'Crecganford' ('Crayford'?) in 456. After the 'Massacre of the Long Knives', where the invading Germanic commander Hengest had his men pull knives out of their sleeves at a truce-meeting with the British leadership and kill Vortigern's councillors, Vortigern was held prisoner by Hengest and forced to surrender at least all of Kent, which as the ancient British tribal kingdom of the 'Cantii' was an authentic Roman administrative unit so this is plausible. When he was released his people repudiated and expelled him and he fled to (probably North) Wales where he later died in a fire. At this juncture, probably ten to twenty years after the initial Saxon landing given all that had happened, Ambrosius, Vortigern's exiled enemy, returned (from Armorica/Brittany?) to take over rule of Britain and fight the invaders. Allegedly he was the younger son of a mysterious 'High King Constantine', for whom no non-posthumous and non-literary evidence survives, who had died or been murdered some time around 430–35. Constantine's eldest son Constans had been overthrown and killed by 'Vortigern', possibly his brother-in-law as the eighth-century Powys royal genealogy preserved on the 'Pillar of Eliseg' near Llangollen names him as husband to the daughter of Western Roman Emperor Magnus Maximus (d. 388) who may have been Constantine's father Ambrosius, then a boy, had been smuggled away to safety; 'Nennius' claimed that Vortigern lived in fear of Ambrosius[20] after he took power around 425, as Ambrosius was the rightful ruler of Britain and possibly an ally of the Roman Empire in Gaul (hence the new king's needing Germanic troops who he could trust better than British ones?). This was the established story of how Ambrosius came to power by the 540s, and was to be embellished by 'Nennius' later and turned into part of the 'Arthurian' epic – updated to use twelfth-century Anglo-Norman terminology – by Geoffrey of Monmouth in the 1130s.

Ambrosius survived as a major protagonist of the post-Roman 'history' of Britain into the medieval stories of Geoffrey of Monmouth in the 1130s as the short-reigning uncle of 'King Arthur'. As mysterious a warlord as that personage but seen as more definitely historical given Gildas' eulogy of him in the 540s, within the lifetime of people who would have known him, Ambrosius was mentioned briefly by 'Nennius' as the ruler who preceded Arthur, with no details of his career. 'Nennius' used to be seen as an objective historian, but recently Oliver Padel has argued that he was creating an inspiring 'myth' of British/Welsh military revival to provide a 'back-story' to his patron King Merfyn's plans. Ambrosius was thus a model of heroic kingship and distinguished Roman Christian origins but less important to him than Arthur.[21] Ambrosius was pushed into the literary background by Arthur from the twelfth century and more or less ignored by subsequent writers (most notably Malory, who concentrated on the reign of Uther Pendragon after him). Arguably, Malory and company were anxious to get on with the 'real story' that their readers or listeners expected, i.e. that of Arthur, and Ambrosius (and Vortigern) now served as a – brief – prologue to this not as part of the main storyline of a post-Roman royal dynasty. Geoffrey and his immediate literary successor, the Channel Islands poet Wace, gave Ambrosius the vital role of leading the 'fight-back' after Vortigern's disastrous reign, but only ascribed a short reign to him; he died early in the war, allegedly at Winchester, and was succeeded by his brother Uther, Arthur's father. Rigorous modern scholarship has been more sympathetic to the literary claims of Ambrosius to have led the British resistance in the later fifth century than to the career of Arthur, restoring him as a central figure in his era. Accordingly he appears in Rosemary Sutcliff's 1950s children's novel *The Lantern-Bearers* as the legitimate and pro-Roman heir to the British over-kingdom, pushed aside by the treacherous Vortigern as a child, who returns to power after the latter calls in the Saxons and is discredited. Ambrosius returns from exile in the mountains of Gwynedd at the isolated hillfort of 'Dinas Emrys', to which he was connected in medieval Welsh myth and leads the British 'fight-back', his officers including the main protagonist of Sutcliff's book, the young ex-Roman officer Aquila who has been kidnapped and enslaved by Vortigern's Saxon allies but escapes to join his 'resistance army'. Ambrosius regains the old British lowland capital, Venta Belgarum (i.e. Winchester) and sets up a kingdom across southern Britain, driving the Saxons back into Kent and eventually forcing a peace-treaty on them. He holds the (real-life) Roman military office of 'Count of Britain', the supreme commander of the Roman forces in Britain pre-410 as stated in the administrative lists of the early fifth-century *Notitia Dignitatum* – as suggested for his career by Robin Collingwood following an 1897 German theory.[16] Ambrosius also appears in Henry Treece's *The Great Captains* and *The Eagle Has*

Flown – as an elderly post-Roman magistrate and national co-ordinator, the predecessor of the rougher and semi-civilised warlord general Artos ('the Bear'), aka Arthur. In Mary Stewart's *The Crystal Cave* the story in Geoffrey of Monmouth is recycled but within a semi-Roman context. This Ambrosius, in Welsh 'Emrys' ('Prince of Light'), is the secret father of her hero Merlin, the bastard son of a South Welsh princess, and is a capable Romanised general and organiser albeit one who dies soon after his return and is replaced by his brother Uther. Ambrosius even has the distinction of being taken up by Hollywood as the hero of the 2007 film 'The Last Legion', based on a highly unhistorical interpretation of the 470s by Vitalio Manfredi which has him as a Roman commander exiled from Italy as the Western Empire ended.

Gildas is the origin of the identification of Ambrosisu as 'the last of the Romans', a man of aristocratic birth whose parents had worn (Imperial?) purple and been killed in the Saxon assault.[22] This may refer obliquely to the stories which survived to Geoffrey of Monmouth's time, where his father Constantine was the post-Roman ruler before Vortigern and the son of Emperor Magnus Maximus (ruled the Western Empire in 383–388).[23] Alternatively, the 'purple' may not be a royal robe but the purple stripe on the toga of a Roman consul – except that a British noble of the post-410 era after the end of Roman rule would not have held a consulship in Rome itself and the title would have had to be a local British rank given to senior magistrates. Nennius refers to his enigmatic 'Merlin Emrys', the 'boy without a father' kidnapped by Vortigern to be sacrificed to secure the foundations of his new fortress at Dinas Emrys in Gwynedd, as 'son of a Roman consul' – but was he using a tradition about 'the' Ambrosius or about 'the' Merlin, the famous magician and prophet? The Medieval Welsh legend called Ambrosius, as 'Emrys Wledig', Constantine's son and Maximus' grandson, or else the grandson of a ruler of Armorica called Gadeon whose father had been the brother of Emperor Maximus' Welsh wife, Helen 'of the Hosts'. Armorica had allegedly been settled by British troops brought in from their island, probably by Maximus in 383 as he invaded Gaul to overthrow Western Roman Emperor Gratian. But it is uncertain in that case where the name 'Aurelianus' came from. Maximus did not have this surname and was supposed by his contemporaries to be a Spaniard.[24] The name '-anus' usually referred to an adoption. Logically, Ambrosius could have been a member of the Roman aristocratic family of the Aurelii adopted by a more distant relative, probably Constantine, or else the latter had some connection to the Aurelii too. He may only have been known as Constantine's son through post-fifth-century guesswork, arising from his being the earlier ruler's heir as head of what could be called the 'Roman party' of fifth century Romano-British nobility opposed to 'Vortigern' the tribal king of Powys.

An early sixth-century South Wales holy man from the kingdom of the Silures in what is now Glamorgan, St Paul Aurelian, also had this surname and so may have been a relative; he seems to have had a link to the kingdom of 'Dumnonia', i.e. Devon and Cornwall.[25] A relative of Ambrosius called Aurelius Cynan/Conan was ruling Gloucester in Gildas' time c.545 and was listed by him as one of the five 'tyrants' who he attacked. (Gildas called him 'Caninus', 'The Dog', presumably an insulting pun on his real name 'Conan'.)[26] The location of these men would suggest that they were probably 'Roman' in culture, Gloucester/'Glevum' being a Roman urban centre close to the 'villa culture' of the Cotswolds and Dumnonia having a major Roman town at Isca/Exeter though also more traditional 'Celtic'/Brittonic farms with 'round-houses' than rectangular Roman villas. Gildas indicates that the current descendants – grandsons? – of Ambrosius had fallen off from his good qualities,[27] which presumes that they (among them Cynan/Conan?) still had political power. There have also been recent attempts by Frank Reno and others to link Ambrosius to various 'Aurelii' prominent in Continental Roman history, though the only Emperor Aurelian (ruled 270–5) came from the Balkans and had no known children. How about the Italian family of the 'Ambrosii', to which St Ambrose (Bishop of Milan 374–97) belonged, particularly as the latter's father was also an 'Aurelius'? So was Ambrosius' father a Roman consul in Italy not a ruler in Britain? The author of one book on 'Merlin' has linked his family to the 'Aurelii' named in the inscriptions on Late Roman silver found buried in Suffolk (the Hoxne Hoard), indicating that they were local landowners who hid their valuables from the Saxon raiders around 400–420. The fact that the powerful Italian family of the Symmacchi, who provided several consuls, also had the family name 'Aurelius' was quoted – with one Aurelius Symmachus being consul in 445.[28] But in that case it is unclear what an Ambrosius related to them was doing in Britain in the 440s to 460s, given that the family were definitively Italian and how limited links to Britain were. Though Gildas' reference to Ambrosius' parents wearing the 'purple' need not mean royal office in Britain this is the likeliest explanation of the term, not a link to the Senate in Rome. Gildas also says that they were killed in the Saxon 'storm' i.e. the invasions of Britain, indicating that they were Britons not Italians.

The dating of Ambrosius has been muddled by the account in the *Historia Brittonum* (admittedly nearly 400 years later), where 'Nennius' dated the 'conflict between Vortigern and Ambrosius' to twelve years after Vortigern's accession, that is, presumably after Vortigern's assumption of the 'High Kingship' in succession to Constantine's son Constans which would be around 425–30.[29] This conflict is linked to the battle between Ambrosius and 'Vitalinus' – taken by 1970s historian John Morris as Vortigern's real name given the muddled details of his ancestors' similar names – at 'Guoloph'. This may be a battle at Wallop, in the Test valley in Hampshire.[30] Vortigern, whose name means 'High King', apparently had a father called Vitalis, so was he really called Vitalinus? But as he was placed in the royal genealogy of Powys in mid-Wales by the 'Pillar of Eliseg', why would this Wales-based dynast be fighting in Hampshire? It would suggest either an invasion of Ambrosius' Romanised region of southern Britain by Vortigern (from Wales?), or Ambrosius' return to Britain across the Channel from exile to a Romanised region to start a revolt. It is assumed that due to his family background Ambrosius represented a 'Roman party', probably of southern British landowners with contacts to the Gallic nobility and the Roman authorities there, who opposed the western British 'hill-country' dynast Vortigern. The hostile attitude of the Catholic Gallic bishop St Germanus to Vortigern – who is left out of his hagiography as this recounts his mission to Britain in 428/9 and Vortigern clearly did not aid him against the 'Pelagian' heretics in Britain – might imply that the Roman church and secular authorities in Gaul backed Ambrosius. But this reading has problems, as 437 (twelve years from Vortigern's accession which 'Nennius' elsewhere dates at 425) is far too early for Vortigern's overthrow – the Saxon revolt against him was in 441/2 according to the Gallic records. The 'Roman party' were defeated at Guoloph by this reckoning and Ambrosius was forced into exile, returning after the Saxon revolt had discredited the usurper. The appeal made by a faction of nobles in Britain to the Roman authorities in Gaul under 'Agitius' (i.e. Aetius, the Imperial commander-in-chief) for aid in 443, recorded in the *Anglo-Saxon Chronicle*, and separately by Gildas,[31] would have followed this defeat. It apparently took place in Vortigern's reign given the 'groans of the Britons' about the oppressive rule of the tyrant. If Vortigern feared a Roman invasion from Gaul, it could explain why he stationed Hengest's Jutes and/or Saxons on the island of Thanet in Kent when they were supposed to be fighting 'Picts' in the North. But confusingly Gildas dates the appeal to a point before Vortigern called in the Saxons – whose revolt is dated to 441/2 or after by the Gallic evidence – yet Aetius is called 'thrice consul' and his third consulship occurred in 446.

This short period of twelve years mentioned between Vortigern's accession and Ambrosius fighting Vortigern is a major problem, quite apart from it pushing Ambrosius forward to a date probably in the 430s which is a long time before the presumed 'British vs Saxon' wars leading up to a 'battle of Mount Badon' c.500. It sounds illogical, as it can hardly accommodate all the events in Gildas' and 'Nennius' stories between (i) the death of Constantine and accession of Vortigern at the start and (ii) the return of Ambrosius from exile to overthrow the usurper. Nor can these 'twelve years' be reckoned from c.425 as the date of Vortigern's accession; the Saxons did not revolt until 441–2 at the earliest as the *Gallic Chronicle* gives that date for the revolt (though that is itself a problematic source) so it is well after c. 437. Indeed, if Bede is correct that Vortigern settled Hengest and his people on the Island of Thanet in Kent in 449/50 their revolt would have occurred after that – though 'Nennius' has the settlement as occurring in 428. Vortigern's expulsion and Ambrosius' return must be set some years after the main Saxon revolt, given the apparent fightback and victories by Vortigern's son Vortimer after the revolt broke out. Vortimer, logically a 'High King' himself if only a briefly-ruling one, then died and his father returned to the throne and recalled Hengest – logical enough if his son's supporters could not be trusted to back him. The implication is that all this occurred quite quickly after Vortimer's victories, but not definitively; presumably Vortigern had retreated in the interim to his homeland of Powys in central Wales and/or the city of Gloucester which was supposedly connected to his family.The return of Vortigern and his recall of Hengest was then followed by Hengest staging another revolt and/or capturing Vortigern by trickery.

Having had to hand over more land to Hengest (i.e. the kingdom of Kent), Vortigern was discredited again and Ambrosius then invaded successfully – which was probably after 450 if the initial Germanic revolt was in or after 441/2, and possibly as late as c.460 if the revolt was after 449/50. The contemporary evidence of the career of St Germanus of Auxerre, a Romano-Gallic military commander turnd bishop who was called on by the Catholic Church in Gaul to help its British counterpart combat the 'Pelagian' heretics there with a missionary visit in c. 429, is also relevant – if dubious for exact dates. His second missionary visit, which is covered by his hagiographer in less detail than the first, was in c.445, and it was presumably this visit which is the occasion when later Welsh stories (first recorded by Nennius c.829) have him clashing with Vortigern and praying for the tyrant's destruction. Vortigern was then killed in a fire at his besieged hillfort, possibly Dinas Emrys in Snowdonia or Doward near Monmouth in south-east Wales, and this event is traditionally linked to Ambrosius' invasion – but only in medieval sources, and it is confused with other stories of St Germanus praying succesfully for the destruction by a miraculous fire of the tyrant 'Benli' (? at 'Moel Fenli' in Powys). So is this 'proof' that the Ambrosian invasion occurred around 445, or putting too much reliance on later myths? To add to the confusion, John Morris and others have suggested an earlier conflict between Vortigern and Ambrosius years before Ambrosius' successful invasion to seize the throne to keep the 'twelve years' reference – possibly a revolt on Ambrosius becoming adult against his brother's supplanter that led to his exile, or that Ambrosius was the son of a second 'Ambrosius' who unsuccessfully led a revolt c.437.[32] In archaeological reality, however, there is no sign of a mass-settlement of Kent (by Jutes, who archaeology shows had Frankish cultural connections, rather than Angles or Saxons) at one 'push', as would be expected had Vortigern really had to cede it all to Hengest in one treaty. Some of the scattered fifth-century settlements with 'Germanic' artefacts are pre-450, the scattered locations across north and east Kent suggest accepted 'incomers' across a wide area not a compact settlement of soldiers in a prescribed and threatened location, and some may even be pre-400.[28] These settlers or traders may well have been officially-sanctioned immigrants from Germanic territories to the later Roman 'Saxon Shore' region before 410, called in to prop up the undermanned Roman army there. If so they could then have aided an incoming 'rebel' commander after the collapse of post-Roman British central authority, without forming part of a coherent 'Kentish state' under one king – see next chapter. But if the Nennian story of Hengest is a myth or simplification, what about that of a wide-ruling 'over-king' aka Vortigern, with a large realm from Powys to Kent, who Ambrosius could be called in to replace? Was this wide-ranging authority really extant in Britain in the 430s and 440s given the archaeological evidence of rapid socio-economic atomisation?

Ambrosius' father could be a Roman-appointed 'king' or governor in the Romanised south of Britain in the late 410s or 420s who was the opponent of the 'anti-Roman' Vortigern. This man might have fought against an 'anti-Roman' or local king from Wales, i.e. Vortigern, in c.437, and been defeated. But this second Ambrosius does not appear in Welsh tradition, where Ambrosius is unambiguously presented as the son of Constantine; no early writer mentions two 'pro-Roman' commanders of the same name a generation apart. If there were two men called Ambrosius and 'Vortigern' fought the elder of them long before being expelled by the younger, why did this fact not survive to the ninth century? More likely, the 'twelve years from 425' claim is a mistake and 'Nennius' was using muddled or inaccurate sources, i.e. whatever was available in early ninth-century Welsh monasteries where records of secular events would be marginal to their main interests. The link to Brittany may be less certain, as some etymologists have speculated that the word used for Brittany – the Welsh 'Llydaw' – was a mistranslation of an early Welsh term referring to Gwent. This latter placing would explain Geoffrey's account of the enigmatic wonder-working boy 'Merlin Emrys', the latter name being 'Ambrosius' in Latin, being found in 'Glevisseg' (i.e. the kingdom of the later fifth-century Welsh dynast Glywys) around Cardiff by Vortigern's emissaries.[33] But was this 'Emrys' the same person as Ambrosius Aurelianus or just some relative with a similar name or an attempt by Geoffrey to link different stories featuring an 'Emrys'? Given the concentration of expatriate British troops settled in Armorica after 383, it is logical that they would provide the nucleus of an army, with a Brittonic-speaking and dynastically British commander, who southern Britons could call on for help in the event of a Germanic mercenary revolt in the 440s.

Literary evidence, albeit only extant from some centuries later and thus open to faulty memories or invention, would place Ambrosius' assumption of power at some time after the Saxon revolt, that is in the late 440s at the earliest. It is more open to doubt if this followed Vortigern's capture by Hengest at the 'Massacre of the Long Knives' and involved (as in legend by the twelfth century) Ambrosius landing with a Breton army, possibly at Totnes, and burning Vortigern in a hillfort. The 'hillfort fire', as we have seen, refers to an unknown ruler within Wales called 'Benli' as well as Vortigern, and its location is unclear as is its link to the second mission of St Germanus in c.445. If Gildas' obscure reference to the battle of Mount Badon, the culmination of the British/Saxon wars, can be interpreted as meaning that the battle took place forty-four years after the start of the British 'fight-back' rather than forty-four years after Gildas' own birth[30] it could suggest that the campaigns commenced as late as around 470. Gildas was writing some time in the 540s, as one of the five kings who he condemned for tyranny and misrule was Maelgwyn of Gwynedd who died in the great plague dateable to 547/9 by Irish records.[34] Whether or not Gildas lived until 570 as one later chronicle has it,[35] if he was forty-four at the time of Mount Badon or if Badon was forty-four years from the start of the wars it is unlikely that Ambrosius was still active at such a late date – or if he was, he must have started his career later than c.445. The tenth-century *Annales Cambriae*, compiled at the court of King Hywel 'the Good' of Dyfed and apparently using much Irish monastic material, dated Badon to 516 or 518,[35] although sceptics insist this is unreliable as it could be a later interpolation into early records.

A tentative chronology can be suggested to fit all this. Ambrosius might have been exiled as a child c. 435, returned to Britain in the late 450s or early 460s, and fought a Saxon war from c. 465/70 (i.e. once he had consolidated his authority in Britain) to the 490s. Geoffrey of Monmouth's account of Ambrosius in the 1130s is also doubtful; he is likely to be wrong in placing Ambrosius' death as within a few years of his return, as this brief a reign would not have been likely to make the major impact on British memory that Ambrosius did. The long(ish) reign of the successful victor over the Saxons in Geoffrey's story should thus be attributed to Ambrosius rather than the obscure 'Uther Pendragon', who 'Nennius' does not refer to as Ambrosius' successor like Geoffrey does. Indeed, if the name 'Uther' is an honorific not a personal name

– 'Wonderful Over-King'? – it might have been originally attached to Ambrosius as the successful war-leader of the 460s and been misattributed to a second ruler. There may be a genuine memory behind the story in Geoffrey of Monmouth's account that Ambrosius had to fight a war with Vortigern's son Pascent, a historical figure of early Welsh tradition recorded as ruler of the Builth area in southern Powys, and his Irish ally 'Gilloman'.[36] Vortigern appears to have had a dynastic link with the ruling Ui Niall dynasty in Tara and a prince appears there with his name in the mid-fifth century, so they may have come to his son's aid.[37] It is possible, as John Morris suggests, that Ambrosius concentrated his campaigns in regions of Southern Britain later lost to the Saxons and planted military colonies of veterans at strategic sites.

Place-names may also provide an 'Ambrosian' link. There may be some connection between Ambrosius and various place-names containing the element 'Ambres-' in southern England, for example, Amberley in Sussex and Amesbury in Wiltshire, if these names are pre-Saxon unlike most southern English place-names (rivers excepted). Amesbury was 'Ambresbyrig' in a charter of 880 and was suggested as an estate of Ambrosius' by J.N. Myres,[38] and Geoffrey has Ambrosius as asking Merlin to build a monument here – unhistorically, Stonehenge – to commemorate the 'Massacre of the Long Knives'. These sites could have been where the monarch fought battles and so was commemorated by the local Britons, owned estates on which he settled his troops, or placed colonies of army veterans to guard strategic points against Anglo-Saxon invasions. Strategically speaking, Amberley in the 'Arun gap' in the South Downs was an ideal 'military colony' to watch for Saxon raiders trying to penetrate up-river into the Weald, with the *Anglo-Saxon Chronicle* placing the founding warlord of the South Saxon kingdom, Aelle, as landing at Selsey ('Seals' Island') in c.477 and his 'son' Cissa taking the nearby Roman town of 'Noviomagus'/Chichester.[39] Even though Aelle's supposed 'base area' around Selsey has never had any contemporary fifth-century Germanic artefacts found, there has been substantial coastal erosion so seaside settlements may have been lost to the sea; there were definitely early Saxon settlements near Worthing so the Arun and Adur valleys were likely routes for raiding and settlement. Similarly, was Ambrosden north-east of Oxford established as a British settlement by Ambrosius to deal with attacks on British areas of Buckinghamshire from the Saxon sites around Wallingford in the upper Thames valley? There are also some 'Ambres' place-names in Essex that could have been settled with troops guarding against raids from East Anglia, while Amberley in the lower Severn valley could guard the Gloucester area.[40] Comparisons have been made with the local militia, based on landed estates and towns, raised by Ecdicius in the Auvergne in southern Gaul to tackle the marauding Visigoths in 469–70. There was a similar concentration of towns and estates in the Cotswolds, where the fortified towns of Bath, Cirencester, and Gloucester only fell to the Saxons in 577; it was possible that Ambrosius, linked by Welsh tradition with local Woodchester, could have raised a fighting-force similar to Ecdicius' there. It is even possible that these large estates in the Cotswolds could have provided horses for cavalry, giving the British an advantage over the Saxons who fought on foot – the Late Roman army was heavily reliant on cavalry and logically the landed post-Roman aristocracy would have had the resources to breed horses on their farms. But this is only a theory; we have no proof that Ambrosius or Arthur was reliant on cavalry who were then mytholgised as the 'Knights of the Round Table'.

The mediaeval story by Geoffrey identified Hengest's killing by trickery of the British nobles of the tyrant's Council in the 'Massacre of the Long Knives' as occurring at Stonehenge. The great circle of 'standing stones' there (presumably the central circle of the monument) was then set up as a monument to the slain at the suggestion of Ambrosius' adviser Merlin, who brought the stones from Kilara Mountain in Ireland. But this is clearly fictional, and the oldest of the stones date back beyond 2000 BC; all are Neolithic and modern archaeology has shown that the site was gradually developed over a thousand years or so using an earlier wooden 'henge' dating from the early fourth millennium BC. The construction may have been intended partly as a memorial, and clearly a distinctive 'sacred space' – the 'domain of the ancestors'? – was separated from the 'secular' lands around it by ceremonial banks and ditches. But this has nothing to do with any fifth-century AD war, and that attribution was evidently mistaken early medieval guesswork. Some scholars have argued that the story is a garbled descendant of a genuine record of Ambrosius erecting a monument to the murdered councillors, traditionally known as the 'Giants' Dance'. This was near a place called Caer Caradoc according to the Welsh *Brut Tyssilio* that Geoffrey may have used as a source.[41] If the name is accurate, the 'fort of Caradoc' presumably means a hillfort remembered as used by Caratacus so it is likely to be somewhere in south/east Wales where the latter staged his resistance campaign against Rome.

Some Welsh sites have been suggested for this place, for example, the stones on 'Mynydd y Gaer' above Pencoed in Glamorgan (by Baram Blackett and Alan Wilson) using the identification of the site's founder as 'Ambrius' in the *Llandaff Charters*. The latter are early twelfth century in their extant form, as reworked for Bishop Urban of Llandaff, but may preserve genuine sixth century details and some names in these charters of early Glamorgan land-grants seem authentic.[42] Alternatively there are the stones at Cerrigydrudion ('Stones of the Heroes') near Llangollen in Powys (preferred by Steve Blake and Scott Lloyd).[43] The site was apparently one of the 'Three Perpetual Choirs' of Britain, 'Cor Emrys', where a rota of monks chanted prayers all day and all night; Geoffrey of Monmouth places the memorial stones set up to the murdered councillors at the 'Cloister of Ambrius'.[44] The antiquity of this concept of a perpetual choir into the fifth century can be verified as it was an Eastern Roman religious practice introduced at a monastery near Constantinople around 400. The attributions of these sites as the place where the murdered nobles were buried may owe more to mediaeval guesswork than reality.

Ambrosius' headquarters is unknown, though it is possible that the garbled mediaeval Welsh legends – taken up by Geoffrey – linking him and his father Constantine as 'High Kings' to Winchester are a mistranslation of older documents or bardic stories placing them at a more geographically feasible town with the same Roman name of 'Venta', i.e. Venta Silurum (Caerwent) in Gwent. Some Welsh traditions also link Ambrosius to Woodchester in the Cotswolds, which would make sense in terms of the likely survival of Romano-British society there in the later fifth century. Similarly, if Aurelius Cynan/Caninus of Gloucester was Ambrosius' relative this would suggest a Severn valley/Cotswold connection.

Other major sovereigns in medieval Welsh writing: are they really historical?

Overlords: exaggerated versions of real men, or just creations of fiction? The examples of Cunedda, Urien, and Coel 'Hen'.

Geoffrey of Monmouth's confused 1130s 'history' of post-Roman Britain continued the story of the 'High Kings' of Britain after Constantine, Vortigern, Ambrosius, Uther and the most famous of them all – King Arthur. His garbled version of the sixth century named all of Gildas' five tyrannical kings as successive 'High Kings' of Britain, ruling in succession. These were: Constantine of Dumnonia (i.e. Devon and Cornwall, plus possibly Dorset); Maelgwyn of Gwynedd; Cuneglasus or Cynglas of (probably) Rhos/Clwyd/Flintshire, Maelgwyn's nephew; Aurelius 'Caninus' ('the Dog', probably a pun by Gildas on his real name, Conan), probably of Gloucester; and Vortipor of Dyfed (south-west Wales). He also included unknown rulers who did not make it into medieval Welsh legends such as Malgo, and made Aurelius Constantine's nephew; after these five, Britain is ruled by later real-life figures such as 'Cadwallo' i.e. Cadwallon son of Cadfan, king of Gwynedd from c. 625 to 634, and his son Cadwallader i.e. Cadwaladwr, ruler of Gwynedd from c.655 to 642. In his version, they rule lowland Britain with London although there are already Anglo-Saxon settlements in the east of the island.[45] This is definitely non-historical, as the Germanic settlements (or at least the use of Germanic cultural goods at residential sites) had spread across most of eastern England by c. 540–550 and across the whole of the south to the Severn plus most of the Midlands by c. 600. This area of what is usually supposed to have had 'Anglo-Saxon' political control included Geoffrey's British 'capital' at London, which in fact was not the thriving town of his imagination but in steep economic decline – the walled Roman city may have been abandoned for the new 'Germanic' trading-settlement on the riverside upstream at the 'Aldwych' i.e. 'old wick', 'old settlement'. Geoffrey's dates and other 'facts' are also wrong where we have other (and earlier) evidence, as with his giving Cadwallon a long reign of over forty years and not mentioning the interval between his death in battle (634?) and the accession of his son Cadwaladr (c. 655) when the usurper Cadfael, remembered in the Welsh 'Triads' as one of the three low-born rulers of Britain, ruled.

Geoffrey's claims to have based his writings on available older sources, especially one 'ancient' book, were a stock means of acquiring 'proof' of authenticity by the twelfth century and are usually rightly treated with much scepticism, especially due to his use of contemporary not post-Roman terminology and provincial and administrative names. Some of his imaginative reconstruction does appear to be based on earlier Welsh myths and can be traced back to 'Nennius' (who also claimed to be using a collection of original sources), for example, his imaginary 'Brutus the exiled Trojan prince' as founder of the royal line of Britain c. 1000 BC and the basic stories of men like 'Llyr' (i.e. Shakespeare's 'King Lear') plus the notion of Caratacus, the leader of the Catuvellauni tribe in south-east Britain in resisting the Roman invasion in AD 43 who later ran a guerrilla war in Silurian territory in SE Wales, as a ruler of all Britain. At best, one or more of Geoffrey's five post-Arthurian 'High Kings' of the mid-sixth-century may have exercised authority over the British rulers of the west – the most plausible candidate is Maelgwyn of Gwynedd (ruled c. 520 to 547/9), whose soubriquet of 'Pendragon' or 'Dragon of the Island' implies that he was recognised as a leader by other British rulers unless this just refers to the island of Mon/Anglesey. Gwynedd was clearly the most powerful state of the mid-sixth century and Maelgwyn had some degree of prestige and possibly military leadership beyond his borders – and by the time that the medieval Welsh 'Triads' were drawn up he was known as the chief elder of over-king Arthur at his court in S Wales. (Modern historians have argued that the 'memory' of Maelgwyn as an over-ruler of Wales may have been exaggerated or even created in the twelfth century and early thirteenth century for political reasons, to 'back-date' and give authenticity to the then overlordship exercised by Gwynedd under Owain Gwynedd in 1137–70 and Llylweyn ap Iorweth in 1194/1212–1240.) Maelgwyn was regarded by Gildas as the greatest of contemporary kings in talent as well as in wickedness, and the monkish polemicist fumed in his writing about how Maelgwyn had allegedly killed his uncle to seize the throne – the word used implies his mother's brother not his father's brother, so if this is correct it refers not to his presumed predecessor Owain 'Dantgwyn' of Gwynedd but to his mother's brother, who would have been ruler of Nant Conwy (i.e. the valley of the River Conwy) and son of king Maeldaf ap Dylan. Maelgwyn later killed his own nephew and married the latter's wife, killed or overthrew assorted unnamed rival princes, and turned to religion and abdicated the throne to become a monk but changed his mind. Geoffrey notably lacks any knowledge of or concern with Maelgwyn's family, such as his great-grandfather the dynastic founder Cunedda (a prince of the Votadini tribe in modern Lothian who moved to North Wales in the early-mid fifth century), his grandfather Einiawn, his father Cadwallon, and his uncle Owain 'Dantgwyn' i.e. 'White Tooth'.[46] This implies that whether or not Geoffrey knew the traditional Welsh dynastic pedigrees of the main kingdoms his concern was a 'national' one, of heroic resistance to the invading Saxons, which would be more interesting to his Anglo-Norman patrons so he concentrated on the 'national leader' Arthur not local dynasts. (This followed the similar concerns of 'Nennius' three centuries earlier.) Nor did Geoffrey bother with the post-Roman dynasts of his own home region, south-east Wales, i.e. Gwent and Glamorgan – though he did place Arthur's court at local Caerleon which followed the situation in the bardic saga of Culhwch and Olwen.

This drastic shift in interest by the most well-connected and influential Anglo-Norman writer with Welsh roots from more historical local kingdoms to a semi- or totally mythical 'over-king' Arthur (and the even more doubtful Uther Pendragon) arguably added to the marginalisation of 'real' Welsh history in the national English, later British consciousness. In Scotland and Ireland some accounts – albeit sketchy – of the earlier medieval kings of the region survived into the writings of later medieval and early modern 'historians' or fabulists, and these kings were presented in folk memory as ancestors of the then ruling kings. (For example, a series of portraits of the early Pictish kings from c. 100 BC to AD 500 were commissioned for the walls of Holyrood Palace under Stuart King Charles II in the 1670s.) But in Wales, as incorporated into England by force in 1284, the government elite were less interested in cultural preservation or links to the past though the local gentry and their client bards and genealogists continued to keep up such stories. In England, the only interest in pre-'Anglo-Saxon conquest' Britain centred on Arthur and his times, as 'Normanised' by Geoffrey and later twelfth-century writers and poets (many of them French), though Roman Britain was more favoured as the British developed their own empire. As a result, the petty rulers of post-Roman Wales tended to be marginalised from recorded history – presumably aided by the mass-destruction of medieval monastic records at the Reformation. Maelgwyn's name and some details of his rule luckily survived due to the mentions of him by his foe Gildas and in Welsh and Irish annals – but other early rulers of Gwynedd were not so lucky. Mystery also surrounds the role of Owain 'Dantgwyn' and his son Cynglas, who Gildas called the 'Tawny Butcher' and the 'charioteer of Dinarth' i.e. 'the Bear's Fortress'. These men apparently ruled the north-east Gwynedd cantref/province of Rhos (and parts of nearby Powys?), and later usurper kings of Gwynedd traced their lineage back to them. But in modern times the name of Dinarth, a hillfort on the north-east Welsh coast, has suggested to Graham Phillips and others that its owner might have been called 'Arth' i.e. 'The Bear', which is close in etymology to 'Arthur', and so been the 'original' for 'King Arthur', the powerful regional overlord and leader of the British against the Saxons in the early sixth century.

So Geoffrey was not using major Welsh records such as the 'established' royal genealogy of Gwynedd, which was extant by the time that the official genealogies of the Welsh kingdoms were drawn up at the court of 'national' ruler Hywel 'Dda', 'the Good' (ruled Dyfed/Deheubarth 905–50, Gwynedd and Powys 942–50) in the tenth century, and he did not use those of Powys, Dyfed, or Morgannwg/Glamorgan either. He does not even mention the contemporary rulers of Morgannwg such as Tewdrig, Mouric, and Morgan, or Vortipor of Dyfed's Roman-named father Aircol ('Agricola') and Irish ancestor Anlach mac Cormac of Leinster from the Dyfed royal genealogy, let alone any of the royal house of Powys from Vortigern's alleged replacement Cadell who are listed on the eighth-century memorial 'Pillar of Eliseg' in the Vale of Llangollen. He was aware of the story, known to Gildas by c.540 so probably accurate, that his King Constantine of Dumnonia had murdered two of his young rival princes in church and named them as the sons of the traitor Medraut who had rebelled against and destroyed King Arthur. But he did not know anything about the royal dynasty of his king Vortipor (ruler of Dyfed), who is commemorated in an extant memorial stone at Castell Dwyran in both Brittonic/Welsh and Irish linguistic terminology (as 'Votiporix' and 'Vortecorigas') and ruled an area in south-west Wales with some Irish settlement, and there is no early Welsh evidence that any of his five kings except perhaps Maelgwyn exercised any authority outside his own kingdom.

Indeed, Geoffrey's version of later sixth-century history has huge gaps that omit what we know from early Welsh genealogies and poems was occurring in northern Britain and he does not mention any of its poet-celebrated major warlords. If Maelgwyn is to be counted as a sort of 'High King' in the 540s the same rank could be allowed a few decades later to his son Rhun (ruled c.550–580), who was able to march his army across and northwards along the Pennines in a major campaign across the then kingdoms of northern Britain, especially Rheged (probably Lancashire and Cumbria) where he evicted a hostile ruler called Eleuther who had raided Gwynedd earlier and was remembered as the father of the poet-prince Llywarch 'Hen' ('the Aged'). Rhun was said to have marched as far north as the Pictish realm beyond Hadrian's Wall from whence his ancestors had come, possibly in support of their King Bridei mac Maelchon – his brother if the unplaced Pictish royal relative 'Maelchon' was Maelgywn of Gwynedd, which was argued by John Morris in the 1980s but is still disputed.[47] Rhun 'the Tall' thus presumably secured the loyalty of those kings whose lands he crossed in the north of Britain, but does not make it into Geoffrey's account of 'High Kings'. If military leadership of a coalition of British kings can be taken as implying some sort of rank as 'High King', then it should also be accorded to Urien or Urbgen of Rheged, who emerged as leader of that kingdom after he and his allies had defeated a rival coalition led by king Gwendolleu of Caerluel (Carlisle) at the battle of Arderydd (probably Arthuret near Carlisle) in or around 573.[48] This battle was indeed referred to as a major event in the surviving poems of the bard, mystic, and probable Druid/'shaman' Myrddin 'Wyllt' ('the Wild'), one of the originals behind Geoffrey's prophet 'Merlin', who was a witness and from his poems is said to have gone mad with guilt at the carnage that he had caused in being a leading instigator of the conflict. The battle and its participants were major events in early Welsh myths and were often referenced in poetry and the *Triads* as were the probably less historical deeds of 'King Arthur', but they do not appear in Geoffrey's work – and neither does the dynasty that produced the rival 'cousins' Urien and Gwendolleu (and Eleuther and Llywarch 'Hen'), that of the early-mid fifth-century northern king Coel 'Hen' ('the Old') who is the original figure behind 'Old King Cole'.

Urien, celebrated in poetry by his bard Taliesin who was a leading figure of early Welsh culture and myth, led a Northern British coalition against the Angles of the kingdom of Bernicia (i.e. the Northumbrian coast from Tweed to Tees) and besieged their king on the island of Lindisfarne c. 589 before being assassinated by Llovan, a villain of Welsh myth sent by his rival king Morcant of Bryniach. Llywarch 'Hen' also celebrated the victories and mourned the death in battle of the next leader of Rheged, Urien's son Owain, who fought the Bernicians in the 590s. These men were important if shadowy figures of British history in the sixth century who were referenced, albeit often with legendary exaggeration, in medieval Welsh literature but did not translate into divergent medieval literature in England (in Anglo-Norman or later in English), largely due to the choice of subjects by Geoffrey for his 'History' in the 1130s which then became the basis for the huge edifice of 'Arthuriana' and the cult of King Arthur. The latter and Geoffrey's version of his career were indeed to be taken by the Anglo-Norman and later medieval English elites as genuine history, and were used for political purposes by aggressive sovereigns like King Edward I who argued that their conquests of Wales and (failed) Scotland were merely re-creating their ancient and 'rightful' realm of Arthur and his ancestors and predecessors. Indeed, as Geoffrey wrote that the first king of Britain, Brutus, had been the father of the kings of England ('Logres'), Wales ('Cambria' under Camber), and 'Alba'/Scotland (under Albanactus) the King of England was the superior of and had the right to demand homage from Wales and Scotland. The unhistorical picture of an ancient realm of all Britain in Geoffrey was used as a justification for medieval English empire-building, as later the war between 'King Arthur' and the dictator of Rome, Lucius Hiberius, was used as an inspiration for Henry VIII as he rejected the authority of the Papacy in Rome and sought to portray himself as an Arthur-like independent 'emperor' in Britain.

The other early medieval Welsh term used to refer to kings exercising some form of authority or prestige over their neighbours was 'Wledig', which as we have seen was also applied to the late Roman ruler 'Macsen Wledig' i.e. Western Emperor Magnus Maximus (ruled 383–88). But this is of uncertain origin and application, and was used for a variety of rulers with varying degrees of authority – some of whom we have independent evidence for, others not. It was used of Ambrosius, and also of his probably slightly older contemporary Cunedda, aka 'Kenneth', ruler of the Votadini tribe in Lothian in the earlier fifth century. The royal

House of Gwynedd was descended according to the genealogies (extant as of the 'official' version created at the court of Hywel 'the Good' of Dyfed, of Gwynedd descent, in the early tenth century) from Cunedda of the Votadini, who was supposed to have been called South to rule in N Wales by the British authorities. The date of this is however unclear; it was 146 years before the time of 'Mailcunus', i.e. Maelgwyn of Gwynedd, who died in the plague of c.547, according to 'Nennius' writing in the later 820s.[49] The Votadini appear to have had a major reputation as warriors and their local late sixth-century descendants were celebrated in one of the very few surviving heroic poems of the era, the *Gododdin* (c.600?), for their last great campaign against the Anglians of Bernicia that ended with defeat at the battle of Catraeth (Catterick?). They also had impressive surviving hillforts, for example, Traprain Law. Cunedda was brought in to reoccupy lands in North Wales lost to Irish settlers, and the archaeological evidence confirms Irish settlement in Lleyn. If this is accurate, he would probably have been a protege of the Western Roman Empire's regent Stilicho (in office 395–408) who is recorded as campaigning in Britain around 399 by his panegyricist Claudian. The use of one body of non-Roman 'foederati' as allies to defeat another body of non-Romans on the frontier, giving them the latter's lands, was a common practice by the undermanned Roman army.

An alternative date suggested on the basis of genealogies would put this at only 106 years, making it in the 440s. This fits better with the established tenth-century genealogy, which has only one generation – Einawn 'Girt', i.e. 'The Impetuous' – between Cunedda and Catwallaun 'Lawhir', i.e. Longhand', who ruled c. 500 as he was Maelgwyn's father and is named by the twelfth-century 'Bruts' as the contemporary of King Arthur who fought at 'Mount Badon' in c.518. This raises the question of which post-Roman ruler in Britain (Vortigern?) devised the strategy of using the warlike Votadini to reconquer Gwynedd from the Irish and had the authority to order or lure him to go south. Given the archaeological evidence of a socially and economically atomised lowland Britain, were there really any authorities powerful enough by the 440s to intervene in both North Wales and Lothian? If the earlier date is correct, Cunedda may have been a subject ally of the late Roman Empire as king of Lothian as this was adjacent to Hadrians' Wall where settlement and so presumably military personnel survived after 400; historians such as John Morris have speculated that his grandfather Paternus' nickname 'of the red tunic' implies some sort of Roman military office.[56] Two generations back from Cunedda brings the date of Paternus into the 360s-380s, contemporaneous with Ammianus' record of the general Theodosius' reconstruction of a system of local rulers as Roman allies after the great 'barbarian' attack on Britain in 367. Mediaeval Welsh genealogists certainly ascribed Cunedda's power to an extensive realm covering all or most of later Gwynedd, as they traced the dynasties of various parts of Gwynedd and the allied principality of Ceredigion (i.e. Cardiganshire) to Cunedda's sons. Thus *Edernyion* was ruled by the descendants of Cunedda's son Edern, *Rhufoniog* by Rhufon and his line, *Dogfaeling* by Dogfael and his line, *Ceredigion* by Ceredig and his line, and *Pwlhelli* by Afloeg's line. The most 'senior' of the principalities, *Meirionydd*, fell to Meirion (Marcianus), the son of Cunedda's predeceasing eldest son Tybion. However, it is uncertain if this is a correct memory of an actual division of the new kingdom among Cunedda's family in the fifth century or a 'post-facto' translation of political links established over generations into explanatory dynastic terms. Could a separate and unbroken sub-dynasty of 'father-son' descent really rule each of the sub-provinces of Gwynedd from the mid-late fifth century right through to the twelfth century, or is this more likely to be political 'spin' establishing a (fictional) legitimate ancestry back to Cunedda for later rulers whose actual ancestors had been forgotten? There was apparent relevance of the contemporary revival of Gwynedd in the 820s under the new dynasty of Merfyn 'the Freckled' to fight the national enemy Mercia in 'Nennius' writings, in creating or exaggerating a story of national success under King Arthur in the sixth century. This is Nicholas Higham's persuasive argument. So it is possible that the concept of a unitary Gwynedd parcelled out among Cunedda's family was invented to justify its 'reunification' by Nennius' patron Merfyn. It has even been suggested that the 'tradition' of the division of Gwynedd among Cunedda's sons was created as late as the 1170s, to provide an earlier precedent for the current division among the sons of Owain Gwynedd. But Cunedda was clearly seen as the founder of the 'national' dynasty that ruled until the death of king Hywel, Merfyn's predecessor, in 825, and this and his dramatic move from Lothian are unlikely to have been invented.

One other 'Gwledic' of medieval Welsh literary myth, Ceredig or Ceretic of the Clyde region, also seems to have been a real person and can be traced in the records.

His kingdom was that of 'Are Cluta' (Brittonic name) or 'Strathclyde' (Gaelic name), the British kingdom of the Clyde valley. This was the former tribal territory of the Damnonii and Selgovae tribes, as listed in the Alexandria geographer Ptolemy's maps of the second century AD. It was the western counterpart of the post-Roman kingdom of the Votadini (i.e. 'Gododdin') to its east, and had its 'capital' or principal royal fortress at Are Cluta (Dumbarton, 'fortress of the Britons'). It was probably reduced to vassalage or established as a new, dependent pro-Roman chieftaincy c.370 by the Roman general Theodosius as he stabilised the area north of Hadrian's Wall to prevent a resurgence of the great Pictish raid of 367. The first definitely recorded ruler, Ceretic, is dateable by a letter of complaint about his raiding by St Patrick c.459; he had kidnapped some of the Saint's Christian converts from Ulster, presumably as slaves, so he must have had a fleet. Patrick duly sent him an angry letter demanding their return or the likely penalty of Divine punishment. His grandfather 'Cinhil' may be the Roman name 'Quintilius' and his great-grandfather 'Cluim' the Roman 'Clemens'. John Morris assumed from the likely time-scale of the genealogy that Clemens was Theodosius' client-king, though this is not definite.[50] Ceretic was known to medieval Welsh genealogists of the Strathclyde royal lineage by the title of 'Gwledic', so he was thus evidently a powerful ruler, probably of all the lands from the Clyde valley and the Antonine Wall south to the Carlisle area.

The title of 'Gwledic' is also used of Coel 'Hen' ('the Old'), who is cited in the royal genealogies of the northern British rulers between the Humber/Mersey and the Firth of Forth, the 'Gwyr a'r Gogledd' ('Men of the North'), as their joint ancestor and some sort of over-king. Given the number of generations from him to dateable later sixth-century rulers such as Gwendolleu of Caerluel and Urien of Rheged, he was presumably early fifth century in dating. As the various kings cited as his descendants ruled a mixture of kingdoms including modern Lancashire, Cumbria, Yorkshire, Durham, Northumberland, and parts of Lothian his authority has been presumed (e.g. by Peter Hunter Blair in *Archaeologiana Aeliana*, 4th series vol 25, 1947 and John Morris in *The Age of Arthur*, Weidenfeld and Nicolson 1973) to have extended from the York region to the Firth of Forth.[51] Peter Hunter Blair reckons that the name given for his father 'Guotepauc son of Tecmant', was in fact part of his own name which was transcribed inaccurately and that 'Guotepauc' is the same as the name of the sixth-century Dyfed ruler Voteporix; thus he could be a Romano-British military official called 'Caelius Voteporix'. As York, 'Eburacum', was a pre-410 Roman provincial capital and military base he has been assumed to have inherited regional military and administrative power in this region, based on the city, and even to have been the leader of what local forces – including those on Hadrian's Wall – were left in Britain after Constantine III took the main army to Gaul in 407. As seen by the recent excavations at the major Hadrian's Wall fortress of Birdoswald, there was a post-Roman residential hall built in the fortress plus smaller local homes and evidence of farming so this – and other fortresses? – remained a nucleus of authority for some decades. Indeed, Coel may have been or inherited the role of the 'dux' (military commander) of this province and commanded the surviving post-407 military units there, though it may be coincidence that the name of the 'Kyle' in Ayrshire suggests that his authority could have extended north-west to this region. This idea of a wide-ranging kingdom or command for Coel may be over-rationalisation of a complex genealogy that owed more to later legends and 'legitimisation' of rulers by giving them illustrious ancestry, and the kingdoms involved were all defunct and in Anglo-Saxon hands well before the extant genealogies were drawn up – in another region of Britain, Wales. But it is politically logical to explain what happened in the former 'military zone' of northern Britain in and beyond the York region, the former lands of the Brigantes ('Bright Ones') tribe conquered by the Romans in the 70s AD. Coel, like Cunedda of the Votadini and later of Gwynedd, was seen in later centuries as a prestigious enough (and still remembered) ruler of approximately the correct date to be placed at the head of local post-Roman royal genealogies.

Genealogies of the House of Coel 'Hen' from the lists in the *Laws of Hywel 'Dda'* (tenth-century king of Dyfed):

1. Bryniach, i.e. approx.. Northumberland and Durham; name then adopted by the Anglian realm of Bernicia from c.600.

Aballac – Eudelen – Endos – Ebiud – Outigern – Titigern – Iutmetal – Grat – Urban – Tetpuil – Teuhant – Tecmant – COEL HEN – Garbiniaun – Dumnugual Moilmut – Bran Hen – Cingar Craut – Morcant Bulc.

2. York, which traditionally fell to the Anglians of 'Deira' on the lower Humber in 580 according to the tenth-century *Annales Cambriae*.

COYL HEN – Ceneu – Gurgust Letlum – Eleuther Cascoed Mawr – Gurci and Peredur.

Genealogies of the House of Coel 'Hen' from the Harleian Mss. 3589, reproduced in 'Y Cymmrodor' no. 9 (1888) pp. 141–83:

(Working backwards:)

(Rheged) URBGEN – Cinmarc – Meirchiaun – Gurgust – COIL HEN

(Lothian) GUALLAUC – Laenauc – Maguic Glop – Ceneu – COYL HEN

(York) GWRCI and PERETUR – Eleuther – Cascord Mawr – Ietlum – Ceneu – COYL HEN

(Pennines?) PABO POST PRYDEIN – ARTHWYS – Mar – Ceneu – COEL

To add to the mysteries of whether this collection of genealogies was based on reality, both Urien/Urbgen of Rheged's father (Cynfarch aka St Cynfarch or Kinnemark) and grandfather (Meirchiaun aka 'Marcianus') were referred to in medieval Welsh tradition as resident in South Wales, not Rheged – so were they disinherited or expelled by rivals? They are presumed to be the 'St Cynfarch/Kinnemark' who had churches dedicated to him around Gwent and the 'Marcianus the Mad' who is referred to as a mentally unstable tyrant ruling around 500 in lands within the later Morgannwg, the tribal kingdom of the Silures. That might fit with the logic of Urien, as a marginalised junior prince formerly living in exile, leading the successful coalition that overthrew the mid-century Cumbrian 'strongman', Gwendolleu of Caerluel, at the battle of Arderydd around 573. But Urien's brother was recorded in these genealogies – which are after all at least 400 years later – as Llew ap Cynfarch, a prince who created a new kingdom for his dynasty in Lothian and is presumed to be the same man as the eponymous 'Loth' or 'Lot' who appears in the (originally seventh-century) *Life of St Kentigern* as the grandfather of that founding bishop of Glasgow. St Kentigern was born to Loth's daughter around 540 and was the contemporary and protégé of Rhydderch 'Hael', 'the Generous', king of Strathclyde from c. 560 to 612. Loth duly went on into Arthurian legend as 'King Lot of Lothian', the husband of King Arthur's power-hungry sister Morgause, and survived as an integral part of the Arthurian myths as far as T.H. White's *Once and Future King* trilogy in the 1930s. But if Loth (aka Llew) was an adult ruler with a daughter able to have children by 540, this makes it unlikely that he was really of the same generation as Urien who was an adult warlord at the peak of his powers between 573 and 589 – a generation later. Some sceptics might argue that Loth was annexed as a suitably prestigious grandfather for St Kentigern in a mythologised hagiography and that this evidence is unreliable, but the story as it survives also includes other details unlikely to be invented such as the Saint's clashes with the mysterious pagan 'holy man' Lailoken ('Twin'), a mystic living in the forests of southern Scotland who has been conflated with Myrddin.

In the context of these genealogies, the sixth-century kingdoms east and west of the Pennines – one line of kings in Elmet (south-west Yorkshire) and another in the East of the county, and several lines in 'Rheged' i.e. Lancashire and Cumbria – seem to have split off from each other over several generations after Coel. Only two of his 'sons' ruled kingdoms, i.e. Ceneu in the lands East of the Pennines and Gwrgust in the lands to the west. After them, the number of kings and kingdoms multiplies – due to several brothers in one family insisting on an equal split of their father's lands? This genealogy could reflect a break-up of Coel's former kingdom under his descendants. The latter could be his genealogical heirs, or else they were his 'political' or military heirs who were later rationalised and 'legitimised' in legend as his family. Thus, Coel is probably to some degree historical in origin as a king of the north based on York, if exaggerated by myth. But other 'Gwledics' are less historical or if they existed have been lost to surviving records, such as the mysterious Amlawdd 'Wledig', only now known as the husband of a daughter of Coel ('Ystradwel', which translates as 'The Wall' – hinting at lands around Hadrian's Wall?) and by her father of the elusive 'Ygyr' or 'Igraine', the mother of King Arthur in literary myth. Another daughter of his was allegedly mother of a hero of medieval Welsh poetry, Culhwch of the poem *Culhwch and Olwen* where he is the cousin of Arthur and seeks his help to carry out 'impossible' tasks laid upon him before he can claim his bride.

The genealogies of the line of Coel also have a hidden clue to one of the mysteries of the Arthurian myths – where the 'dynasty of the Grail' in medieval British and Continental literature comes from. The literary story of the Arthurian 'Quest for the Holy Grail' only appears in the works of the French poet Chretien de Troyes in the second third of the twelfth century, despite all the enthusiasm of some modern Arthurian investigators for finding the 'original' behind it (or even the Grail, the cup said to have been used by Jesus Christ at the Last Supper and then used to catch drops of His blood at the Crucifixion). The notion of a cup – or to be precise, a cauldron – with mystical Otherworldly origins and the power to indefinitely nourish those who drank from it – has been demonstrated as being 'Celtic' (that is, Brittonic/Irish) in origin, and the connection of Arthur and his followers to a quest in search of a magical cauldron is Welsh not French – the early medieval Welsh poem about the *Spoils of Annfwn*. It was also a part of pre-Christian not Christian myth, and featured gods, demigods and the 'Celtic' Otherworld. However much it was Christianised in the twelfth century and thirteenth century, it was based on an 'original' story in ancient British culture, and some of its obscure names are also definitively British and crop up in the early Welsh royal genealogies. Most notably, the semi-historical king 'Peredur' of York, a descendant of Coel who by the time of the *Annales Cambriae* in the tenth century was said to have lost his capital to the invading Anglians of Deira around 580, appears to be the 'original' of the Grail-finder 'Sir Perceval'. This gives us a clue as to where another part of the Grail stories – the line of holy 'Grail-Keepers' connected to the relatives of Christ – came from. The ancestry of Coel, presumably via the tribal kingship of one of the Northern realms, is traced back in the genealogies compiled at the court of Hywel 'the Good' in the early tenth century to the mythical 'Aballach' – who was supposedly a first-century AD ruler connected to the family of Jesus Christ. This dynasty was thus the pre-Anglo-Norman version of the later 'Grail Dynasty', keepers of the Holy Grail from the time of Joseph of Arimathea, as this included a mysterious 'King Evelake'. Aballach was apparently related to Joseph, and his sister was the supposed ancestor of the South Wales ruler Eudaf 'Hen' ('the Old'), father of Helen 'of the Hosts' who married Emperor Maximus. As Peredur of Eburacum/York was a descendant of Coel 'Hen' he was thus connected to the family of Aballach – hence the tradition of the 'Grail-finder' being of the 'Grail Dynasty' which was utilised by later mediaeval writers. In fact, the enthusiastic modern writers who regard this dynasty from Aballach as a 'fact' preserved in medieval Welsh documents ignore the political propaganda value to contemporary rulers of stressing the antiquity and Biblical-connected holiness of their ruling families – Hywel 'the Good' of Dyfed in particular was a keen Christian devotee who went on pilgrimage to Rome c.930 and laid out imitations of the Holy Places around Jerusalem at his sanctuary of the cult of the Cross at Nevern. The 'holy Palestinian antecedents' of the dynasties of the north of Britain, with or without Joseph of Arimathea, have to be seen in the context of medieval Welsh politico-religious 'spin' as well as authentic genealogical memories.

Chapter Two

Hengest, 'King Stallion/Gelding': Founder Of Kent. Did He Ever Exist?

When we come on to consider the early Anglo-Saxon kingdoms in Britain, we have the same problem as with Vortigern, Uther, and Arthur and to a degree Ambrosius. Did the supposed founders of the kingdoms in the fifth century and sixth century ever exist in real life, or were they legendary? Were stories about them constructed in later centuries by enthusiastic poets (usually for oral recitation in the halls of the warrior elite) and 'determinist' Christian Churchmen, to support a political purpose and glamorize and legitimize the ancestors of their current kings? This duly plays into the whole question of how authentic or 'rigorous' early writing of 'history' was in the early medieval centuries, and to what extent it was a branch of literature and served the purposes of propaganda or projecting the author's contemporary society and its beliefs back into the past. Modern (post-Second World War) historians have taken a dim view of the objectivity of these early sources and the whole notion of a 'reliable' history based on written sources and genuine oral memories, and accordingly the 'history' of this early period has seemed a great deal less certain than it once did.

The most extreme sceptics and proponents of rigorous science-based enquiry, indeed, have even argued that we cannot be certain that existing (mostly post-1200) copies of 'earlier' written works, British/Welsh and Anglo-Saxon alike, were accurately copied by scribes and so preserve the exact details written down in lost, earlier copies of the works. Mistakes and 'embroidering' of original texts took place, and so a chain of faithful transmission of details cannot be taken for granted – and hence only the 'hard facts' of archaeological data are reliable. This may well be too gloomy a view of the accuracy and professionalism of copyists, but when we come to the basic economic and social situations of Britain in the early post-Roman centuries the archaeology shows that the traditional literary/'historical' stories are at odds with 'facts on the ground'. As mentioned earlier, work on the botanical data of what plants were growing in the fields of 'post-Roman' and 'Anglo-Saxon' England has shown that there was no abrupt break in occupation of farmland in the fifth century, as would appear from Gildas' apocalyptic statements of mass-invasion, massacre, destruction, semi-genocide, and the Britons hiding from their attackers in hills and caves. By this reckoning, the Late Roman farmland would have reverted to scrub for a number of years until re-settled and re-used by incoming Germanic farmers, and there would be no continuity of occupation. But this does not happen, fields were not left unused to revert to scrub, and the boundaries of late Roman estates can be seen behind the boundaries of 'Anglo-Saxon' villages as far apart as the Fens and the Cotswolds – and some sites, for example, the crucial Fenland one excavated at Mucking, show apparently coeval 'British' and 'Anglo-Saxon' settlement in the same community. As a result of these excavations and a new view of whether the arrival of 'Germanic' goods and systems of burial across eastern England in the fifth century need mean mass 'invasion' as opposed to trade and new fashions of living, it is possible to argue that the narratives in Bede and the *Anglo-Saxon Chronicle* of the creation of new kingdoms by invaders are at best an over-simplification owing much to later literary myth. Similarly, when we come to the finds made in specific areas of 'Anglo-Saxon settlement/conquest' in the *Chronicle* we do not find a cohesive 'bloc' of new Germanic villages created within a short space of time across a region, as would be expected if it was indeed overrun and settled as in the literary record. There are extensive 'Germanic' settlements (as defined by the goods discovered there and the methods of burial) from the fifth century in the upper Thames valley around Wallingford and Abingdon, centred on Sutton Courtenay, but no literary record of any 'Anglo-Saxon conquest' or kingdom in the region that early – and there was a 'British' enclave to their north-east, around Verulamium/St Albans and Bedford, that appears to have lasted as a British 'state' until conquered by the West Saxon ally Cutha c. 571 (as in the *Chronicle*). Given the location of 'advancing' Anglo-Saxon sites moving further west through the sixth century, the main settlement- or trade-route in this period appears to be the Icknield Way, with a route south-west from the heavily settled regions of the Fens and East Anglia to the upper Thames – and in the South there is no archaeological record of 'settlement' at the time of the supposedly expanding West Saxon kingdom in Hampshire c.500. (See next chapter.) There are evidently major gaps in our written 'evidence' and contradictions with archaeology, and this is even apparent in the first kingdom to be created according to later literature – Hengest's (Jutish not Anglo-Saxon) realm of Kent.

Hengest was traditionally held to be the founder of the kingdom of Kent, which unlike all the other Anglo-Saxon states (apart from Wight) was 'Jutish' by race as defined by Bede. The latter (writing on Tyneside in Northumbria in the 730s) divided up the incoming Germanic peoples who settled in Britain in the fifth century and sixth century into the famous three peoples of 'Angles, Saxons and Jutes'.[1] This has been followed ever since as the defining statement on the origins of the 'English' (from the word 'Angles') although in fact the more contemporary if more physically remote Eastern Roman historian Procopius, writing in Constantinople in the 540s, referred to Angles, native Britons, and Frisians[2] – i.e. presumably those settled in the Frisian Islands, who could have been linked ethnically or culturally to any of the above. This categorization agrees over there being different origins for the peoples settled in different areas of lowland southern Britain, though not if this was primarily geographical – and the 'peoples' then settled in separate areas as located by the names of the new states, e.g. those of the West, South, Middle, and East Saxons and the East and Middle Angles. Did the Jutes come from Jutland, the Angles from the 'angle' between Germany and the Jutland peninsula, and the Saxons from the later region of Lower Saxony in north-west Germany? It agrees with the differences discovered by archaeologists between the burial-practices and types of jewellery used by the 'Angles' (that is, the peoples of the Midlands, East Anglia, and the Humberside in Yorkshire), the Saxons to their south in Essex, Sussex, and Wessex, and the Jutes who Bede placed in Kent and the Isle of Wight. The fifth-century and sixth-century 'Germanic' archaeological discoveries in the two latter areas have definite similarities, and differences from the intervening 'South Saxon' region in Sussex – so this has been taken as confirming Bede's accuracy.[3] But Bede did not produce a definitive account of the early 'migrations' to Britain, as it has been noted that he did not include a separate, non-English tradition preserved in the Continental Saxons' later region (at the abbey of Fulda) that there had been a 'reverse migration' of Saxons out of Britain to Germany some time in the mid-sixth century to defeat their rivals the Thuringians, leading to new settlement up the Elbe valley. Also, the supposed differing styles of 'Germanic" jewellery starts to appear in Eastern coastal sites dateable to well before the supposed 'invasions' of around 430 to 460: was it also worn by Late Roman soldiery and their womenfolk (of partly Germanic origins)?

Bede is our main early source for details of Hengest's career, and was as fond of dramatic narratives featuring major characters as Gildas with an equally didactic Christian tone. Though he was writing in Northumbria nearly 300 years later, in the 730s, he was an assiduous collector and checker of facts and was a prestigious figure at a major monastery (Jarrow) with international links. So he would have had access to Church records in Kent, where the first Anglo-Saxon archbishopric was based at Canterbury, and probably also to the traditions of the royal court of the local Kentish kingdom. (The latter would mainly have been oral 'sagas' recounted at feasts by the kings' celebratory 'scops' or poets, with heroic exaggerations and a mixing up of stories.) Bede was a protégé of leading local churchmen such as his own abbot, the late seventh-century writer, book-collector and theologian Benedict Biscop, and though he did not travel himself a number of the senior figures of contemporary Northumbrian monastic life made it as far as Rome, in their search for manuscripts and holy relics. Indeed, despite the disruption of mid-late seventh-century Mediterranean trade and other travel by the Arab invasions, links with the surviving eastern half of the Roman Empire were maintained and Bede and other writers in Britain were aware of which Emperor was reigning and what was going on in the Eastern Church. The first great centralising Archbishop of Canterbury who reorganised the structure and official 'rulebook' for procedure in the English Church across the island, Theodore of Tarsus (in office 669–690), was indeed a Greek refugee from the Arabs, born in St Paul's home town in what is now south-east Turkey (ancient Cilicia). Bede was fond of stories of miracles and Divine intervention and made the most of miraculous happenings involving live and dead saints (including saintly kings) in his *History of the English Church*. He also played up the narrative as a 'positive' and 'determinist' story of the triumph of the Roman Church mission sent to Kent by Pope Gregory 'the Great' in 596–7 and its heirs, possibly as a riposte to the 'defeatist' story of Britain's ruin presented as the early part of the period's definitive narrative by Gildas in the 540s. Bede's story was concentrated on the achievements of the Roman Church, so he did not mention any surviving post-Roman Christians (of British/Welsh origin) living in Kent when Gregory's missionaries led by St Augustine arrived, though it is probable that there were some such people and that they may have used the church of St Martin in Canterbury.[4] He does mention the earlier arrival of a Catholic cleric, Bishop Liudhard, from the Frankish Merovingian kingdom in Kent c.581 when king Aethelbert married a Frankish princess, Bertha, as recorded by the 590s Frankish historian Bishop Gregory of Tours,[5] but not any converts. Bede's Kent in 597 is a pagan 'tabula rasa' awaiting the Word of God as delivered from Rome; and he does not mention any surviving Christians of British origin in the kingdom of Northumbria when it is converted by Roman Christian missionaries led by Bishop Paulinus from Kent in the later 620s. The role and importance of pagan rulers like the ferocious Penda of Mercia (ruled c.626 to 655) in Anglo-Saxon history is downplayed, and they appear as the villains set against his Christian heroes.

Bede's work thus leaves important but inconvenient facts out in the interest of a coherent and determinist narrative, and he is nowadays reckoned as less reliable than once supposed – which has effects on his reliable knowledge and useage of details of fifth-century Kent too. But he knew how to assess and balance sources and has written documents as well as oral narrative to rely on, and his 'determinist' narrative of inevitable (Catholic) Christian triumph across England is generally taken as largely accurate apart from his deliberate sidelining and 'down-playing' the importance of both pagan and British ('Celtic') Christian 'outsiders'. His story of the foundation of the first Anglo-Saxon kingdom, Kent, by the brothers Hengest and Horsa, the Jutish sons of Wihtgisl,[6] was clearly what was known or believed to have happened in the fifth century as seen by the early eighth-century locals. He also refers to the later line of kings, including Aethelbert (the late sixth century 'Bretwalda', a sort of over-ruler, who the ninth-century *Anglo-Saxon Chronicle* has ruling from c.560 to 616/17 and who invited the first Catholic Christian mission to England in 597) as descended from Aesc/Oesc, also known as 'Oeric', son of Hengest.[7] The dynasty were known as the 'Oescings', which has been used as evidence that they traced their origins to the obscure Aesc, not the far more 'high status' and heroic Hengest – referenced in other, heroic stories of mainland Europe, as we will see later – the latter was a late and bogus addition to the royal genealogy. For that matter, even Aesc might be a version of the shadowy Saxon founder prince 'Ansehis' who according to a story which reached the Italian 'Ravenna Cosmographer' had brought his people to Britain, not necessarily a real man.[8] Bede alleges that the initial force of three shiploads of mercenaries defeated the Picts, as they had been hired to do, but then induced their inviter 'Vortigern' to hire more of them and spread the word about the fertility of Britain and the weakness of its inhabitants to encourage more of their countrymen to join them. Once they were strong enough they revolted in alliance with the Picts, and overran much of the island of Britain. Chaos, massacre, and devastation then followed, as in the sixth-century Welsh account by Gildas (Bede's main source for this?), and the disaster was blamed on the sins of the British but it did not lead to the invaders overrunning more than the south-east of Britain in the short term.[9] The Britons under Ambrosius defeated the invaders, but the return of peace was followed by renewed civil wars and immorality among the next generation plus a failure to bother with converting the incoming Saxons – inviting merited divine punishment by further Saxon successes.[10] Bede's account is clearly based on the work of Gildas, as seen in Chapter One, and his dating of the initial Anglo-Saxon-Jutish arrival was as being some time after the c.429 first missionary expedition by St Germanus (which he also paraphrases).[11] His version was supported by other – ninth-century – Welsh and English sources, i.e. the 820s work of Gwynedd historian 'Nennius' and the annalistic account in the ?890s *Anglo-Saxon Chronicle*, though the former is now reckoned to have relied on him and not on independent writings as its main source.

In all these accounts Hengest was supposed to have been the first Germanic captain to come to England and settle there, though archaeology shows that there were Germanic artefacts and so presumably Germans in south-east Britain before 410 – possibly as hired mercenaries on the 'Saxon Shore' there.[12] The main areas of early Germanic 'finds' from the late fourth or early fifth centuries (mostly in burials) was in northern and eastern Kent, near the Roman ports and fortresses of Dubris/Dover, Rutupiae/Richborough, and Reculver. The existence of the ruins of a major archway at Richborough (legendarily linked to Hengest's 'brother' Horsa as mentioned by Bede) has been suggested as indicating that this was a Roman monument to the landing of the main Roman invasion force there in AD 43. Notably, if the incoming 'Germans' – whose grave-goods show similarities to those in Jutland – received lands extending to a compact and autonomous district this is not reflected in the archaeology, where early 'finds' are more scattered, and it did not extend over all of the later Kent (especially the wooded inland south-west areas). The extent of 'Kent' as an administrative region in the fifth-century, before and in the time of Hengest, is unclear but Julius Caesar's account of his invasions of Britain in 55 and 54 BC, which the Britons fought to a standstill, calls the local peoples the 'Cantiaci'. The same name was known to the first-century BC historians and geographers Strabo and Diodorus Siculus.[13] The name 'Cantii' was used for the people of this region by the Alexandrian geographer Ptolemy in his map of Britain in the second-century,[14] so the name of 'Kent' was clearly adapted from a British one by the 'incomers', as was 'Bernicia' from 'Bryniach' in the north. Whether there was one extant province or kingdom – and how far this extended, for example, to London – and if this was transferred 'en masse' to the 'incomers' as in 'Nennius' is more doubtful. The usual Roman procedure was to create local administrative districts in the lands of and named after the regional tribes who they had conquered there, as in both Britain and Gaul where this preserved the structure and identity of the pre-Roman polities. The physical survival of the local elites as a Romanised and landholding 'ruling class', ready to re-emerge as the new leadership after Roman rule ended, is more obscure but logically possible – and as the names of pre-Roman tribal states in Britain were resumed by the post-410 governments they were clearly proud of their ancient identity. This would presumably apply to whoever ran the administration of the land of the Cantiaci after 410, probably from the old regional capital of Durovernum/Canterbury – whether or not any surviving Roman military structure remained on the 'Saxon Shore'.

It would be the normal late Roman practice to give lands near their military garrisons to incoming non-Roman mercenaries or 'foederati' ('federates' i.e. allies), and so presumably land would be granted to any such German mercenaries hired by the local regime – including Hengest. As referred to already, by the 420s to 440s there were plenty of settlers (scattered so clearly locally-tolerated) in the region of south-east Britain using Germanic goods and burying their dead according to Germanic 'pagan', not indigenous British Christian, customs. This extends to

East Anglia, Lincolnshire, and in particular the region of the Fens (a major and drained Roman corn-growing area) so there was not one sole region of settlement as implied by Bede and Gildas – and the number of Germanic sites in this region implies a substantial settlement but there is no record of who ruled them. The earliest 'English' kings mentioned in the extant records are mid-late sixth-century, a full century after the earliest 'Germanic' goods in the region (e.g. brooches), as dated by their style. There are also some archaeological finds in East Anglia similar to those in Kent, though this is known as an 'Anglian' not 'Jutish' region from its regional name and Bede's division of the incoming peoples into separate 'Angle', 'Saxon', and 'Jute' groupings. For that matter, careful modern examination of crucial early 'Anglo-Saxon' farming sites in this region such as Mucking shows that there is no clear distinction (or an obvious time-lapse) between 'Romano-Briton' and 'Germanic' settlement there, nor a notable difference in goods or farming-practices. The wooden halls once seen as the 'trademark' residences of 'Anglo-Saxon' incomers could be built or used by Britons too – so was there really a dramatic break in continuity of occupation?

Hengest – to use the traditional name for whoever commanded the main force of Germanic mercenaries in the kingdom of the Cantiaci in this period – was thus not the 'first settler' or commander of the sole 'incoming' force of mercenaries, as claimed in the later stories. Nowadays even the basic theory of the invaders being mercenaries who revolted against their employers is questioned and some prefer to see 'peaceful acculturation' by a mixture of incoming traders from Germany and locals who adopted their goods and customs out of 'fashion' as the influence of Rome faded – though this ignores the statement in the *Gallic Chronicle* that Britain passed into the hands of the Saxons in (?) 441–2. It is not clear either who brought these incomers to Britain, as the later stories in Gildas, Bede, 'Nennius', and the ninth-century *Anglo-Saxon Chronicle* all refer to 'Vortigern' (i.e. the 'over-king' of Britain) doing this but there is no proof that such a man existed or at least held wide authority as opposed to being a remote ancestral figure known by the time the Powys 'Pillar of Eliseg' was put up in the eighth century as their dynasty's founder. It is not clear that any such ruler wielded power over the majority of lowland Britain in the 430s or 440s, or that he had dominion over the local British kingdom of the 'Cantii' i.e. 'Kent'. By the ninth century the author of the *Historia Brittonum* ('Nennius'?) in Gwynedd was referring to the local ruler as 'Gwrangon', who Vortigern displaced to give his lands to Hengest so he was clearly seen by that time as the region's overlord.[15] But was Vortigern brought in to add lustre to Hengest's achievement in setting up a new kingdom, by showing him as both seizing and being given a legal title to the region by the man reputed to be the 'national' British leader, not just some local warlord? And was 'Nennius' just using a local, Kentish myth or hero-saga which he had heard about from visiting Anglo-Saxons in his native Gwynedd by the late 820s? (The earlier 820s had seen large-scale 'Anglian' Mercian invasions of that kingdom.) The archaeological evidence for lowland Britain is for political and presumably social atomisation after c. 410, with a sharp decline in non-local trade, a virtual end to building in stone, a complete end to coinage (suggesting a lack of metals or skilled metalworkers), and a collapse even of local pottery industries in southern Britain, e.g. the New Forest. Dating the end of the useage of buildings is notoriously difficult, but clearly the larger ones in both rural areas (e.g. the 'villa economy' with its large estates) and towns were abandoned so people did not have the resources or security to carry on as before. This is not a world with a secure and powerful regional kingship of a respected 'High King' across southern Britain, as implied in the early twelfth century stories of Geoffrey of Monmouth and his sources – and 'Vortigern' is linked by the later genealogical records of Powys to that kingdom in central Wales, a long way from Kent.[16] Could an over-king with such a wide 'reach', a man able to call in an important Germanic captain of mercenaries to defend the SE of Britain and make the locals accept him, exist in the chaotic and decentralised fifth-century Britain that we know of from archaeology?

The legend of Hengest and his foundation of Kent is unclear beyond essentials, with different versions none of which is contemporary, and some of it is shared with 'stock' Germanic hero-tales. The latter have duly been listed and analysed by modern experts such as David Dumville and Patrick Sims-Williams, showing that the 'legend' seems to be just that – an assembly of stories also told of other subtle and crafty heroes who led their peoples to success in new lands and outwitted more powerful rulers.[17] The idea of the new kingdom being founded by brothers appears as early as the twins Romulus and Remus who by the third century BC were agreed as the founders of Rome and appear as such in the late first-century BC histories of Livy, and in Germanic terms two brothers also 'founded' the Goths, conquerors of Italy and Spain, in Jordanes' sixth-century *Getica*. As seen, the dynasty of Kent that ruled to the mid-eighth century was called after his 'son,' or 'grandson' Aesc/Oesc not the founder himself, which is not quite unique as the Ostrogoths (East Goths)' royal line of the 'Amalulfings' was traced to Amal the great-grandson of the people's founder. It may mean that Hengest was later annexed from legend by enterprising dynasts as a prestigious ancestor and Aesc c.500 was the real founder.

Notably, no early 'founder' kings in the fifth century and early sixth century are recorded for the nearby kingdoms of 'Saxon' Essex and 'Anglian' East Anglia, though the archaeology shows extensive early settlement there – so the absence of a reliable and historical 'founder king' for the Kentish kingdom from the period of settlement would not be unusual. This adds to the argument that settlement – assuming that the influx of Germanic goods points to incoming migrants as opposed to trade and cultural changes in 'fashion' – was usually small-scale and relatively peaceful, and large-scale invasions by nucleated bodies of warriors led by a 'hero' owes more to later legends. A successful kingdom, such as that of the later sixth-century Aethelbert of Kent who became the 'Bretwalda' (a term used by Bede,[18] of uncertain origin implying some sort of leadership of a coalition of kingdoms by an overlord) needed a suitably heroic founder. Hengest's name translates as 'Stallion' or 'Gelding', which could be a nickname but also appears to have been the ancient Kentish standard of a white horse; his so-called 'brother' Horsa translates as 'Mare'.[19] The horse was a sacred emblem to many Germanic peoples, and survived as the Saxon (and in due course Hanoverian) regional emblem in later Germany. Many modern historians declare that these names add to the theory that Hengest probably never existed; a legendary Germanic hero known for his prowess and cunning was brought in from sagas to give extra lustre to the founding of the kingdom. For that matter, they argue that the idea of early 'history' of a polity as the deliberate result of literary creation to boost a political 'message' was the norm in this period, not analysis and the sifting of evidence.

The written evidence for Hengest is all of later date, with an independent Continental reference to him in the so-called 'Finnsburg Fragment', a part of an old Germanic poem discovered by the English scholar George

Hickes and published in 1705. In this, Hengest is a warrior in the service of a (half-Danish?) warlord called Hnaef, prince of the 'Hocings' ('people of Hoc', his father), who takes over command of the latter's warband after he is killed when a brawl or dispute breaks out during his visit to the Frisian warlord or king Finn at the latter's eponymous hall, Finnsburg. From a reference to the saga of Hnaef in the surviving Anglo-Saxon heroic poem it appears that Hnaef's sister Hildeburh is Finn's wife in this saga, so Hnaef is visiting his marital kin when some sort of brawl occurs during their banquet. He is killed, but most of his warband manage to drive Finn's men out of the hall and hold it against them for several days; Finn cannot evict them and does not want to lose more men so he negotiates a peace-settlement. Hengest, as the new commander of the warband, agrees to stay on at another hall in the district, but later kills Finn in a clash and is persuaded by his homesick men to leave for their (and his?) homeland, Denmark – which includes the peninsula of Jutland where presumably the 'Jutes' originated. This Hengest was thus a heroic commander of mercenaries of part-Danish/Jutland origin and he led a successful battle against a Danish ruler, Finn, some time in the fifth century – but was he 'the' Hengest? Some modern experts in ancient Germanic sagas, most notably the world-famous fantasy writer Professor J R R Tolkien and Scott Gwara,[20] regard the two figures as being one man, and the latter dated the battle at Finnsburg to the 450s. Given that the story is referenced in the later Anglo-Saxon epic *Beowulf*, its events must predate those of the latter saga, which is set at around 500 as the hero is said to have fought in a dateable invasion of Francia by the Danes around 520 mentioned by Frankish historians. Others are not so sure and think that the two Hengests are separate figures. But 'Hengest' was a name that attracted heroic stories, and the relevant question is whether he was annexed for the identity of the unknown founder of the 'Germanic' – and culturally Jutish, not Saxon – settlements in Kent at a later date as more prestigious than the minor figure Aesc.

The earliest English version of Hengest's arrival is the story in Bede (c.731), who presumably derived it from oral Kentish accounts known to the monks of Canterbury. He dates the arrival of the first Germans (three ethnic groups – Angles, Saxons, and Jutes) at 449–50, the consulship of Marcian and Valentinian. A force of mercenaries, led by Hengest and Horsa, sons of Wihtgisl, came to aid the British king 'Vortigern' against the raiding Picts, and achieved great success but outstayed their welcome, brought in their countrymen, and eventually revolted against their employer.[21] The various versions of the *Anglo-Saxon Chronicle* (later ninth century, written in Wessex) agreed that Hengest and Horsa were brought in during the reign of Eastern Emperor Marcian and Western Emperor Valentinian (449/50 to 455/6) to defeat the Picts in the north but revolted and seized their own kingdom. The version in the Bodleian Library names their place of landing as Ebba's Creek (Ebbesfleet near Sandwich, Kent), as in Bede. The continuing story then has them fighting Vortigern at 'Aeglesprep' or 'Agelesford', which has been traditionally interpreted as Aylesford, in 455; Horsa was killed there, and Hengest and his son Aesc then 'took the kingdom'. (Aesc is alternatively called Hengest's grandson, and supposedly lived to 512 which makes this unlikely.) In 456 they won a victory at 'Crecganford', supposedly Crayford on the River Darent, and the British fled to London leaving all Kent to them. A further victory followed at 'Wippa's Creek' in 465 and after a final victory in 473 the 'Welsh' (the word used here for the first time, meaning 'Foreigners') fled 'like fire'.[22]

The *Historia Brittonum* (Gwynedd) version of the events by 'Nennius' in the 820s is similar in overall structure but dated differently. This dates the Germanic arrival as 428, three years into Vortigern's reign which began in the consulship of Western Emperor Valentinian III and Eastern Emperor Theodosius II, i.e. 425. It has Hengest arriving with three ships to fight the Picts and being granted land at 'Ruym', 'river island' (i.e. the river-surrounded island of Thanet in Kent, next door to the Roman fortress at Richborough and Reculver?). The date is twenty years before Bede's. In due course Hengest persuades Vortigern to allow him to bring in sixteen more ships – and his daughter Ronwen (Rowena), with whom the king becomes besotted. Hengest arranges their marriage, and is granted Kent; forty more ships arrive under his son Octa and their kinsman Ebissa and are sent north to fight the Picts. The Germanic revolt follows, with Hengest and his brother Horsa being driven back to Thanet thrice by Vortigern's son Vortimer and besieged there. A long war occurs with the main battles of the campaign at 'Derguentid', 'Episford' or 'Rithergabail' ('Horse Ford'), and by the 'inscribed stone' on the shore of the Gallic Sea. Horsa falls at Episford, and after the final battle Vortimer evicts the Saxons. He soon dies and is buried on the seashore;

Vortigern invites the Saxons back. This time the treacherous Hengest invites Vortigern and his nobles to a parley where both sides promise to come unarmed, and the Saxons pull knives out of their long sleeves on Hengest's signal to kill all the Britons except Vortigern. He is taken hostage and forced to hand over more territory (i.e. all of Kent?) before he is released, and is deposed by his countrymen. This detailed story may derive from a British written source, but equally likely from legend; some modern historians think that 'Nennius' acquired it from Kent as the Saxon name of the battle of 'Episford' is given first and then translated into Welsh. Its independence from the Bede/*Chronicle* version cannot be verified.[23] The clues in the names of the battles have been reinterpreted in modern times to assert that they need not refer to Kent at all and could be related to warfare on the lower Humber, using alternatives of the ninth century Nennian translated names used in the later *Brut Tyssilio*, for example, 'Rhyd y Pyscod' ('Fishford') for Episford and 'Sathnegabail' i.e. 'Station of the Ferryboat' for Rithergabaill ('Ferriford' on the Humber?). This region was also settled by Germanic incomers in the fifth century and has river names like 'Derwent' that could be an alternative version of the battle of 'Derguentid' or 'Darenth' (and is nearer the presumed sites of conflict by the incomers with the Picts).[24] But the 'Gallic Sea' reference seems to indicate a battle near a Roman memorial near the Straits of Dover (Richborough?), so whoever informed 'Nennius' of the contemporary Anglo-Saxon myths of Hengest's wars clearly meant them to be in Kent. The Yorkshire links seem rather to come from whatever source Geoffrey of Monmouth used for his supposed war between Hengest and Ambrosius culminating in the battle of Conisborough, and the medieval Welsh 'Bruts' similarly refer to this war – but cannot be proved to have used reliable or pre-Galfridian sources for it.

The archaeological evidence for extensive early Germanic settlement in Kent seems to show widespread undefended villages in the first half of the fifth century – and even perhaps a few artefacts from earlier. The fact that 'settlers' lived close to towns such as Canterbury would imply that it was by arrangement with the locals, but there is no evidence of the seizure of or settlement of the 'invaders' in the towns as would be assumed by the stories in Gildas, Bede and Nennius. There is no evidence of the battles and massacres alleged by the *Chronicle* (and by Gildas on the British side). According to this interpretation the whole story of

'Hengest' was a later fabrication, imported from a Continental saga to give a heroic past to the Kingdom of Kent. If there was a real 'founder' of Kent in the 420s to 450s in the sense of a mercenary captain with a British employer decades before Aesc reigned c.500, he may have been unrelated to him. The difficulties extend to the ethnic (or cultural) identity of this leader, though the traditional name for Hengest's father cited by Bede and 'Nennius', Wihtgils/Wihtgisl, sounds 'Jutish' i.e. from the Danish mainland. It has a similarity to the names of the dynasty of Wight, also settled by 'Jutes', as will be seen in the next chapter – their co-founder was a 'Wihtgar' according to the late ninth-century *Chronicle*. But this has been alleged to have been a 'back-formation' by later propagandists to play up the link between the two kingdoms, and may not be genuine.[25] The accompanying argument by Patrick Sims-Wiliams that Bede does not specifically say that Hengest fought in Kent, only that he founded its dynasty, seems however less probable given the strong tradition linking the two. Nor can the use of glamourizing myth by the early settlers (deriving from a practice by their Continental ancestors?) to link their royal families to the ancient founder-gods of the Germanic peoples, most especially Woden ('ancestor' of the royal houses of Kent, Wessex and Northumbria plus others), be used to imply that because one ancestor was invented the entire family trees were fake. Adding the gods to a royal family tree to make it seem more glamorous and worthy of loyalty has been a common practice of 'pagan' tribal monarchies across the world, and as a general rule the further back in time from the composers the more likely the names are to be fictitious. But we cannot say for definite when the 'addition' of the early names in the Kentish royal family tree occurred and if it included Hengest. His generic name as a male horse (either 'Stallion' or the less glamorous 'Gelding') is one argument that he was an invention, but this is not conclusive. His name may have been forgotten and only his 'war standard' remembered. The story of the circumstances of his arrival in Britain and subsequent revolt is logical. The practice of using Germanic 'federates' was common practice in the fourth century and fifth century. Logically, 'Vortigern' could even have placed Hengest in Kent c.450 to oppose a crossing from the Continent by his Roman enemies, backers of his nemesis Ambrosius; a mercenary settlement on Thanet was militarily valuable.

The *Chronicle* states that Hengest died in 488,[26] which is not beyond the bounds of possibility for a young war-leader of the 440s but is unlikely for a man who entered Vortigern's service in 428. The entry may rest on a vague memory that he ruled for forty years (a suspiciously round number, also used for the reign of Wessex's founder Cerdic). Indeed, even the notion of his successor Aesc founding a permanent kingship is dubious, as no records survive of the supposed reign of the latter's immediate successors (?Octha then Eormenric) and the next definite 'king', Aethelbert, Eormenric's son, emerges in mid-century, succeeding in 560 or 565 according to different reign lengths and accession dates in different versions of the *Chronicle*. It is not clear at this early date if the Kentish 'state' (if it can be called that) needed a permanent ruler, i.e. 'king', to administer justice and lead religious rites or just a leader in time of war like other early Germanic states. Famously, the first (first-century AD Roman) writer to analyse Germanic society, Tacitus, says that the German 'tribal' states of his time only elected 'kings' for wartime and relied on civilian 'judges' in peacetime – so was this also the practice in those new proto-states in Britain which were not at war? If Aesc can be dated at around 490–510, Hengest was clearly supposed to have been one or two generations older. In the twelfth century Geoffrey of Monmouth has him being defeated, captured, and executed by Ambrosius at 'Caer Cynan', probably Conisborough in Yorkshire, on uncertain evidence.[27] Hengest remains as much an object of controversy and denial of his existence as does the British 'Arthur', and in both cases centuries of literary invention are to blame. Like Arthur he entered national mythology as a symbol of the heroic origins of the British (or English in this case, though if he existed at all he was not an 'Angle'). The tale of his supposed invasion became fixed in nineteenth-century nationalist history-books, and in the US in 1776 Thomas Jefferson proposed putting him and the even more dubious 'Horsa' on the new nation's state seal to symbolise their English origins.

Chapter Three

Cerdic of Wessex: Man of Mystery

A Question of Ethnic Identity. A British Name for a Germanic Dynast and a Multi-Ethnic Kingdom?

There are major controversies in the accuracy of the traditional account of the 'West Saxon' dynasty and its kingdom. They ultimately proved to be the last Anglo-Saxons to hold out against the Vikings in the 870s thanks to Alfred, and led the reconquest of England in the early tenth century. Their state formed the kernel of the new kingdom of England, with their royal line surviving as rulers of the country to this day. Equally importantly, they were the patrons of the major surviving chronicle-history of the Germanic peoples, the (presumed) late ninth-century *Anglo-Saxon Chronicle*. The victors against the Scandinavians wrote the 'official' history of all the Germanic peoples in England, with the heroic past of their royal house duly being played up. The other kingdoms only appeared in the work for especially important events, mostly already 'featured' in Bede's *Ecclesiastical History* or otherwise connected to the Christianization of England; the feats of pagan kings ignored or denounced by Bede (e.g. Penda of Mercia) were thus marginalised. More is thus known of the West Saxon version of their early history than that of most of the other Anglo-Saxon kingdoms, and a full list of their early kings' military successes was maintained – unlike our knowledge of other major kingdoms such as Mercia or East Anglia. But their origins were somewhat less clear than the *Chronicle* presents. Is this version of events no less dubious than the Kentish legend of Hengest? And can we trust such 'determinist' heroic stories about the early kingdom?

Cerdic and his origins

The ruling house of the West Saxons, known by Alfred's time as the 'Cerdicings', traced their descent from Cerdic – an alleged Saxon descendant of the god Woden, but with a British name.[1] The line of kings was traced back in the various versions of the genealogy presented by the *Chronicle* and by Alfred's biographer Bishop Asser to a son of the god, called 'Baeldeg', who was elsewhere cited in Anglian genealogies as the ancestor of the kings of Mercia and East Anglia – though the length given to the genealogy varied. The idea that 'Cerdic' was a Saxon name is due to its early nineteenth-century revival by the anachronistic Sir Walter Scott for the name of the stalwart Saxon father of his hero in 'Ivanhoe' (slightly altered to the unhistorical 'Cedric' – due to a spelling-mistake?). The other contemporary fifth-century British 'Cerdics' – or 'Ceredigs' – included a mid-fifth-century Welsh prince, alleged founder of the eponymous 'Ceredigion' (Cardigan), and a ruler of Strathclyde who St Patrick corresponded with c. 460 about his slaving-raids on northern Ireland. Cerdic's successor and supposed son or grandson Cynric had an Irish name ('Cunorix'?), which confuses matters further and suggests a multi-ethnic origin. The dynasty were also known as the 'Gewissae', both in Bede's account of the conversion c. 640 and in the ninth century at the time when our current main source of information, the *Anglo-Saxon Chronicle*, was compiled.[2] The genealogy in Asser's version made the eponymous 'Gewis' a son of Brand, son of Baeldeg, son of Woden; the *Chronicle's* version was longer but contained suspiciously rhyming pairs of names that 1950s analyst Kenneth Sisam has suggested were invented by heroic poets. When the extant version of the *Chronicle* was put together at King Alfred's court in the 880s or 890s the kingdom was facing invasion and probable annihilation by the Scandinavian 'Great Army' who had already overrun Northumbria (867), East Anglia (869/70) and Mercia (875 division, with the invaders taking the eastern half). The embattled West Saxons, who had fought the army to a standstill in 870–1 and driven off invasions again in 876 and 878, needed to present their royal lineage as impeccably Saxon as a force for unity, not half- or fully-Welsh/British. This was particularly so as Alfred was seeking to act as leader of all the surviving Saxon and Angle peoples not under Scandinavian rule, and was father-in-law and ally to the new ruler of the surviving half of Mercia, 'ealdorman' Aethelred. He was also recognised as honorary overlord by the surviving Anglian mini-state of Bernicia in northern Northumbria. The royal houses of Mercia and Northumbria were all Germanic in their claimed descent, with the god Woden stated as their ancestor – the West

Saxons needed to be similarly Germanic too. Their 'official' genealogies notably gave their royals' ancestry close links to the dynasty of Bernicia, which may suggest an early alliance given that many genealogies were constructed to express 'political' as much as genealogical facts.

The name of 'Gewissae' given to the kingdom in sixth- and seventh-century literary references is of uncertain provenance and is not Germanic. 'Gewis' does appear in their royal genealogy as an ancestor, as 'Icel' does in the ancestry of the Mercian royal house the 'Icelingas' ('people of Icel'), but the word is more commonly identified as a term for a grouping that became rationalised as a man's name. It may mean 'confederates' and if so would indicate a body of warriors in Cerdic's service who came from different – British, Saxon, and Jutish? – origins. This notion of a mixed warband of differing ethnic origins was normal for the mixed-up political world of post-Roman chaos in fifth-century Western Europe, with many German warriors rising to high rank in the later Roman Empire (including the West's regent in 395–408, Stilicho) and Romans taking service with emerging non-Roman warlords as their empire collapsed. (Attila the Hun had a Roman secretary, Orestes, whose grandson was the last Emperor of the West.) Both Romans and Germans settled in Gaul fought for the Western Roman commander-in-chief of 433–54, Aetius, against Attila in 451; a mixed warband serving a commander of mixed British/Germanic origin in England around 500 was logical. Indeed, it has been argued that the designation of the 'Saxon Shore' for the coast of south-eastern Britain in late Roman military 'command zones' means that it had Saxon settlers there, as mercenaries, as well as its facing a threat of Saxon invasion. These men could have fought for Cerdic – and the Westernmost 'Saxon Shore' fortress was at Portus Adurni, probably the surviving Roman fort of Portchester Castle, which was close to Cerdic's area of activity and saw a 'Saxon landing' in 500 according to the *Chronicle*.

Does the word 'Gewissae' suggest a geographical or a 'group identity' origin? It has been suggested by modern Welsh scholars that there could be a connection between the 'Gewissae' and the south-east Welsh principality of 'Ewias', west of the lower Wye in Herefordshire. This was the region of 'Ergyng', so-called from its presumed origin as the dependant administrative territory of the Roman town of 'Ariconium' south-west of Hereford. Certainly, Geoffrey of Monmouth (from this region himself) gives the title of 'Dux Gewissae', 'leader of the Gewissae', to an obscure South Wales ruler of c. 410 called Owain, alleged son of Emperor Magnus Maximus (ruled 383–8), who has no apparent connection with the royal line of Wessex. He also named Vortigern as their ruler – implying a link to the lands that Vortigern was supposed by the time of the eighth-century Powys monumental 'Pillar of Eliseg' to have inherited from his father-in-law Maximus. The implication is that the title was a British/Welsh one, and possibly linked to the kingdom of Maximus' wife Helen's father, known to later Welsh legend as 'Eudaf Hen'. Eudaf's kingdom, in turn, might be linked to the lands of southern Powys, 'Gwerthyrnion' north of the middle River Wye, which descended to Maximus' daughter Severa and her husband 'Vortigern' according to the eighth century Powys monument the 'Pillar of Eliseg'.[3] Alternatively, the garbled and inaccurate version of Maximus' career in the 'Tale of Macsen Wledig' in the twelfth-century Welsh 'Mabinogi' legends (known since their nineteenth-century translation by Lady Charlotte Guest as the *Mabinogion*') call Maximus' father-in-law the local ruler at Caernarfon, the Late Roman fortress of 'Segontium' in North Wales. Whether 'Dux Gewissae' was a title implying any geographical location, it would seem that Owain and Cerdic both held it. So were they related, and could Cerdic's father – 'Elesa son of Esla' in the West Saxon genealogies – be linked to Ewias or to Vortigern's line in Powys? Vortigern's son apparently transmitted the family claim to the principality of 'Gwerthyrnion', modern Radnorshire around Builth Wells, to his descendants as late as the ninth century – and this region is close to (north of) Ewias. Geoffrey did not concern himself with Saxon history and makes no reference to the use of the title by the rulers of the West Saxons, suggesting that he acquired the information from some ancient Welsh or Breton source where the name 'Gewissae' appeared as that of Owain's lordship – probably in South Wales.

The clues to the mystery of the British connection of the 'Gewissae' and of Cerdic may lie in the names involved. The alleged descent of Cerdic from 'Woden' only means that by the ninth century the West Saxon royal house sought to put themselves on an equal dynastic footing with those other Anglo-Saxon dynasties that made this claim. The 855 entry of the *Anglo-Saxon Chronicle* gives Cerdic as son of Elesa, son of Esla, son of Gewis the eponym of the 'Gewissae'.[4] But Cerdic's elusive father 'Elesa' might have been a similarly-named son of 'Vortigern', king of Powys in the early fifth century, or the elusive Saxon warrior 'Osla of the Knife' who appears by the twelfth century in Welsh literary myth as a foe of 'King Arthur' at the battle of 'Caer Faddon'[5] (which might be the legendary battle of Mount Badon, Arthur's greatest victory). Was the Saxon connection an invention of the later dynasty in order to bolster its credentials to rule other Saxon kingdoms? Certainly, the vague borders of the post-Roman royal 'Celtic states' mean it is plausible that Powys then included Ewias, which is directly adjacent (south-east) to that part of Powys which remained in the realm of Vortigern's son Pascent's family (the area around Builth Wells, on the upper Wye). The name of Powys means '*Pagenses*', i.e. 'People of the rural district attached to a Roman city', and the city in question may well have been Gloucester whose legendary rulers were linked to Vortigern's family.[6] Possibly Cerdic was an exiled member of the region's dynasty, son of a disgraced princeling who fled abroad to become a Saxon mercenary commander in the mid-fifth-century – a foe of Ambrosius? There were assorted roving bands of Saxon plunderers at large in central Gaul in the 460s, including one grouping on the Loire who became embroiled with the local expatriate Britons in Armorica and the elusive British king 'Riothamus' (a name possibly meaning 'High King'). Alternatively, 'Gewissae' may have derived from 'Guentissae' i.e. the people of Gwent to the south-west. Vortigern's son Vortimer was supposed by medieval times to be the father of a princess, Matriona/Madyrn, who married into their royal house – and the local kingdom was thence called the 'Garth Madyrn', 'garden of Matriona', i.e. her inheritance. It would be logical for a British princely adventurer connected to this family who had lost out in an internal power-struggle to flee and take command of a German warband to set up his own kingdom. This is the suggestion of the only historical novelist to tackle the career of Cerdic, Alfred Duggan (an Oxford contemporary of Evelyn Waugh).

'Osla of the Knife' has been suggested as 'Elesa' (or his father 'Esla').[7] If he was an adult battling Arthur around 500–20 at 'Mount Badon' it seems too late for his son to be an independent kingdom-founder in c.494 or 514, the dates of Cerdic's landing in the *Anglo-Saxon Chronicle*,[8] unless Cerdic was attacking the South coast to assist his father's coalition of invaders, and if 'Esla' or 'Osla' had led a major Saxon coalition his fame should have been great enough to survive to the ninth century to be included in the *Anglo-Saxon Chronicle*. Given the fondness of the *Chronicle*'s writers for glorifying the dynasty of Cerdic, Esla/Osla would have made a good first holder of the 'Bretwaldaship' – the mysterious title of obscure origins given to a series of Saxon kings who held authority over several rulers, starting with Aelle of the South Saxons c. 491. Or did Cerdic and his decendants prefer not to play up Esla's role as he had been a mercenary not a 'king' ruling a definitive territorial state, and he had been defeated by the British? It is possible that Cerdic had some sort of dynastic claim on Ewias, from which he or his father had to flee in a dynastic conflict, and he or his heirs thus used the name in their dynastic title. This is the theory put forward by Chris Barber and David Pykitt in *Journey to Avalon: the Final Discovery of King Arthur* (1993).[9] But Cerdic – or his father – could well have been given his British name by a British mother, the father being some obscure Germanic warrior (in British service?). Nor is it clear if there is any significance to the fact that the bogus dynastic descent from 'Woden' created by the time of the *Chronicle's* composition places his ancestors as closest-connected to the ruling house of Bernicia. All that can be said is that the 'official' origins of the family as stated in the ninth century do not tell the full story.

The problem of the 'Anglo-Saxon Chronicle' as evidence for Cerdic: dating and settlement.

The *Chronicle* is dated to nearly four centuries after Cerdic's time, and it is unlikely that written evidence could have survived that long (probably in a monastery as monks were more likely to be literate) in an era of frequent wars and plundering. Oral evidence has a tendency to be embellished and 'improved', and the *Chronicle* was written at a time of the West Saxons' fight for survival against the invading Scandinavian 'Great Army' that had temporarily expelled King Alfred from his kingdom in 878 and still posed a major threat. It retails the basic story of their heroic past and long wars for survival, and naturally in this version of history the founding king of Wessex would have to be a respectable Saxon, descended from the founder-god Woden, not an 'alien' Briton. It shows signs of heavy editing (e.g. in omitting most of the history of kingdoms hostile to or ignored by the West Saxons), and it cannot be ascertained how much material was altered or even invented for political reasons when its current version was composed in the later ninth century at the court of King Alfred. Most scholars assume it to have been a work of 'Alfredian' propaganda designed to glorify Alfred's dynasty at the time of the Viking invasions, possibly commissioned by the king personally. Dorothy Whitelock has disputed this. As it stands, it has a list of Cerdic's alleged achievements:

494/5 'Landing' with son Cynric at 'Cerdicesora' (Cerdic's Shore'). (Five ships.)

500/01 Cerdic 'takes the kingdom'.

508 Cerdic kills the British ruler Natanleod and takes the land as far as Cerdicesford.

514 The 'West Saxons' land at Cerdicsora. (Three ships.)

519 Cerdic and son Cynric 'take the kingdom' and win battle at Cerdicesford.

527 Victory at 'Cerdic's Leag/Leah' or (the 'Peterborough' version of Chronicle, Bodleian Mss. Laud 636) 'Cerdic's Wood'.

530 Victory for Cerdic and his allies Stuf and Wihtgar at 'Wihtgaresbyrg' on the Isle of Wight, which is conquered.

534 Death of Cerdic; succeeded by Cynric.[10]

The lengths of reigns given to early West Saxon rulers are suspiciously synchronised; it is not clear whether Cerdic 'took the kingdom' in 495 or nineteen years later, and the entry for the landing is repeated. Possibly the editors of the *Chronicle* mixed up his own landing as an individual captain, in 495, with that of a second force of 'West Saxons' nineteen years later – two of the copies of the *Chronicle*, the manuscripts from Corpus Christi College Oxford and Peterborough, refer to the commanders in 514 as Stuf and Wihtgar.[11] These two, Cerdic's 'nephews', ended up ruling Wight. It has been suggested that the synchronicity of the rival dates (495 and 514) is due to the habit of early writers of compiling annals on the basis of the Church's nineteen-year 'Dionysian cycles' of Easter dates. Thus, the landing of Cerdic could have been alternatively recorded in entries in the Church tables as occurring in the 'cycles' beginning in 494/5 and 513/14 and the ninth century Alfredian-era reviser who compiled the *Chronicle* had not known to which 'cycle' it belonged so he entered it twice.[12] David Dumville, for example, in his article on the Alfredian-era 'Genealogical Regnal List ' in *Anglia*, volume IV (1986), argues that the regnal lists could even be interpreted as placing Cerdic's likely arrival-date at the start of the next 'cycle' after that, in the period from 533/4.[13] It has also been suggested (by H. M. Chadwick, 1924) that the concept of 'Anno Domini' and 'Anno Passionis' were mixed up – dating by the latter reckoning would be about thirty years later than by the former. He and other writers also maintain that Cerdic's historicity could be dubious and that legends surrounding him were created to account for place-names (e.g. Charford).[14] But it is likely that even 400 years later the dynastic annalists could call on genuine memories/records of who had founded the kingdom – the Saxons did not conveniently 'latch on' to an appropriately heroic figure at the expense of reality, or Hengest rather than his presumed son, Aesc would stand as the nominal founder of the Kentish ruling house, the 'Aescings'.

Also, different versions of the *Chronicle* give slightly different lengths for the reigns of the early kings, for example, the 'Winchester' Mss. in Corpus Christi College, Cambridge gives Cynric's son Ceawlin 17 years and the latter's nephew Ceol 5 but the 'Peterborough' Mss. in the Bodleian, Oxford gives them 30 and 6 years respectively.[15] Ceawlin's overthrow and expulsion from his kingdom, apparently by Ceol and his brother, is 'fixed' at 591/2 – so does the '30' claim refer to him assuming some degree of kingly authority but not sole rule in c.561, a fact which the compiler of the 'Winchester' manuscript was unaware of? Nor is it clear why the *Chronicle* should link Cerdic's supposed grandson, Cynric, with his first campaigns in the 490s (or 510s) when he is supposed to have died as late as 560. Cynric's name was British in origin too – 'Cunorix'. Cerdic's son in the regnal lists, Creoda, is not mentioned in this tradition or accepted by all accounts as a reigning king – though it may be that the *Chronicle* writer simply mixed up the names of Creoda and Cynric. The confusion may have arisen as Creoda predeceased his father, and the chronicler knew that Cerdic was assisted by a colleague so he assumed that to be his ultimate successor Cynric. If Cynric, Cerdic's grandson, was ruling from c.534 to 560 it would be more logical to assume that he was not born until after 500.

Another mystery is why the *Genealogical Regnal List* of the dynasty should present Cerdic as 'taking the kingdom' in 500, six years after his landing[16] – did this imply a formal assumption of a kingly title, or a seizure of enough land to constitute a separate kingdom? Did he 'take the kingdom' from another person – and was that person British or Saxon? Why was this person not named – or does 'take' mean 'set up'? And where was this kingdom, which if it was 'West Saxon' and near his landing-place has left no archaeological record? Was it the British 'civitas' of Winchester, or the Jutish 'province' west of Southampton Water recorded by Bede? It is suspicious that a version of the *Chronicle* gives six years as the time between Cerdic's landing and 'taking the kingdom' and six years between Hengest doing the same two actions in Kent – and exactly equal forty-year reigns for both Cerdic and Hengest. This could be coincidence, but looks more like borrowing details to make up for the real ones being unknown.

Cerdic's career shows him as progressing through conquest of parts of Hampshire where there is no archaeological evidence of Saxon presence that early apart from apparently peacefully-established settlement close to British-held Winchester. Even these sites bearing Germanic goods, for example, at the early 'Saxon' village of Twyford, believed to denote the presence of Germanic 'federates' in the service of the authority at Winchester, may be evidence of no more than enterprising local post-Roman Britons trading with the Continent or of a group of Germanic traders. It is now argued that sites bearing 'Germanic' goods need not be inhabited by ethnic German 'incomers'. There is also the question of a considerable amount of culturally 'Jutish' settlement in the western part of southern Hampshire, i.e. the New Forest area, which was called by the Jutish name 'Ytene' and known to be 'Jutish' in the eleventh century. There was also a distinct 'Jutish' cultural style to artefacts found at villages in the Meon valley in south-east Hampshire, the separate 'people' of the 'Meonwara' (whose name suggests a distinct sense of identity from that of the Saxons around Winchester), and the incoming Germanic Isle of Wight inhabitants of the sixth century were called 'Jutes' by Bede. If Cerdic was either a 'Saxon' or leading a predominantly Saxon warband/army, then he 'must' have been ruling over a combined Saxon and Jutish 'state'. The *Chronicle* presents Cerdic as fighting at the 'Natan leaga' (probably Netley Marsh near Totton rather than Netley near Hamble) against the eponymous 'Natanleod' in ?508 and at Cerdicesford (Charford on the River Avon according to the chronicler Aethelweard) in ?518.[17]

It is also possible that if the locality of the landing-site at 'Cerdic's Shore' was around Ower at the western side of the mouth of Southampton Water, isolated by the estuary and the local boggy moorlands of the New Forest from any British authority and its troops at Winchester, Cerdic may have chosen this site as difficult for his foes to attack. There was one local Roman road from the head of Southampton Water running down to the coast around Lepe (now mostly lost to bog and urban development), but it was a good area for defensive guerrilla warfare – as noted by novelist Rosemary Sutcliff who had her version of Cerdic (a son of Vortigern and Hengest's daughter Rowena) holding out there from King Arthur's troops.

O.G.S. Crawford, in an article on 'Arthur and his battles' in *Antiquity* in 1935, suggested a logical procession by Cerdic, expanding his lands west along the Roman road – the 'Cloven Way' – from the head of Southampton Water to the Avon.[18] This suggests a sensibly logical strategic pushing of his frontiers westward – though unfortunately no evidence has been found of early Saxon or Jutish remains in the area. The name of 'Natanleod', Cerdic's foe at ?Netley, sounds Pictish, deriving from Nechtan, and it is unclear what a man with that name would have been doing ruling in south Hampshire around 500 – though he could have been an adventurer who had carved out his own realm far from 'home' or a commander recruited by a wide-ranging British warlord like Ambrosius or 'Arthur'. Another battle, at 'Cerdices leag' in 527, is less easy to locate though Crawford suggested a site on 'Grim's Dyke' west of the Avon, along the Roman road from Charford.

It is perfectly plausible for Cerdic to have been fighting at Netley around 508 and further west around Charford around 518 to consolidate the borders of a realm based on the New Forest or Southampton areas. The battles are possibly at the time recorded by Gildas as the period of peace following Mount Badon,[19] which has been used as an argument for erroneous dating – but they may have been minor skirmishes which he did not know about. Crawford suggested a link with some of the evasive 'twelve battles' between the British warlord 'King Arthur' and the Saxons around 500. If Cerdic was buried at 'Cerdic's barrow', this indicates that he ruled as far as the extreme North of Hampshire and would indicate that he ruled the whole county.[20] If the Roman administrative divisions of the region reflected the 'tribal' make-up of the area at the Roman conquest (as was usual) and this was still in place in the fifth century, Cerdic would have ruled the area controlled from the pre-Roman tribal capital, 'Venta Belgarum' (Winchester), which may be more or less modern Hampshire. The fate of the other Roman town in the area, further north but within Hampshire – Calleva/Silchester, capital of the pre-Roman 'Atrebates' – is unclear but this town, unlike Winchester, was abandoned. It is thus possible that Cerdic took over the administrative district of the Roman and post-Roman 'civitas' (administrative city) of Venta Belgarum, i.e. Winchester, along with its Romano-British residents – if the town was still occupied, which archaeology has no yet confirmed. Ruling a mixed population, he and his successors had no claim on an exclusively Saxon name for their realm – hence the use of the (?dynastic) attribution of 'Gewissae'.

Early English archaeological sites in the district are few, but they confirm Bede's assertion that the area to the west of Southampton Water where Cerdic landed (the New Forest, recorded as 'Ytene' by Florence of Worcester) was a 'provincia' of the Jutes – as was the Isle of Wight, supposedly conquered by Cerdic and his nephews Stuf and Wihtgar in ?530 and granted to them from ?534. In this case, archaeology cannot be used as a guide to the whereabouts and extent of Cerdic's 'kingdom' as it included peoples using Jutish, Saxon, and post-Roman British goods. The etymology of these names is however somewhat dubious, particularly the coincidence of the name 'Wihtgar' with the Isle of Wight and of a supposed British chieftain 'Natanleod' with 'Natan leaga'/Netley. 'Wihtgaresbyrg' is probably the Saxon name for Carisbrooke Castle, the principal late Roman fortification on the island and so a logical place for a battle – but it may only be guesswork that it was called after a 'Wihtgar'. It is even more so with the supposed naming of Portsmouth after 'Port' in the *Chronicle*'s 501 entry. The latter name is less likely as an individual's than as that of a Roman place-name, possibly connected to the local site 'Portus Adurni' which seems to have been a walled settlement and may be the 'Saxon Shore' fortress at Portchester. As with Carisbrooke being the site of the battle on Wight, it was a logical site for a battle between invaders and defenders but the origin of the name is less certain. Not knowing the origins of the name 'Portsmouth' in the ninth century and lacking knowledge of the Roman nomenclature, a Saxon annalist thus guessed that it came from a personal name and logically made that 'Port'.

Even if Cerdic did fight at Portsmouth and on the Wight, the names of his allies and enemies seem to have been invented to account for place-names that derive from other sources (e.g. the fortress captured by Wihtgar, 'Wihtgaresbyrg', from the Roman name of the island, 'Vectis'). Wight was only conquered by the West Saxon king Caedwalla in 686, when Bede relates that the last – pagan – King Arwald was killed and two princes who fled to the adjacent 'Jutish province' on the mainland were caught and executed.[21] It has been suggested that the *Chronicle* entries for Wight, particularly concerning Stuf and Wihtgar, were incorporated into the West Saxon 'heroic narrative' of conquest after the annexation, or even by King Alfred in the ninth century as his mother Osburh was related to the Jutish dynasty of Wight. Making the founders of the kingdom of Wight Cerdic's nephews thus implied that their uncle was their senior (and overlord) and gave the Cerdicing dynasty a claim on the island. The first two rulers, and 'Port' of Portsmouth whose arrival is included in the *Chronicle,* may in reality have been unconnected with the house or career of Cerdic.The inclusion of Aelle's major exploits in Sussex in the Chronicle – his landing in 477, victory at 'Mearcredesburn' in 485, and capture of Anderida/Pevensey in 491[22] – may be due to ninth-century West Saxon annexation of that kingdom and so acquiring an interest in its past history by 'co-opting' its elite. It has been guessed that Cerdic might have started his career as a warrior in Aelle's service and so included his exploits in his dynasty's memories of their origins. The capture of Anderida in 491 mattered enough to the Wst Saxons to be remembered, unlike other exploits of early Saxon commanders across southern Britain.

The overwhelming mass of Saxon residential sites from the sixth century are in the upper Thames valley, particularly around Abingdon and Oxford. This used to be assumed as evidence of a large-scale Germanic immigration up the Thames, by-passing the British 'enclave' in the Chilterns.[23] Nowadays it is not even clear that the use of Germanic goods denotes Germanic settlers – though it is a logical assumption. In any case, the *Chronicle* makes no reference to the peoples of the upper

Thames area until Ceawlin's campaigns c.580. This would suggest that they were diffuse leaderless groups of farmers, they were peaceful settlers (or a mixture of Saxon and British villagers) who did not establish their sites by conflict and thus had no need of a 'warrior aristocracy' with heroic traditions to be passed down to later generations, or they had rulers who were not connected to Cerdic's dynasty and so were expunged from the West Saxon royal records used in compiling the *Chronicle*. The claim that their leader under Ceawlin, Cutha the conqueror of the Chilterns (c.571), was Ceawlin's 'brother' is unlikely given the dissimilarity of the two men's names – it is more likely to reflect a political alliance.[24]

Can the two be reconciled? It has been suggested that Cerdic, whether or not a rebel British warlord (or one with a British mother) in command of Jutes and/or in the service of a British authority at Winchester, established a multi-ethnic lordship and his successors in the mid-sixth century then linked it up with the predominantly Saxon but leaderless settlements in the Thames valley. This was the solution put forward by R. G. Collingwood and J. N. Myres in *Roman Britain and the English Settlements* (1937). The *Chronicle* has Cerdic's 'grandson' Cynric advancing through Wiltshire, to Old Sarum (Searubyrg) in ?552 and Barbury (Beranbyrg) in ?556.[25] Certainly, the first important ruler of an expanded kingdom appears to have been Ceawlin, Cynric's 'son', the first West Saxon ruler to be called '*Bretwalda*' by Bede.[26] But did the later 'Saxon' identity of that kingdom hide a far more complex real-life origin, and how ethnically 'Saxon' was its royal family? In a way, this question about its dynasty's origins may serve as a microcosm of the real mixed Brittonic and 'Anglo-Saxon' ethnic origins of the southern English, as suggested by recent investigation of their 'DNA'. Just how far was an 'Anglo-Saxon' identity, for kings or ordinary citizens, a simplistic cultural 'construct' not a proveable ethnic origin?

Chapter Four

Early Mercia – An 'Anglian' Kingdom? Partly British, and a Welsh Not An English Ally?

A s seen in the preceding chapters, even where we have the supposed names and details of the careers of the 'founders' of Anglo-Saxon (or Jutish in Kent) dynasties their probable history seems a good deal less clear or ethnically exclusive now than it did a century or two ago. The way that 'history' and what we would now think of as 'literature' (in the early mediaeval period, mostly oral) were conceived of in the period when the kingdoms were established was not the same as it is now. The 'founding sagas' of kingdoms were not necessarily based on reality as opposed to inspiring heroic myths, and their purpose was to legitimise the rulers and elites at the time when they were composed (e.g. by showing their heroic ancestors in the best possible light) and to inspire their audiences. Tales were told of the founders and other important ancestors that could incorporate details taken or adapted from earlier legends of other heroes, and unifying personalities could indeed be invented where needed for a current political project – to express the current 'unity' of a people by giving it a glorious and purposeful past. Given the similarity of details for the careers of rulers of different kingdoms, even in the supposedly 'historical' *Anglo-Saxon Chronicle* for the fifth century and sixth century where Hengest and Cerdic both land at one date, 'take the kingdom' at another, and reign for forty years, the modern mythographer and sceptics have had a field day denying the historicity or plausibility of these 'records'. Even in the case of monastic writers with a tradition of more 'objective' written history from ancient Greek times to fall back on, they had a 'determinist' project to pursue of showing the forward march and triumph of the (Catholic) Christian Church and the workings of Divine providence in the defeat of the pagans and victories of the virtuous. As we have seen, modern analysts have shown that the British/Welsh 'historians' had their own agendas. In the case of the Anglian historian Bede, he used his sources with more demonstrable carefulness and weighed up evidence but still played up his Catholic heroes, saints and kings alike, and ignored or minimised the careers of pagans.

This has tended to obscure the history of the major kingdom in the Midlands that dominated southern England from the mid-seventh century to the early ninth century at the expense of Bede's own Northumbria – Mercia, ruled in the crucial earliest period of its dominance from c.625 to 655 by the pagan warlord Penda. The latter was the – frequently successful – foe of Bede's heroes in Northumbria, kings Edwin (ruled c. 617 to 633/4), Oswald (ruled 634/5 to 642), and Oswy (ruled 642 to 670/1), and until Oswy killed him and brought his 'empire' (with its thirty or so sub-rulers) down at the battle of Winwaed in 655 Mercia often had the better of their conflicts. Penda killed Bede's Christianizing hero-king Oswald at the battle of Maserfelth/Maes Cogwy (Oswestry?) in 642, aided by the 'Celtic' Christian Welsh princes of Powys, and was arguably a stronger ruler over much of southern England for longer in the period from 634–55 than the Northumbrian rulers who Bede accords the title of 'ruler of Britain' – which is presumably the rank of 'Bretwalda' ('wide ruler' or 'Britain-ruler') used for the list in the Wessex-based *Anglo-Saxon Chronicle*. The specific word 'Bretwalda' is only used in ninth-century West Saxon sources, which has led to suggestions that it was a local invention, possibly used to glorify their first such ruler – Egbert, who ruled Wessex from 802 to 839 and took military supremacy in England from Mercia in battle in 825. Bede never concedes the title of senior ruler of Britain, or the rank of pre-eminent king in southern Britain, to Penda despite his victories. Nor does he do so after the failure of his own sovereign Oswy of Northumbria's attempt to break up Mercia in 655–8 when its resurgent kings, Penda's sons Wulfhere (ruled 658 to 674/5) and Aethelred (ruled 674/5 to 704), defied Northumbria successfully and defeated various rulers in southern England without any Northumbrian intervention. Their power and claims were ignored by him and his 'heroic narrative' of Christian triumph concentrates on Northumbria and where appropriate its missionaries in the south, although unlike Penda these kings were evangelising Christians.[1] The *Anglo-Saxon Chronicle* ruthlessly marginalises Mercian history throughout the seventh, eighth and early ninth centuries despite – or more likely because – it was usually stronger than the kingdom of Wessex, in which the *Chronicle* was written for King

Alfred in the later ninth century. Mercia was not finally defeated in a major battle and eclipsed by Wessex until Egbert's victory at Ellandun in 825, but its history is usually only covered when it impinges on that of Wessex.

The sources are thus inclined to marginalise or play down the importance of Mercia, which provides us with a major problem in analysing its real history and importance and the careers of its rulers. If any chronicles or heroic sagas once existed recounting its history, these have failed to survive with the exception of a few hagiographies and the *Tribal Hidage*, a late seventh century (?) administrative list of its sub-provinces and their acreage.[2] Indeed, it is not even clear that the latter (which concentrates on listing the amount of tribute due from various regions to an unknown administration) is Mercian rather than East Anglian or southern Northumbrian, as it lists Mercia among the tribute-payers along with the constituent regions of most of its neighbours. This 'Mercia' is listed at a relatively smallish 30,000 'hides' of land, parallel in size with Kent and Sussex and much smaller than Wessex which has 100,000 'hides', so it is presumably 'central' Mercia, the nucleus of the kingdom, not all the extended later kingdom – and when Bede refers to the size of the central Mercian 'state' annexed or made vassal to Oswy of Northumbria in 655–8 he puts this at 7,000 'hides' north of the River Trent and 5,000 South of it.[3] We have a reverse problem for Mercia to those for Kent and Wessex – the absence of much early documentation, accurate or otherwise, for its history. Does the absence of material reflect the absence of identifiable leadership in the period when the first Germanic settlements were being established in the Midlands? Or does it reflect rather the non-survival or marginalisation of its ruling families, so there were no men (and it usually was men who led and determined public policy in this age of warfare though later Christianity gave women high status as queenly patrons and abbesses) who had an interest in keeping up the memories of their fifth-century and sixth-century predecessors into later centuries?[4] Did the emerging dynasty of Penda in the seventh century deliberately ignore the traditions of other once-important local dynasts, in the interests of ruthless and politically necessary centralisation around their own power? In that cause, did this aggressive dynasty even create its own fictional genealogy which traced its leaders back – as usual for an emergent Anglo-Saxon kingdom – to the prestigious supreme pagan war-god Woden, to legitimise its demands for obedience? Were its defeated and marginalised rivals really just as ancient and worthy of respect, but were obliterated from the records?[5] Or does the modern argument among scholars that an absence of reliable (or any) names for early regional kings means that none that existed apply here? In that case, the 'sub-states' named after regional 'peoples' and/or geographical features, of which Mercia has many, were formed by agreement among local groups of settlers as a matter of administrative, judicial, military and economic convenience requiring co-operation for security and success. There were no long-term leaders, merely war-leaders appointed for campaigns when needed, and a similar form of co-operation on a larger scale was involved in the 'creation' of a new kingdom of Mercia.

The archaeological evidence for Mercia – a name which means 'The Mark' aka 'Frontier', i.e. the frontier between the Anglian settlers identified by Bede and the British/Welsh – suggests a considerable degree of settlement in the lower Trent valley in the later fifth and early sixth centuries, probably linked to a similar high degree of settlement to the east in Lincolnshire (the then separate kingdom of 'Lindsey' whose ruling dynasty had a mixture of Anglian and British names) and the Fens. This settlement then spread gradually westwards into Leicestershire, Nottinghamshire, Northamptonshire, Warwickshire and Staffordshire in the mid-late sixth-century, and NW over the upper Trent into Derbyshire and the Peak District. There are no accounts of any conflicts between these Germanic 'incomers' and the local British in the *Anglo-Saxon Chronicle*, which concentrates on warfare in Southern Britain involving the kingdoms of the West Saxons (or 'Gewissae') and their neighbours in Sussex and Kent plus occasional information about the West Saxons' later allies in Northumbria. Mercia and its eastern neighbours East Anglia (apparently a merger of the lands of the Anglian 'North Folk', i.e. Norfolk, and 'South Folk', i.e. Suffolk) and Essex are neglected, and Mercia is only referred to when its first clashes with the West Saxons occur in the Cotswolds in the mid-620s. Given the division of Mercia in the later seventh century into a multitude of local regions, their names mostly based on geographical identity rather than the identity of founders or dynasties, it is usually now presumed that the Midlands kingdom formed from a 'coming together' (voluntary or enforced by one leadership?) of these regional kingdoms into one state.[6]

This was presumably for purposes of mutual aid and military alliance, though its dating is unclear and some historians have used the (later) medieval charters across the Midlands that refer to sixth-century events (foundations, battles, conquests, and other 'records' of Anglian expansion moving Westwards) as proof of a coherent and co-odinated gradual move Westwards by incomers, culminating in the creation of a 'state' around 585 to 590.[7] Others argue that this later material is largely mythical.

The creation of a coherent state was probably aimed against the British to the West, but it soon had another context entirely – inter-Anglian warfare. This arose from the strong enmity from c.610 between Mercia and its Northern Anglian neighbours in Northumbria, a state formed by the merger of the fifth-sixth century settlements of 'Deira' in Yorkshire and the younger state of 'Bernicia' North of the Tees by the Bernician warlord Aethelfrith in c. 604. As the latter forcibly unified the Anglian and conquered the British kingdoms of the North in a series of campaigns from c.593 to 604 and then moved south-west to fight the British of North Wales successfully at a battle around Chester or Bangor-on-Dee around 615/16, did this threat as much as wars with the British impel the Mercian peoples into unity? And without the continuing looming threat of Northumbrian aggression under Aethelfrith's successors, his wife's brother Edwin in 617–33/4 and then his own sons Oswald and Oswy, would Mercia have failed to consolidate under one successful dynasty?

There are major questions concerning those 'mini-states', later absorbed into larger ones, whose names seem more clearly to indicate a geographical not a personal identity. The greatest number of these in any of the Anglo-Saxon kingdoms are in Mercia, suggesting that this did indeed have a separate development from its (smaller) neighbours. But was the creation of Mercia a result of these kingdoms coming together voluntarily for their defence, or of a 'push' by one particularly aggressive and talented dynasty – that of Penda's family? Given Mercia's size compared to the relatively small and compact kingdoms of Kent, Sussex, and East Anglia, forming a 'coalition' of settlers from disparate local mini-states to use their resources together seems logical, whether or not in response to an outside threat. One clue here is the nature and approximate dates of the ruling dynasty of Mercia, whose 'founder' was said to be Creoda in the 580s although the dynastic ancestor after whom it was named was the even more obscure 'Icel'.[8] The 'definitive' version of the family genealogy recorded by the eighth century gave five generations from Icel to Penda, who was killed in 655 aged around fifty – Icel, Cnebba, Cynewald, Creoda, Pypba, and Penda.[9] As with Kent (and the Goths on the Continent), the man after whom the dynasty was named was not the first to rule the 'state' according to surviving records; but in this case the founder was later, not earlier than the first ruler of the kingdom. The dynasty of the 'Icelingas' does not go back as far as those of Kent, Sussex and Wessex, as if there was approximately thirty years per generation Icel was alive around c. 480 to 500; the kingdom was only created c.580 by his great-grandson Creoda, according to later royal genealogies and the dubious medieval Midlands charters. It was not coeval with settlement, presenting different problems from the situations in Kent and Wessex; did the early settlers have military leaders at all, were these men later forgotten and if so why, and was settlement a haphazard affair involving local initiatives by small groups of households not larger warbands? The archaeology shows widespread Germanic settlement in the lower Trent valley by the early sixth century, but there is no record of who ruled these areas at the time.

As seen from the later seventh century 'Tribal Hidage', the kingdom included such distinct peoples based in distinct areas as the 'Pecsaetan' (the Peak District), 'Wreocensaetan' (the Wrekin, east Shropshire), and 'Arowsaetan' (River Arrow, Warwickshire), along with the 'Hecani' or putative 'West Mercians' of Worcestershire. In the south-east were the 'Cilternsaetan' of the Chilterns, and in the East were the 'Gyrwe' of the Fens. These appear to be based on geographical identity, which begs the question of whether the locals had seen themselves in that context as a separate 'people' from their arrival or if that identity was created for them in the seventh century by the new kingdom of Mercia for administrative convenience. In the cases of certain of these 'provinciae', as Bede calls them, there is an apparent link to a previous Roman unit, for example, the 'Wreocensaetan', based around Viroconium/Wroxeter by the Wrekin which was still inhabited in the sixth century, and the 'Magonsaetan' of western Herefordshire based around Magnis (Kenchester).[10] There is also an argument among modern analsyts about whether they took over coherent Roman units, such as a town with its dependent rural territory or a large rural estate. This seems to apply in the Cotswolds where the Late Roman estate boundaries can be seen to survive into Anglo-Saxon estates and villages, and also to former Roman towns in the East Midlands such as Great Chesterford in the Fens. Does it apply to the territory around Magnis/Kenchester in western Herefordshire too, or to the post-Roman British/Welsh kingdom of 'Ergyng' in south-west Herefordshire which seems to reference the name of the local Roman town, 'Ariconium'? It probably applies to their acquisition of a new 'Anglo-Saxon' (actually Anglian) identity in that the latter used an extant geographical name, and implies that the older post-Roman name was known and was worth using so logically some of the original inhabitants stayed on to coexist with new 'Germanic' arrivals. The proportion of the two ethnic (or cultural?) groups is unclear, but the names used for local sites seem to be mainly Germanic so they probably provided the bulk of and linguistic preferences of the elite.

But were all the rulers of these new mini-states ethnically 'Anglo-Saxon', or local Mercian? There is a question here over the surprising names of the kings of the two main West Mercian sub-kingdoms, 'Hwicce' and 'Magonsaetan'. The seventh-century kings of Hwicce – based around Winchcombe in Gloucestershire, a long way from Bernicia – have Bernician names, (e.g. Eanfrith and Oswald). Is this coincidence, or were they Bernician in origin – refugees from the ruthless state-builder Aethelfrith (ruled Bernicia c.593 to 617, all Northumbria from c.604) who sought new lands in a distant kingdom? His takeover of his Anglian neighbours in 'Deira' south of the Humber was apparently by force, killing or expelling its rulers, and the refugee prince Edwin, son of king Aelle and brother of king Aethelric, took refuge in (Welsh Christian) Gwynedd and later in (Anglian pagan) Mercia, on the latter occasion marrying its king Ceorl's daughter. Presumably fearing a Mercian invasion to restore Edwin to power, Aethelfrith then forced Ceorl to exile Edwin on pain of attack; he fled to East Anglia whose king Raedwald successfully invaded Northumbria in ?617 and restored him by killing Aethelfrith in battle near Doncaster. Did other foes of Aethelfrith flee into Mercia and end up ruling a new mini-state there, and was this by permission of its kings or as independent actors?

The first recorded king of the Herefordshire/Shropshire region, Merewalh, was supposedly a son of Penda of Mercia but his name means 'noble Welshman'. Was he a son of Penda by his legendary Welsh wife, Heledd of Powys, or a Welsh adopted son or stepson? The royal charters show that Merewalh's family claimed to be kin to Penda's family, and to the Mercian royals' Kentish 'in-laws'. Merewalh, who ruled for around thirty years, was succeeded by a son called 'Merchelm', i.e. 'Helmet of the Mercians/the Frontier', which suggests his intended role as a protector of the western frontier of Mercia; the royal family's saintly womenfolk played a major role at the local abbey at Much Wenlock. The state appears to have centred around a Roman administrative unit, that of the town of 'Magnis', Kenchester, near Hereford, and there is no archaeological evidence of Germanic settlers pre-650 so it was probably ethnically mainly British/Welsh. The survival of pre-Anglian land units and Christianity is very likely, but a British identity and a definite early linkage of Merewalh to the town of 'Magnis' and its district of 'Magonsaetan' (as opposed to the Anglian 'Hecani' around Much Wenlock) has been doubted by Margaret Gelling.[11] The close links of various Anglo-Saxon royal dynasties and secular and religious elites over a wide area – a contrast to usual assumptions of intense parochialism in an era of poor roads and unrest hindering travel – can be illustrated by the way that the royal abbesses of Merewalh's dynasty, for example, St Mildfrith, interacted with their Kentish relatives on the Isle of Thanet in distant Kent, and the importation of the ex-bishop of Mercian-sacked Rochester to be the first Anglian Christian bishop of Hereford by the man who had done the sacking in 676, King Aethelred (ruled 674/5 to 704).

No lines of rulers, hereditary or otherwise, are recorded for the Mercian sub-states although they presumably supplied most of the 'duces' – 'governors', not of royal rank, by the normal Latin translation – recorded in the Mercian hegemony by Bede for the year 655 when these various sub-rulers marched into Northumbria in Penda's invading army. Most of the thirty sub-kings who he says fought for king Penda at the battle of Winwaed near Leeds[12] must have come from within Mercia, given that his non-Mercian allies (e.g. East Anglia) still had full royal status. It may be that they were 'decentralised' local kindreds who only needed a ruler in times of war – as the earlier Germanic peoples recorded by Tacitus in Germany in the first century only elected special war-leaders and otherwise relied on 'judges'. Notably, there are no recorded kings for Kent in the three or four decades before the accession of king Aethelbert c.560 or in Sussex in the century or so after the conquests by Aelle c.477–90 – in both cases, times of peace. (But were the records lost rather than the central power of kings lapsing?) Alternatively, the triumphant central kingship of Mercia established c.580/90 may have suppressed all record of its defeated local rivals, and no lists of kings have survived to be recorded in later books.

However they were governed, such 'mini-states'were at serious risk of being conquered by aggressive, predatory neighbours with larger armies with determined leadership, as the Franks did to the Thuringians in Germany in the sixth century and the Saxons in the mid-late eighth century. The most famed warlord of early Mercia, Penda, may well have conquered his Midlands rivals from the local 'peoples' during his reign from c.625 to 655, and Caedwalla of Wessex similarly suppressed assorted sub-kings recorded for mid-seventh-century Wessex during his dynamic reign in 685–8. The pagan warlord Penda achieved a clear military ascendancy for Mercia in central England from the 620s to the 650s, as the catalogue of his victories shows, though Bede did his best to downplay his power and importance (no doubt due to religious antipathy). Similarly to his treatment of Cadwallon, Bede portrayed him as a violent and treacherous warlord intent, as a heathen, on wiping out the Christian Northumbrians in 655, with his defeat being due to Divine favour to the virtuous king Oswy.[13] His obscure 'Icelingas' dynasty traced its royal line to a fifth-century Continental king called Offa of the Angles,[14] however much this was propaganda rather than fact and intended as a 'political' claim in order to demand the loyalty of the Anglian peoples in England to the Mercian kings. But it had not made any impact in the sixth century when Mercia appears to have been a mixture of small groups of settlers identified as 'peoples' by their geographical areas (e.g. the 'Pecsaetan' of the Peak District, 'Wreocensaetan' of the Wrekin, 'Arowsaete' of the Arrow valley, 'Cilternsaean' of the Chilterns, and 'Gyrwe' of the Fens). The creation of Mercian power is obscure but appears to have been mainly Penda's work, given how little is known of his forebears; the nomenclature of his immediate family suggests that their 'power-base' was probably Warwickshire where the name of the village of Pebworth may be linked to his father, king Pybba. There was an early grouping of Anglian villages in the region, centred on the Avon valley, by around 600. By the same reckoning, his ancestor Cnebba could be linked to Knebworth in Hertfordshire and by this reckoning their kin could have moved West as opportunities for seizing new lands arose – and the Warwickshire link could account for Penda's first appearance as a warlord fighting the West Saxons over the Cotswolds at Cirencester c. 628.[15] But this linkage of names may be coincidence.

The south-east Midlands seems to have retained a degree of local self-identification as a separate political unit, the kingdom of the 'Middle Angles' which Penda gave to his eldest son Peada in 653. There were also separate, smaller regions – originally named after a specific local group of settlers? – such as the 'Spalde' around Spalding and the 'Hicce' around Hitchen, which from their location seem to have been incorporated into the later lands of the 'Middle Angles', plus the elusive 'Faerpingas'. The 'original' area of Mercia as identified in the 'Tribal Hideage', i.e. that not covered by the named local regions around it or with separate local names for its peoples, seems to have been in east-Northamptonshire, Leicesterhshire, and Nottinghamshire. But it is unclear if this was the authentic political nucleus of a kingdom that was set up in or near the 580s, the lands ruled by the 'Icelingas', to which other lands around it were added later as satellites. There is also the question of other, originally distinct territories beyond central Mercia that were later in the seventh century ruled by subordinate allies of the Mercians, usually relatives of their royal house. The best-known of these is 'Surrey', the 'South Region' – probably of a very obscure kingdom of the 'Middle Saxons' in what is now Middlesex, whose kings (if any) are unknown. Frithuwold is the only recorded king of Surrey, as known from charters of 673–5. At the time he was the sub-king there for its overlord Wulfhere of Mercia (ruled 658 to 674/5), whose sister Wilburh was his wife. Surrey had been settled back in the later fifth century or early sixth century from the archaeological record, and may have existed as a kingdom – a vassal of the East Saxons in the sixth century and later of Kent. However Frithuwold is unlikely to have had a hereditary claim except via female descent, as land-grants for South-East Mercia in the seventh century show that a family with alliterative names similar to his held estates in Buckinghamshire, within Mercia, and the similarly-named (early eighth century) St Frideswide had royal relatives ruling around Oxford. Frithuric, possibly his father or brother, granted land at Breedon-on-the-Hill in Leicestershire to a monastery c.675/90. If the family dominated that area they were probably of 'Middle Angle' blood and/or allegiance, sub-kings of Penda in the 640s to 655. Frithuwold was probably Wulfhere's nominee to rule the middle Thames Valley, as an important and loyal local noble. He granted Chertsey Abbey an important charter in 673/5. His daughter (St) Osyth, whose strong religious interests may have been inherited from him, married Sigehere, king of the East Saxons from c.663 and another protégé of Wulfhere; their son was the saintly Offa who abdicated to journey to Rome. Frithugyth, who married king Aethelheard of Wessex (a Mercian ally from c.726), may have been Frithuwold's younger daughter or grand-daughter. The Surrey kingship was duly suppressed by Mercia around 700 and disappears from history – with its more extensive neighbour in the Cotswolds to the West, Hwicce, following suit later that century

The first king of Mercia was Creoda, son of Cynewald, son of Cnebba, son of Icel (first of the dynasty in England). The extensive nature of Anglian settlement across the Eastern Midlands in the sixth century and the existence of many separate 'peoples' in the seventh century suggest that the Anglian advance from the Fens was a piecemeal matter but not whether it was mainly peaceful or if not whether settlement was made by small groups of families or larger units. Did the latter (e.g. the 'Pecsaetan' of the Peaks or the 'Wreocensaetan' of east Shropshire?) come together for wars or administrative arrangements and 'law-giving' assemblies by mutual agreement, and live separately the rest of the time? Or was there constant conflict and a 'winner takes all' situation that the stronger warlords triumphed in? The eventually dominant Icelingas may have suppressed records of their rivals, but it is assumed that those few 'peoples' named after an individual assumed the appellation from a war-leader. The name 'Mercia' means 'Mark' or 'borderlands' (as later taken over by Mercian scholar J.R.R. Tolkien for his Saxon-like kingdom of Rohan). Logically the requirements of anti-British warfare on this frontier, and later rising tension with expanding Northumbria once the latter overran Deira in c. 604, led to some warlord – probably Creoda – assuming authority as leader of a coalition of minor kingdoms. As seen by Bede, the northern frontier of Mercia by c.617 was the (lower) River Trent. The probable date for the establishment of one kingdom is the 580s, with some putting the 'accession' of Creoda (formal assumption of leadership of a coalition?) as c.589. The *Chronicle* gives his date of death as 593; it is assumed that his son Pybba, father of the first great Mercian king Penda, succeeded him. But Pybba died within a decade or so and was not succeeded directly by Penda, so presumably the latter was either under-age or lacking in military backing at the time (c. 605?) so an adult war-leader with greater support took over.

This man was Ceorl, an obscure king of the Mercians in the early seventh century who is not in the recorded dynastic descent of the Icelingas. His predecessor was presumably Pybba, father of Penda; it is not clear if Ceorl was a usurping sub-king who took power on Pybba's death or if he was chosen as king as a proven warrior unlike Pybba's young sons. According to Bede he was the king who gave refuge to the exiled Deiran prince Edwin, enemy of Aethelfrith of Northumbria, c.615/16. Presumably the two men formed an anti-Northumbrian alliance against the threat posed by Aethelfrith, with Edwin intended as a Mercian candidate for the throne of Deira, as Edwin married Ceorl's daughter Cwenburh.[16] But within a year or so Aethelfrith compelled Ceorl to expel his son-in-law. It was Raedwald of East Anglia who aided Edwin in killing Aethelfrith and installing him in Northumbria in ?617,[17] and Edwin's accession would have ensured better relations with Mercia. Ceorl's date of death is unknown, as the length of his successor Penda's reign is disputed; the most probable version gives Penda a 30-year reign from 625/6 as in the 626 entry of the *Chronicle*.[18] This entry also names dynastic founder Icel's (Continental resident) father as Eomer – a name used by J. R. R. Tolkien for his king of Mercia-like 'Rohan'.

Two great warlords and regional strongmen: so why were they not counted as 'bretwaldas'? Penda and Wulfhere.

Mercia only emerges into the limelight of history under its greatest early ruler, Penda son of Pybba, who ruled it from around 625 to 655. The most distinctive and successful of the early Mercian kings, he may not have been the founder of its political unity but he did establish its military greatness as a worthy rival to Northumbria – who his predecessor Ceorl had shrunk from confronting over Edwin's presence at his court c.616. Arguably Mercia dominated the 'South-Humbrian' peoples in the seventh century as Northumbria dominated the 'North-Humbrians', though the useage of the former term as a means of reference to the peoples of the region is rare[19] so it never became a distinct and accepted region as Northumbria did. Penda was unlucky in receiving a bad press as a a pagan from Bede, whose Christian Northumbrian royal heroes were his foes. He was at least as powerful as the presumed 'Bretwalda'/over-king (as named by Bede) Oswy in 642–55, though he has been omitted from the list of such overlords in Bede's work and in the *Chronicle*, and already by this date he had been able to bring down the previous Northumbrian 'Bretwalda' Oswald (Bede's main Christian warrior-king hero) in battle in 642[20] so he was militarily his equal. The 'kingship' which he took over from Ceorl some time after 620 was more properly an over-kingship over many junior rulers and 'peoples', based on geographical districts, whose multiplicity is preserved in the 'Tribal Hideage'. Penda may already have been a sub-king when Pybba died c.605 and been superseded by an older rival. Ceorl was reigning around 616–17 when Edwin of Deira took refuge at his court, and Penda probably reigned for thirty years in which case his death-date of 655 would make his accession-date as 625. To confuse matters it seems that one source claimed that he reigned for fifty years, but this may be a reference to his becoming a sub-king, succeeding his father Pybba in a local kingship but not as supreme king,[21] or a simple mistake arising from his living for fifty years – another apparent mistake refers to him as aged fifty at his accession which would make him active and fighting until he was eighty.[22] He first appears in the *Chronicle* in 628 as (probable) victor of a battle over kings Cynegils (ruled from c.611 to 643) and Cwichelm (his sub-ruler and probably his son) of the West Saxons at Cirencester.[23] He need not have been 'over-king' of Mercia by this date, only the local king of the Cotswolds area (presumably annexed by Ceawlin of Wessex after his local victory at 'Deorham'/Dyrham in 577 and lost to Mercia since). Bede implies that his reign began with his assisting Cadwallon to overthrow Edwin of Northumbria in 633/4 and lasted twenty-two years to 655,[24] but this may relate to his period of full power if it was this campaign that secured his position within Mercia. A claim has been made that he and Pybba may have had estates on the Warwickshire Avon, around Pebworth, and that Penda emerged as a successful war-leader in this area. If so, the extension or confirmation of Mercian control of the Cotswolds would have served to win him adherents and a reputation as a warlord, before or after his assumption of the central kingship of Mercia.

Mercia was weak enough in 626 for Edwin of Northumbria to march across it unhindered to attack Wessex after an attempt to assassinate him arranged by its king Cwichelm who sent an assassin with a poison-smeared short sword.[25] The assassin was barely foiled, by the self-sacrificing bravery of a thegn called Lilla who was duly commemorated with a still extant memorial cross. There was clearly no attempt by any Mercian ruler to stop Edwin's advance and aid the West Saxons, though the two kingdoms fighting together might have won and if they acted separately Edwin was capable of 'taking them out' one by one as the opportunity arose, especially as Penda was a pagan and (at least as recounted by Bede) Edwin could already be counted on as pro-Christian due to his recent marriage to Aethelburh, daughter of the late first Christian king of Kent, Aethelbert (d 616/17). The conversion of Northumbria and its king to Roman Christianity did not accompany his marriage to a prestigious Christian princess and the arrival of a bishop to minister the sacraments to her and her co-religionists, in which Edwin's Kentish marriage had followed the precedent of Aethelbert's Frankish marriage c.581. But Edwin had been living among ('Celtic' rite) Christians in Gwynedd as an exile in the early 610s before he arrived in Mercia – the later Welsh sources indeed say that it was a 'Celtic' Christian bishop from Rheged, ex-King Rhun, who first baptized him. He was familiar with Christianity and the benefits it offered a king (e.g. Church patronage for his rule and membership of the international European comity of 'civilised' nations with the Franks and Spanish Visigoths), and was probably held up in converting himself and his kingdom by fear of a 'patriotic' backlash from conservative nobles who did not want to incite bad luck from the old gods. According to Bede, it was the 'double miracle' of Edwin's narrow escape from a Wessex-sent assassin and the birth of a daughter to his new wife in 626 that persuaded him to consider converting; it was confirmed after Bishop Paulinus told him that a mysterious dream which he had had of a stranger offering him future triumph and restoration to his throne (in return for following his counsel) at the lowest point of his exile was a vision of Christ. This was the 'spin' put on it anyway.[26] As seen from the pagan court of Mercia, Edwin might well turn into a devout son of the Church who sought to win God's favour by converting his neighbours too, and he was already an ally of Kent and had a grudge against Mercia for refusing to support him against Aethelfrith in c.616. But whoever was in command in Mercia, either Ceorl or Penda, allowed Edwin free passage to attack Wessex – either there was an interregnum before the selection of a new king or the current ruler dared not risk his army against the seasoned war-winner Edwin with his tough Northern troops.

At this stage Mercia would appear to have been a loyal (?) ally of Northumbria and to have recognized Edwin as its overlord or at least not stood in his way when he was challenged. But this changed later in the 620s, as the kingdom of Northumbria made a bold but ultimately unsuccessful attempt to overrun Gwynedd in North Wales – which Edwin would have known from his exile there. Edwin had evidently acquired a fleet, probably based in the Dee or Mersey, as he occupied the island of Mon/Anglesey and appears to have conquered the Isle of Man (also ruled by the Britons) too.[27] From the Welsh poems that celebrated his foe Cadwallon ap Cadfan of Gwynedd, the latter was at one point forced to seek shelter on the island of Priestholm off Mon as Edwin overran his lowland domains, and some time after this he had to flee to Ireland. But he returned with reinforcements, evicted Edwin from Gwynedd, and pursued him back into Northumbria in a campaign of 'fourteen battles for Britain' – and in a dramatic 'volte face' Mercia became his ally. For the first known time an 'Anglo-Saxon' kingdom fought in alliance with a British/Welsh state against a fellow-Anglian one, which raises the question of whether this sort of strategy of 'my enemy's enemy is my friend' was more common than is usually assumed in post-Roman Britain. Were all the 'Anglo-Saxon' and 'British' states normally formed into two opposing power-blocs with a major element of ethnic hatred (plus 'Christian vs pagan' rivalry until the Anglo-Saxons converted to Christianity)? Or is this just assumed on account of the basic details of major wars between them, which were in fact less common than supposed, surviving in the records? Was the overall strategy of regional dominance what mattered, resulting in each major regional state surrounding itself with a bloc of dependent allies that could include those of 'rival' ethnic groupings (or at least with an elite from that background)? As we shall see, Mercia is a major candidate for this form of regional politics that challenges some basic assumptions about the mutual hostility of a steadily 'advancing' Anglo-Saxon and steadily retreating 'British' society. The Mercian alliance with Gwynedd in the early 630s is the first known instance of this – and in the 640s it was to be allied with another Welsh state, Powys. Northumbria too had its British/Welsh links, in this case vassal sub-kingdoms in the Pennines (e.g. Elmet in south-west Yorkshire) and possibly a vassal Rheged into the early seventh century – plus its post-Edwinic rulers Oswald and Oswy having spent over a decade in exile at the Gaelic monastic missionary centre of Iona in the Hebrides and been converted to Christianity. Oswy had one British wife, Riemmelth the heiress of Rheged, plus one Irish princess as his wife or mistress – and Penda had a part-Welsh 'son' with a Welsh name, Merewalh.

Penda was in control of Mercia by October 633 (or possibly 634), when he was the ally of his sister's husband Cadwallon of Gwynedd in a conclusive war with Edwin. Edwin was killed at the battle of Hatfield Chase near Doncaster, a site implying a Northumbrian/Mercian war over control of Lindsey east of the River Trent. Edwin's elder adult son Osfrith was killed too; his younger brother was take captive by Penda, presumably held hostage, and later allegedly murdered in violation of an oath.[28] This crushed Northumbria and broke it up temporarily into its constituent parts, with Penda dominating south of the Trent. This was probably when Mercia finally took control of Lindsey, and in the 640s Penda was able to invade East Anglia several times to punish its Christian kings. Cadwallon ravaged Deira and seems to have been aiming at evicting its Anglian population, which may imply a desire to restore the local British kingdom as his allies – if Bede is to be trusted given his aggressively pro-Northumbrian stance. Bede called him a nominal Christian by faith but as bad as any barbarian by his murderous habits and massacres of civilians.[29] Cadwallon was however killed by the Bernician heir (St) Oswald, son of the late Aethelfrith, in battle in Bernicia, at Heavenfield (Hallington) on the Tyne near Hexham, a year later – with Bede celebrating the way in which the devout Christian convert Oswald planted a cross as his standard on the battlefield and sought and received Divine backing, like the Roman Emperor Constantine 'the Great' defeating the pagans at the battle of the Milvian Bridge in 312.[30] In fact, as Bede conveniently downplayed, Cadwallon was a Christian too, allied to the pagan Penda – and neither of those two warlords saw religion as a barrier to strategic alliances. Oswald revived Northumbrian power in 634/5 to 642 and formed an alliance with distant Wessex to the south, visiting it for the conversion of its king Cynegils to Roman Christianity, marrying his daughter, and presumably aiming their alliance at Mercia.[31] But Penda remained unchecked until 642, though the losses that the Gwynedd army had suffered in its defeat by Oswald were evidently serious enough to ruin it as a military 'Great Power' and it dropped out of regional warfare for decades. Possibly this led to Penda seeking a more useful alliance with Gwynedd's now better-resourced Southern neighbour, Powys, which then included the upper Severn valley around Shrewsbury and the post-Roman hillfort of the Wrekin – one of these is probably the elusive 'Pengwern' headquarters of Penda's ally King Cyndylan of Powys in the era's heroic Welsh poetry. Given the amount of poems written in celebration of the accomplished war-leader Cyndylan, whose men were hailed as the 'heirs of Arthur', and of his alliance with Penda (which was clearly not seen as something to deplore despite his being an Angle and a pagan), the army of Powys must have had good leadership and a strong 'esprit de corps'. Some uncertainty surrounds whether these poems were in fact written in the mid-seventh century and sung by bards at the court of Cyndylan and after its downfall, as they allege, or were in fact ninth century; the ascription of them to the Rheged poet-prince Llywarch 'Hen' is dubious as he was active in the 590s and he would have had to be very old to be celebrating Cyndylan's court in the 640s or 650s. But in any case this was an era of a – second – major alliance between Christian Britons and pagan Angles, which stands on its head the idea that there was inevitable and unceasing war between the two rival ethnic and cultural groupings.

At some time Penda seems to have allowed his brother Eowa to become co-ruler, but it is not known if this was voluntarily (to secure a loyal deputy when he was campaigning far afield?), to satisfy the requirements of local custom for several co-rulers, or an imposition by Edwin or Oswald who sought to weaken his power.[32] Possibly the fact that the Welsh sources, 'Nennius' in the ninth century and the *Annales Cambriae* in the tenth century, regarded Penda's reign as lasting for ten years from the battle of 'Cocboy'/Maserfelth refers to his sole rule; until 642 he had had Eowa as co-ruler and from 653 he had his son Peada.[33] In the 640s Penda's next major ally was also British – and Christian – i.e. Cyndylan, prince of Powys, while he was raiding (Christian) East Anglia to kill two kings, the ruling Egric and his predecessor Sigebert, in one battle and then evict their devout successor Anna for allying with Wessex against him as if he not Oswy of Northumbria was its overlord.

The complicated picture of Anglian/British relations in the 640s and 650s West Midlands (co-existence not confrontation?) may also include a British principality at Lichfield, ruled by Morfael, and the enigmatic name of Penda's 'son' Merewalh, ruler of Herefordshire and southern

Shropshire. Twelfth century Welsh literature made Penda marry Cyndylan's sister Heledd; this may be based on reality. The Welsh lament for Cyndylan says that he fought as an ally of Penda,[34] and the Mercian/ Powys alliance may explain why in 642 a major war with Oswald saw the Northumbrians marching into Shropshire – to attack Powys as well as Mercia? Penda routed them at Maserfelth (Oswestry) on 5 August, killing Oswald who was apparently dismembered and strung up on a tree in a contemptuous pagan ritual riposte to his Christianity. The one major Mercian loss at the battle was Penda's brother Eowa. From 642 to 655, Penda was the main military power in southern England. He was able to raid deep into Northumbria to humiliate Oswald's brother Oswy c.644, reaching as far north as Bamburgh which he set afire (the wind put the flames out in time).[35] This argues for confidence and impressive logistics, even if his host moved fast and lived off the land and Oswy wisely shirked battle. He had married a sister off to Cenwalh, king of the West Saxons from 643, and when that king repudiated her for another woman c.645 Penda invaded Wessex and drove him into exile in East Anglia for three years.[36] Probably in retaliation for East Anglian aid to Cenwalh, Penda then invaded that kingdom around 650 and drove king Anna into exile; the latter was able to return, presumably when Penda went home, but was killed in a second Mercian attack around 653. His brother Aethelhere succeeded him, as a Mercian vassal. Logically this would make Penda, not the new king Oswy of Norhumbria, overlord of the kingdoms South of the Humber – but he is not given any ranking as a 'bretwalda' by Bede in the 730s, which may reflect opinion about Penda in the Northumbrian court and Church rather than the actual politics of the mid-seventh-century. Just how reliable is Bede's list of 'overlord' kings?

An uneasy treaty with Northumbria in 653 saw Penda's eldest son Peada, new king of the 'Middle Angles', marry Oswy's daughter Aelfflaed (Elfleda) and Oswy's son Alchfrith, sub-king of Deira, marry Penda's daughter Cyneburh.[37] The peace did not last, though it is uncertain if Peada's conversion to Christianity and importation of Northumbrian missionaries infuriated his father on religious grounds, as treachery to the ancestral faith. Bede claims that he despised those who converted as traitors but did not ban it.[38] Behind Bede's story of his widespread ravaging in Northumbria in the next few years – and refusal of offers of vast amounts of gold to desist – it is evident that he did not feel safe until

Oswy was destroyed. Another massive invasion of Northumbria in 655 involved thirty 'duces' including the ruler of the East Angles, plus troops from his Welsh allies, and penetrated as far as Bernicia again. Oswy's nephew Aethelwald of Deira joined the invaders despite Penda having killed his father Oswald; did Penda offer him his father's and uncle's throne? Oswy avoided battle, but Penda could find enough supplies to keep his army active and eventually the two men came to terms. A treaty was agreed, probably with Oswy's son Egfrith as a hostage as he was at the Mercian court at the time of the battle which followed, and Penda was returning south when hostilities resumed. Possibly encouraged by heavy rain to intercept the Mercians and prevent Penda getting away with his loot, Oswy attacked Penda at the river Winwaed (?near Leeds) on 15 November 655 and secured a crushing victory; Penda and Aethelhere were among the many casualties, with numerous men drowned in the swollen river. Mercia was left at Oswy's mercy, though he retained Peada as his sub-king of the Middle Angles for some months.[39] Penda was probably aged around fifty (one unreliable source says eighty), and had had a remarkable career of success which was minimalised by his Christian detractors. He was unfortunate to be the last successful pagan warlord in England, the arch-foe of Bede's heroes, and for no Mercian narratives of events to survive, though his toleration of his eldest son's conversion and his two Welsh Christian alliances show that he was not a militant foe of the new faith when this would conflict with political advantage. He laid the foundations for the domination of the southern English by Mercia in the later seventh and eighth centuries despite his personal destruction in the disaster of 655.

The same dominance of southern English affairs can be ascribed to Penda's second son Wulfhere, who was not regarded as 'bretwalda' either. The second of three sons of the great warlord, he and his brothers were left at the mercy of Oswy of Northumbria when he killed their father at the river Winwaed in November 655. Oswy allowed Wulfhere's elder brother Peada, his own son-in-law, to retain the kingdom of the 'Middle Angles' (south-east Mercia), where the younger boys presumably fled, but all Mercia was annexed on Peada's murder at Easter 656. Oswy sought out Wulfhere to kill him, but he was hidden by loyalists and re-emerged three years after the Winwaed disaster (i.e. autumn 658) to lead a national Mercian rebellion. Oswy's governors were driven out, and Wulfhere restored the independence of Mercia which Oswy had to accept.[40] For all practical purposes Wulfhere was as dominant in southern England after c. 660 as Penda had been, with clear military primacy over Wessex. Raiding South to or from 'Ashdown' (the Berkshire downs) in 661 to drive back king Cenwalh, he was able to hand over parts of eastern Hampshire to his ally Aethelwalh of Sussex and to compel the kings of Wight to transfer their allegiance from Wessex to Sussex. Several West Saxon sub-kings seem to have been killed, with Cenwalh humiliated by the loss of territory,[41] and Wulfhere was clearly aiming to build up Sussex at Wessex's expense and cut the latter's resources down to size so he could not be challenged again. Sussex was seen as his regional 'proxy', and was built up accordingly – but was to fall victim to the raiding Wessex prince Caedwalla after Aethelwalh's death. He also formed an early alliance with king Earconbert of Kent, whose daughter Eormenhilda he married, and was overlord of Essex by c.663. He was able to install the ex-bishop Wine of Wessex in the see of London c.670. His local control was probably exercised by his brother-in-law Frithuwold, who appears as his sub-king of Surrey by 674 and seems to have been Mercian in origin.[42]

Wulfhere may have converted to Christianity at Peada's Christian court, which had been converted from Northumbria; his choice as the first bishop of newly-Christian Mercia c.658 was the Northumbrian Trumhere. His own religious links were mainly with the see of Canterbury. Either he or Penda installed loyal dynasties of long-lasting sub-kings in their south-western territories – the possibly Northumbrian line of Eanfrith and Eanhere in Hwicce and the possibly half-Welsh line of Merewalh (?his half-brother) in Magonsaetan. He also assisted the new, Anatolian-born Archbishop Theodore of Canterbury in summoning the first synod of all the bishops in England at Hertford, within Mercia, in 672.[43] In 673 Wulfhere was confident enough of his influence in Kent to demand the regency for the under-age new king Eadric, Eormenhilda's nephew. This had to be conceded initially, but within a couple of years locals rallied round Wulfhere's rival Hlothere, the late King Eadric's brother. Kentish troops may have been needed to assist his invasion of Northumbria in 674, a first direct challenge to Mercia's one-time conquerors arising from a confrontation over control of Lindsey. Oswy's son and successor Ecgfrith, who had once been a hostage at Penda's court, defeated the invasion and regained Lindsey, and the resulting battle between Wulfhere and the new

King Aescwine of Wessex at 'Beda's Head' probably implies a West Saxon attempt to take advantage of this.[44] Revolt in Kent on Hlothere's behalf against the pro-Mercian regency followed. Wulfhere died unexpectedly before he could retaliate, late in 674 or early in 675; if Bede is correct that he reigned for seventeen (full) years, as opposed to ruling into his seventeenth year, it may have been later in 675.[45] He was probably in his mid-thirties. His brother Aethelred succeeded him. As powerful a king in southern England as his father though usually unwilling to confront Northumbria, he had as much right as Oswy to be accounted senior ruler South of the Humber but was literally sidelined by Bede despite his role as a major Christian patron. Arguably this reflects anti-Mercian prejudice and a determination by Bede to show that Northumbria was the rightful and consistent leader of the southern as well as northern Anglians, Bede having grown up in the 670s at the time of Ecgfrith's wars with Wulfhere and his equally devout successor Aethelred. So has reliance on the Anglian world of the seventh-century as seen from Tyneside in the 730s (and from Wessex in the 890s) distorted the real picture of inter-state relations in this era? The real importance and centrality of Mercia – and its militaristic elite culture? – are well illustrated by the 2009 discovery of the 'Staffordshire Hoard', not far from its principal royal centres of Lichfield and Repton. The collection of valuable and intricately-carved objects dug up include goldwork with a variety of Christian and non-Christian themes and many which seem to be hilts from swords, though it cannot yet be definitively dated within the seventh and eighth centuries – it may have been a collection of loot belonging to a senior warrior from Penda's or Wulfhere's army (or an invading Northumbrian?).[46]

Chapter Five

Bernicia, Deira And Early Northumbria: Another Kingdom Of Mixed Heritage?

The records are equally miminal and the 'real history' obscure for the emerging Anglian kingdoms of the 'Northumbrians', i.e. the peoples north of the River Humber. In this case, there was a union of two earlier kingdoms around 600 as in Mercia – slightly later than the traditional date for the foundation of the latter, and possibly partly a reaction to it – and another case of an aggressive new state (with two initially rival dynasties, not one as in Mercia) subsuming various local Brittonic kingdoms which evidently became its vassals and probably contributed more to the new kingdom's personnel and culture than has usually been assumed. As with Mercia, the main surviving literary accounts on the Anglo-Saxon 'side' are the 730s work of Bede (a 'local' from Bernicia in this case so better informed and not intrinsically hostile to its rulers) and the later ninth-century *Anglo-Saxon Chronicle* – West Saxon, but based in a kingdom that had been a Northumbrian ally in the seventh century and preserved more of its history and even its basic royal lists and 'dates'. It was embarrassing for the devoutly Christian Bede that the early successes of the warlords of Bernicia North of the Tees – which unified the two kingdoms into Northumbria by force c. 604 – were carried out by pagans, but he gave more detail for the run of victories by unifying King Aethelfrith 'the Crafty' (ruled Bernicia c. 593 to 617 and all Northumbria from c. 604 to 617) than he did for the Mercian pagan unifier Penda. He seems to have looked on Aethelfrith as a sort of Anglian version of King Saul of Old Testament Israel, i.e. the pagan but admirably successful predecessor of the holy and more divinely-favoured King David (i.e. Edwin of Northumbria, who converted to Christianity). In his opinion, Aethelfrith conquered more of the enemy (i.e. the Britons) and ravaged more territory, like a ravening wolf, than any other Anglian warlord. Saul was a sinner who turned against God and ended up killed by the national enemy, as Aethelfrith was killed by the East Anglians in ?617 after failing to insist that their king Raedwulf expel the refugee Deiran prince Edwin whose kingdom Aethelfrith had overrun, but the young rival who had fled abroad in fear of his wrath – Edwin, the new David – restored the nation's power and success and won favour with God as His champion.[1] Thus Bede was able to put a positive 'spin' on the history of pagan Northumbria, although his account of the period from its initial settlement ('547' in the *Chronicle*) to the 590s was minimal, and as with 640s-650s Mercia we have a literary version of the British 'side of the story' of the endemic regional warfare too.

In this case there was no long-term Anglian-British alliance but constant military struggles, and we possess (later copies of) the Welsh poems composed by the bards belonging to the courts of the Bernician kings' British enemies – the poems of Taliesin, bard to King Urien of Rheged (as mentioned earlier, killed by a British rival around 589 while besieging the Bernicians on the island of Lindisfarne), and the poems of Llywarch 'Hen', bard to Urien's son Owain (killed around 594, possibly at the battle of Catraeth). These poems, plus *the Gododdin* by Aneirin (c. 600?) which commemorates the heroic but disastrous campaign of a collection of noble British warriors from the north against Aethelfrith's Bernicia at the battle of Catraeth, was long assumed to be an authentic and crucially early collection of evidence of this period and its society from the British point of view, as seen in studies from the 1920s to the 1960s. More sceptical analysts of the texts such as David Dumville would now place some or all of it in the ninth century, compiled by the heirs of the defeated North Britons in exile in Wales or their local admirers and so subject to mythologization from a viewpoint 200 years after the events in the same way as the Ancient Greek myths of the Trojan Wars. The details of sixth-century battles and kingdoms in the *Historia Brittonum* of 'Nennius' c.829 and later the *Annales Cambriae* and Irish chronicles may also have been influenced by myth and political 'spin' building up the 'glorious past' of the 'Men of the North' and their heroic struggle against Bernicia – though some experts still assert that some of the poems attributed to Taliesin, Llywarch Hen, and Aneirin use genuine late sixth early seventh-century wording so are contemporary.[2] But in either case, it does give a 'snapshot' of the heroic society and fierce rivalry between Briton and Angle – and among the Britons – in the period, and adds to the lack of much archaeological evidence of early Anglian settlements north of the Tees in confirming the long wars and decades of insecurity. In this situation an expert and cohesive Bernician 'war machine' was built up ready to take on and often overwhelm its southern neighbours after victory over the Britons and their neighbours of Dal Riada by c.604 – and the lack of any large 'bloc' of Anglian settlements in these early decades may imply that many defeated Britons were forcibly enrolled in the new state as Aethelfrith's and later Edwin's vassals. But the dominant language of Northumbria within reach of the new 630s Christian missionary base at Lindisfarne was certainly Anglian (i.e. Germanic), as Bede says that incoming Dal Riadan missionary leader Bishop Aedan (Gaelic-speaking) had to rely on King Oswald to translate for him into Anglian when he was preaching to the local thegns when he first arrived.[3]

The various British kingdoms of the north between the Humber and the Forth that may have emerged from the post-Roman dominions of Coel 'Hen' (see Chapter One) had by the mid-late-sixth-century split up, and were remembered in the later Welsh legends of the 'Men of the North' ('Gwyr a'r Gogledd') as being ruled by the descendants of Coel. One major kingdom was Rheged, probably in Cumbria and Lancashire and ruled successively by Urien ap Cynfarch and his son Owain after the eclipse of the rival kingdom of Caerluel/Carlisle at the battle of Arderydd/'Arthuret'(?) around 573; another kingdom was based in York until the declining city fell to the Anglian settlers on the lower Humber (the kingdom of 'Deira') around 580. A British kingdom survived in Elmet in south-west Yorkshire to be annexed as a vassal by Northumbria in the early seventh-century, though as with Rheged we cannot be certain how long its kings survived as sub-kings of the Northumbrian kings; it still had a British ruler, Dunaut, around 600 and the later Welsh account of Cadwallon of Gwynedd's war of 633/4 with Edwin of Northumbria refers to it taking place in Dunaut's kingdom. Another minor sixth-century Yorkshire kingdom was ruled by the mysterious 'Arthwys son of Mar' (whose name sounds like 'Arthur' but there are no Arthurian legends linked to him) and Pabo 'Post of Britain' (presumably meaning 'Strong Defender' as with a post holding up the roof of a residential hall) was also overrun.

Finally there were the kingdoms north of the Tees, the semi-forgotten 'Bryniach' in Northumberland which gave its name to Bernicia (did the latter claim to be its heirs?) and the kingdom of 'Din Eidyn' around Edinburgh whose ruler Mynyddog 'the Golden' was reputed by Welsh poetry to be a generous host and who recruited the legendary band of British heroes who were killed by Aethelfrith at the battle of Catraeth around 595–600. The latter campaign, commemorated within a few decades in heroic poetry (the '*Gododdin*') with an echo of the Ancient Greek saga of Troy was a band of the region's most notable heroes joined up for an attack on a neighbouring kingdom and most ended up dead in a bloodbath, immortalised the most famous campaign of the era for centuries. But as with the Mycenaean Greeks at Troy, it was the swansong of an era and the kingdoms involved soon collapsed or were overrun, in this case by expanding Northumbria, and it is still unclear if 'Catraeth', an Anglian fortress attacked by the Britons who were heavily defeated, was Catterick in Yorkshire as the name implies. Or was the war intended to forestall Aethelfrith taking over the resources of his Anglian neighbour Deira and so becoming too powerful for the Britons to match? The latter were inclined to internal rivalries and petty jealousy, as in the Arthurian stories of 'Arthur' being overthrown in a rebellion led by the 'traitor' Medraut or Modred (aided by Maelgwyn of Gwynedd?), and indeed Urien was recorded in Welsh tradition as having been murdered during the siege of Lindisfarne c.589 by an emissary sent by his rival, king Morcant of Bryniach – whose kingdom was soon to fall to Bernicia. This tendency towards British civil wars had been deplored by Gildas in the 540s, though we do not know where he was writing (one later hagiography made him the son of a Clyde region chief, Caw), and he implied that it had disrupted an era of peace from invasions after the battle of 'Mount Badon'.

The literary evidence may have exaggerated the scale and heroic qualities of the later sixth-century northern British wars, and the surviving royal genealogies were written down (copied accurately or altered for political reasons?) in Wales in the ninth century so sceptics claim that this evidence is not a contemporary record but subject to later mythologization.[4] But it is clear that the Britons were a formidable if often disunited foe for the Bernicians and the archaeology shows only a few definite Anglian settlement sites on the Northumbrian coast north of the Tees during the sixth century. The kingdom of Bryniach, its main foe whose name it took, was presumably based at the major regional hillforts of Traprain Law and

Yeavering Bell, and with only a few scattered references to the wars in the *Chronicle* and Bede it may be that most of the Brittonic population of the region were forcibly enrolled in the new kingdom of Bernicia as vassals of Aethelfrith and his predecessors and its British – and Christian? – components have been played down in a 'narrative' on both sides of the wars that preferred to present an unsubtle picture of conquest on one side and ruin on the other.

It appears from the sources that the 'family' (dynastically linked or not) of 'founder' warlord Ida of Bernicia battled the local British kingdoms through the later sixth century. Its history and kingship then is obscure, but its surviving genealogy and occasional references in the *Anglo-Saxon Chronicle* suggest that it was established by Ida c.547 and based on the coastal rock-fortress of Bamburgh (allegedly called 'Din Guari' as a British fortress and then renamed after Bebba, wife to his son Aethelric). The date of '547' for the conquest and fortification of Bamburgh[5] is a very rare mention of northern affairs in the Southern-based *Chronicle* for this period, though notably Northumbrian history has more entries than Mercian history and this presumably reflects the seventh-century alliance between Wessex and Northumbria – a logical time for details of early Northern political and military developments to have been transmitted to Wessex. The Irish chronicles speak of a major plague in Britain and Ireland in 547 or 549 and the (later) *Annales Cambriae* in Dyfed say that king Maelgwyn of Gwynedd died in that outbreak, so logically an epidemic and losses of personnel in Bryniach could have left the fortress of Din Guari undermanned and enabled an ambitious warlord with an eye to the main chance to seize it. It was many miles from the then Anglian settlements on the lower Humber, the nucleus of the very obscure kingdom of Deira which was said in a note in Nennius's history to have been ruled by a king called Soemil (great-great-great-grandfather of Ida the Bernician founder) some time in the fifth century when 'Bernicia was separated from Deira' which may mean that a breakaway settlement was established north of the Tees.[6] Possibly Ida, presumably of royal Deiran blood or one of their 'in-laws' if his connection to their dynasty is not just later prestige-seeking propaganda, was a restless warrior or pirate captain with ambitions that felt constrained in this region and sought a new field for his activities which he could dominate. Bernicia seems to have been restricted to a few embattled settlements on the coast for decades, though the picture of ceaseless Anglo-British hostility may have been distorted by the surviving sources being mainly British heroic poetry that concentrated on crisis not co-existence and the *Chronicle's* concentration on the importance of Bamburgh may have marginalised other, non-celebrated settlements.

Ida's father Eoppa, mentioned in the *Chronicle* and in a fragment of chronicle derived from Bede now preserved in a monastery in Berne,[7] may be connected to the 'Ebissa' remembered in legend as a fifth century Germanic warlord operating in the north-east and later linked to the campaigns of Hengest's son Octha who was said to have campaigned in the region until his father died c.488 and then gone south. (Ebissa duly made it into Geoffrey of Monmouth's 'history' as a warlord who fought Ambrosius and Uther in the later fifth century, but it is unclear how historical this is.) In fact, as we have seen, Hengest's successor and alleged son was Aesc or Oesc, not Octha. According to the royal genealogy of Bernicia Ida died after a twelve-year reign, which would 'officially' make it 559 but may have been in the 560s.[8] He was not succeeded immediately by any of his (six or twelve?) sons, suggesting that they were under-age; Glappa was the next king. Not listed as one of Ida's sons, he succeeded him; it is possible that although Ida had a multitude of sons none were adult or militarily experienced enough to lead in the fierce warfare with the local British of Byrniach, and that Glappa was an older kinsman or allied war-band commander who took control by agreement or usurpation. He either reigned for one year or five, which may mean that after a year he had to share power with his eventual successor, Ida's son (?) Adda. He probably died in the mid-560s, and was succeeded by Adda who reigned for around seven years.[9] The latter would bring us to around 568.

The Bernician king-lists and early dating are complicated both by different versions giving different lengths of rule to various kings and a different order of succession, and the possibility that as the lengths of their reigns do not add up correctly to the length of time between the 'foundation' c. 547 and Aethelfrith's death c.617 several kings ruled simultaneously. Multiple rule was more common in the mostly peaceful, nucleated states of south-east England, for example, Essex and later Kent, but is possible for a land of scattered settlements needing their own warlords or a group of rival leaders who would not concede power to one man. There is also the question of muddle between the Aethelric of Bernicia, father of Aethelfrith and son of Ida, and his contemporary Aethelric of Deira – and to add to confusion the *Chronicon ex Chronicis* gives the Bernician ruler a reign of two years in Bernicia and five in Deira, either mixing up the two men or alleging that it was Aethelric not Aethelfrith who conquered Deira.[10] The lengths of reign as recorded in whatever sources were used by the twelfth-century historian Florence of Worcester in the *Chronicon ex Chronicis* was:

Adda 7; Glappa 5; Theodulf 1; Freothulf 7; Theodric 7; Aethelric 2; Aethelfrith 24.[11]

The conquest of Deira, however, was placed by the *Historia Brittonum*, nearer to events than Florence, at twelve years into Aethelfrith's reign, so if he ruled for twenty-four years and was killed in 617 this would set his accession at 592/3 and the conquest of Deira at 604.[12] There was also Hussa who ruled for seven years, apparently before Aethelfrith. To add to the problems, the genealogical lists do not name Theodulf and Freothulf (as well as Glappa) as members of the dynasty of Ida, so they may have been independent or usurping regional commanders; the same applies to Hussa who Florence does not mention.

It is however agreed that Aethelric was a son of Ida and so a brother of Adda, presumably younger as he ruled later; and Aethelfrith was Aethelric's son and if he reigned for twenty-four years came to power around 593. Hussa is very obscure, not placed in the genealogies as a son of Ida, and presumably a senior warlord of the hard-pressed coastal kingdom who assumed leadership by agreement or by a coup against the 'legitimate' line. Alternatively, he may have ruled with and eclipsed one of Ida's sons at a time when the kingdom was divided. His seven-year reign is usually placed before that of Ida's son Theodric, who ruled for seven years and preceded Aethelfrith's father Aethelric. Aethelric (probably) ruled for around seven years, Aethelfrith succeeding c.593, so by this reckoning Aethelric took the throne around 586. This was the time of the major wars with Rheged and Bernicia must have been under serious military strain given the resources and 'esprit de corps' of the warbands of Rheged, but we have no idea of the course of the campaigns or which of the Bernician kings were killed in which battle, though at least one was killed by Owain of Rheged. One version has Hussa as Aethelfrith's immediate predecessor, in which case he not Aethelric would have fought Urien of Rheged in the late 580s and his son Owain in the early 590s.

His reign is usually assigned to the late 570s to early 580s. Hussa's son, Hering, was recorded as leading an army against the British in 603;[13] the family had enough military and landed power to remain a source of military leadership under the rule of Aethelfrith.

Aethelric is alternately given as ruling in the 570s, i.e. after Adda, or immediately before his son Aethelfrith, i.e. from the mid-late 580s. The sketchy dates given in the *Chronicle* for royal reigns from Ida's arrival in the north (c.547) to Aethelfrith are at variance with other sources. Several kings may have reigned at once to account for the 'overlap' in the tally of years reigned in this period – or some non-dynastic rulers have dropped out of the extant records. Aethelric may thus have been co-ruler for several years with Theodric, king in the 580s, possibly an older brother whose realm was severely threatened by British counter-attack under Urien of Rheged. The extreme pressure which Bernicia was under from Urien and his son Owain probably continued into Aethelric's reign. If he, rather than his 590s namesake of Deira (?the man overthrown or killed by Aethelfrith of Bernicia in c.604 as the states were unfied), was the elderly and unfortunate ruler called Aethelric referred to by William of Malmesbury in his 1120s history[14] this would fit in with the contemporary British poet Taliesin's panegyrics to Owain's successes against Bernicia. Owain's principal Anglian enemy was 'Fflamddwyn', 'the Flame-Bearer'[15] who presumably had a name for burning places; if this was Aethelric he must have been an active and feared foe. This Anglian ruler was killed in battle by Owain some time before 593/4. Assuming that he was under-age in the late 550s as he was not a contender for the kingship for another thirty years but he had an adult son in c.593, he was probably in his forties or early fifties. He has probably been mixed up with his contemporary King Aethelric of Deira, the other Anglian constituent part of Northumbria and son of the latter's most renowned King Aelle. The latter was well-known enough in the Southern kingdoms to have his accession-date of '560' noted by the *Anglo-Saxon Chronicle* in Wessex, along with that of King Ceawlin of Wessex the same year, with them both cited as ruling for thirty years which coincidence may have helped in making his accession memorable.[16] However, his date of death is unclear as one source puts it at 588 and Bede has him still ruling when St Augustine landed in Kent in 597 – though this has been suggested as a mistake arising from Aelle having been alive when the first Catholic bishop, i.e. Kentish queen Bertha's Frankish chaplain Liudhard, arrived which was earlier (c. 581?).[17]

The Winchester version of the *Chronicle* also gave Aelle's legendary ancestral line in the 560 entry,[18] an honour only accounted to very few non-Wessex rulers (e.g. the Kentish dynasts) so he may have been a West Saxon ally – but it is not clear if his father Yffi and other ancestors reigned in Deira or not. (They were traced back to the god Woden as usual for pagan dynasts, but via the same ancestor as the West Saxon royal house.) The ancestor who 'separated Deira from Bernicia' was named in the 820s Welsh work of 'Nennius' as Soemil, five generations back from Aelle – late fifth century? – and five from Woden, but this is well before the settlement of Bamburgh. Does it refer to the first Northern settlements set up independently of Deira? The number of late fifth-century and sixth-century Anglian-style grave-goods and other discoveries made around the lower Humber and in the vicinity of York and Leeds suggests that the kingdom of Deira, centred there across the river from Lindsey, was both older (by a century or so?) and more populated than Bernicia, which may account for Ida leaving c.549 to set up his own state. It was supposed in the Welsh annals to have annexed York in c.580,[19] ending the post-Coel British kingdom there; the evicted kings were supposed to be Peredur (the 'original' of the Arthurian hero Sir Perceval) and Gwrci. In the 1840s and 1850s some early Anglian cemeteries were found in close proximity to York, suggesting either that the early post-Roman British kingdom there accepted incoming mercenary settlers (agreeing with Gildas' and Nennius' account of Hengest's mercenaries being sent North c. 430–40 to fight the Picts?) or that when the Anglians took York they set up a local base. The continuity of British into Anglian residence with no break at certain sites, for example, Driffield, also suggests peaceful 'mixed' settlement not eviction and a temporary break in use of land. But even if the kingdom of Deira – source of the 'not Angles but Angels' slave-boys who Bede recounts as Pope Gregory seeing in a slave-market in Rome before he decided to convert their fellow-countrymen[20] – was reasonably large and powerful by c.600 it fell victim to Aethelfrith of Bernicia, who presumably had a more war-ready army after his long and successful wars in the north.

From British literary sources it is clear that the kingdom of Bernicia came under threat of extinction in the 580s and early 590s from the coalitions built up by its British neighbours, warlords Urien and Owain of Rheged – and that its survival owed as much to its kings' tenacity as to the fortuitous assassination of Urien c.589 by a jealous British rival, Morcant. The string of Germanic coastal settlements from Bamburgh along to the Tees would hardly have defeated the British state commanding the resources of Lancashire, Cumbria, and south-western Scotland (plus occasional outside allies, as seen in the Catraeth campaign c.595/600) but for determined and skilful leadership. The skill, cohesion, and 'esprit de corps' of the warriors of Rheged under Urien and Owain is apparent from the poems of Taliesin and Llywarch 'Hen', and in the *'Gododdin'* (on the Catraeth campaign) the poet Aneirin presents a picture of a body of heroes from across northern Britain recruited to aid Rheged. Given the post-Roman heritage of the local British kingdoms based around Hadrian's Wall, a major area of Roman military concentration, it has been speculated that the British had the advantage of cavalry.

There was nothing inevitable about the Bernician defeat of Rheged in the mid-590s, when Owain was killed (possibly at Catraeth), or its subsequent defeat of the veteran Gaelic warlord Aedan of 'Dal Riada', the Irish settlers' kingdom in Argyll, at 'Degsastan' (?Dawston in Liddesdale). The Bernician kings built up a war-machine which Aethelfrith, then used to take over neighbouring Deira c.604, annex many northern British kingdoms into one large state, and 'found' Northumbria. The founder of the united state of Northumbria and the first known Anglian king to reach the Irish Sea, he was evidently a talented general and a charismatic leader. He was the son of Aethelric, ruler of Bernicia ?in the early 590s and a younger son of the dynastic founder Ida; he was probably born in the late 560s or early 570s. Aethelfrith succeeded (?his father) c.593 at a time of danger for the Anglian people from Owain of Rheged. He soon managed to turn Bernicia's fortunes around – against a much more experienced enemy – and inflicted a decisive defeat on Rheged and its ally Mynydog of Din Eidyn (Edinburgh) at Catraeth c.595/600. The site of the battle has been debated but was probably Catterick; the British had assembled a force of experienced mercenaries recruited from all over the North. Much of the central-northern Pennines area was either overrun by Bernicia or reduced to vassalage. Bernicia now became the dominant power of northern Britain. Aethelfrith was to win the sobriquets of 'the Ferocious' and 'the Crafty', suggesting a military reputation for a mixture of direct aggression and subtle tactics. The threat which his power posed instigated King Aedan mac Gabhran of Dal Riada, to bring an army Southwards from Argyll to challenge him c.603. The battle between Aethelfrith and a Dalriadan-British coalition at 'Degsastan' (?Dawston at Liddesdale) saw heavy losses for both sides; Aethelfrith claimed the victory and Dal Riada did not challenge him again. In 604 Aethelfrith overran his weaker southern neighbour Deira beyond the Tees, probably killing its king Aethelric and driving his brother Edwin (born c. 585?) into exile in Gwynedd. This victory provided the crucial cement for the newly dominant power among the northern Angles, permanently united in one state stretching from Forth to Tweed; those British rulers who survived (e.g. in Rheged and Elmet) were vassals. Aethelfrith had two wives – Bebba, mother of eldest son Eanfrith, and Acha (mother of Oswald and Oswy), daughter of King Aelle of Deira and possibly acquired as a mean of legitimizing his rule there.

The Anglian state now threatened to cut off the Britons of Gwynedd from their kinsmen in the north, quite apart from tension arising from the presence in Gwynedd of Edwin. Probably in 613 to 616, Aethelfrith advanced west to the Dee and fought a major battle with king Selyf ap Cynan of Powys at Chester; the victory, where Selyf was killed, consolidated control of Cheshire. Before the battle Aethelfrith massacred a large number of monks from the nearby British monastery of Bangor-on-Dee who had gathered near the battlefield to pray. Edwin now fled to the court of Ceorl of Mercia, who married him to his daughter but was intimdated by Aethelfrith into expelling him.[21] He went on to Raedwald of East Anglia, the main military power in Southern Britain, who refused a bribe to murder him. Raedwald took up Edwin's cause and marched North in 617; the two states were probably contending for control of Lindsey. The East Anglians withstood Aethelfrith's attack on the River Idle near Doncaster and he was killed. Raedwald then assisted Edwin's return to York to take over all Northumbria; Aethelfrith's sons fled to Dal Riada.[22] But despite Aethelfrith's defeat and death his state survived, soon regaining military pre-eminence, and ultimately his heirs not Edwin's were to rule it.

Edwin seems to have been able to use his years in exile from Northumbria across north-west Britain to his advantage, in learning how to tackle the armies of the local British/Welsh kingdoms successfully (especially Gwynedd) and probably knowing the geography for future battles and attracting local clients. He extended his new kingdom's power across the region, campaigned with initial success in the coastal plains of Gwynedd as far as Arfon, and secured an even greater empire which from its extent and the lack of any archaeological evidence of Anglian settlement there must have relied on a number of British sub-kings. His realm included the Isle of Man and Anglesey/Mon, so he must have had a fleet and if so was the first Anglian ruler to appreciate naval power and probably established a base on the lower Dee or Mersey. He fully incorporated the eastern Pennine British kingdom of Elmet (around Leeds) in Northumbria, either reduced Rheged to vassalage or annexed it (ex-king Rhun became a bishop and was said in Welsh tradition to have baptised him), and as a former refugee in Wales knew enough of Welsh war-tactics and their kings' capabilities to take them on successfully. He temporarily expelled Cadwallon, son of his ex-host Cadfan of Gwynedd, from his kingdom c.628 and was probably the first Anglian ruler to march along the North Wales coast as far as the Menai Strait. His marriage to Aethelburh, the daughter of Aethelbert of Kent, in 625 brought a Roman Christian mission under Paulinus, first bishop of York, to his court – York had been a Roman provincial capital and seat of a bishopric under the Late Empire and Pope Gregory had intended to set up a see there in his plans of 596–7. According to Bede, Edwin finally agreed to become a Roman Christian and accept baptism from Paulinus after a year or so of carefully weighing up the options and preparing the ground among his noble elite – the depth of traditionalist attachment to their old pagan religion brought from Germany is unclear but Edwin was clearly careful to bring his nobles 'on board'. He may have been in a weak position among the fierce, war-experienced nobles of Bernicia who had had decades of warring on the northern British Christians under his predecessors and may well have regarded their gods as having brought them success – especially as Edwin was a Deiran not a Bernician by birth and had overthrown their great war-leader Aethelfrith with 'foreign' East Anglian help. Bede alleges that he finally decided to convert after he survived an assassination attempt by a West Saxon agent at Easter 626 and his wife gave birth to a daughter on the same day (see previous chapter), and though Bede's stylised account of the Northumbrian nobles debating the 'pluses' and 'minuses' of conversion and deciding to convert in 627 may be a 'good story' of 'what should have happened' not a verbatim memory it would indicate that the king allowed his elite to decide without any open pressure. The episode probably occurred at a Roman-style 'arena' which could seat a large number of attendees, with the king presiding and at the most 'nudging' the guests in the right direction. Then, if Bede is correct, the former pagan chief priest Coifi – who from his office would have been a high-ranked noble – ceremonially broke with religious 'taboos' and desecrated his own shrine by riding a horse into it and throwing a spear, showing that the old gods were powerless.[23]

The conversion of an increasing section of the Northumbrian elite and their subordinates followed with mass-baptisms led by Edwin's children – though Bede typically does not say whether or not there were already many 'Celtic' Church Christians of British descent in the kingdom, as must have been the case in the former British sub-kingdoms e.g. Elmet and Rheged. The term 'Celtic' is a modern one, covering the post-Roman Churches of the British Isles in the lands ruled by Brittonic/Welsh kingdoms plus Ireland and from the 560s Dal Riada; they had differences in some rites from the Roman practices but were in fact fully Catholic in theological terms. (It has been a modern anti-Catholic assumption by some observers that their greater 'devolution' to decision-making by local kingdoms' churches based on monasteries not centralised orders sent from Rome implies greater 'democracy' or humility than Roman Christianity, but this is exaggerated.) Whether or not Bede ignored a 'Celtic' Church contribution to the evangelisation of Northumbria in the 620s and avoided mentioning any local British clerics' involvement in the formerly British-ruled regions, Edwin chose to align himself with the Roman Church and its mission in Kent. He thus brought himself into the comity of Christian states linked to the Papacy rather than to the surviving, less centralised post-Roman Church in Ireland and Scotland, orientating Northumbria towards the Continent not the Atlantic fringes. The fact that he built a large new church for Bishop Paulinus in the main ex-Roman city, York,[24] implies his south-facing diplomatic 'profile' and his Deiran, not Bernician, dynastic origins – so was hostility to the conversion more serious in the less 'settled' north that had a more hostile relationship with the Britons (and Rome)? His diplomatic as well as religious 'volte-face' from the previous isolated, pagan condition of Bernicia made him the heir to Aethelbert of Kent, his father-in-law, as well as to the great exemplar of an expanding Catholic-orientated Christian monarchy, Clovis the Frank. But, unlike Francia, the Northumbrian state was not able to achieve permanent military supremacy over its local rivals.

Edwin's campaigns against Gwynedd ended in disaster as his victim Cadwallon returned from exile in Ireland with more troops, won back his kingdom, and then invaded Northumbria with aid from the pagan Penda of Mercia, as seen above. Edwin's death in battle against Cadwallon at Hatfield Chase near Doncaster in autumn 633 or 634 (aged forty-eight) led to Northumbria breaking up temporarily.[25] Aethelfrith's eldest son Eanfrith, who had fled to the Pictish kingdom to the north (and as we shall see had married a Pictish princess) regained Bernicia while Deira, ravaged by Gwynedd, was temporarily kingless and then passed to Edwin's nephew Osric. Eanfrith duly fell victim to Cadwallon too, presumably on suspicion of his reliability and/or his Pictish links. Soon the kingdom was reunited by Aethelfrith's younger sons, Oswald (d.642) and Oswy (d.670), who were Christians like Edwin but had been converted in exile at the remote island monastery of Iona in Dalriada.[26] This great kingdom of contemporary western Scotland, centred in Argyll ('Coast of the Gael'), had been founded by Irish settlers c.500 (traditionally led by an Ulster prince, Fergus mac Eric) and its church was run by a mission following the 'Celtic' Irish Christian customs which had been set up in 563 by the northern Irish prince St Columbcille/Columba at Iona. It was the vigorous and far-sighted statesman Columba, an energetic traveller and evangeliser across huge tracts of difficult mountain and seaside territory in Northern Britain, who inaugurated the practice of anointing a king with holy oil to show Divine and Church backing and thus cementing the alliance of Church and State. His biographer Adomnan, abbot of Iona a century later, records that he consecrated the Dalriadan king Aedan c. 574. This practice – based on the Old Testament anointing of Saul by the prophet Samuel – was now imported to Northumbria and England. But the existence of a major Christian mission at Iona, ready to assist the exiled Oswald and Oswy, owed a great deal to the minutiae of 550s Irish politics rather than a 'master-plan' of expansion by the Irish Church which was anyway decentralised into separate organizations in each of the five main kingdoms under the nominal leadership of the archbishopric of Armagh in Ulster. Columba, a great noble from the ruling dynasty of the Irish 'High Kings' (the 'Ui Niall') who alternated the latter's throne between one Ui Niall branch ruling in western Midhe and one branch ruling at Ailech in Ulster, had led a coalition of disgruntled local kings to defeat the centralizing 'High King' Diarmait mac Cerbhaill around 560. He and his allies had defeated the latter and wrecked the centralised power of the kingship to reassert the autonomy of the five provincial kings (of Ulster, the two parts of Midhe, Leinster, Munster, and Connacht) and make the 'High King' at most a 'first among equals' – at least as remembered in later tradition which may have been as inaccurate as Anglo-Saxon 'foundation myths'. He was however a confrontational and controversial personality with many enemies, and he had apparently been encouraged (or ordered) to leave Ireland and undertake a mission to Dalriada in expiation of the bloodshed which he had caused.[27] But for the revolt against Diarmait, would Dalriada have been Christian and missionary monks been available at Iona?

The divergences of Irish Church practices (e.g. in the clerical tonsure and the date for celebrating Easter) were imported into Northumbria under Oswald after his defeat of Cadwallon and assumption of the throne in 634/5, as the latter resumed Edwin's conversion of the region but brought in missionaries from his own place of exile, Iona. These were headed by a new, Iona-taught 'Celtic Church' bishop based in Bernicia, Aedan, and Edwin's bishop Paulinus had fled to Kent when his patron had been killed and failed to return, so the see at York lapsed. The new Northumbrian Church with its Iona-taught practices served by the mid-seventh-century to emphasize a difference in tone from the Roman Church practices used in Kent and from Wessex's conversion in the mid-630s there too, and the rigid hierarchy and increasing centralization of the Papacy in Rome in the seventh century prevented any long-term co-habitation. As seen by the list of questions on doctrines and practices which Bede lists St Augustine as submitting to his superior in Rome in the late 590s and the detailed way that Pope Gregory replied, Rome had rules for everything – as was to be expected of an institution set up under the centralised bureaucracy of the later Roman Empire – and expected to be obeyed. The Irish Church, divided into five provinces under loose leadership from Armagh, and its daughter-Church on Iona had no legalistic central authority issuing directions to its subordinate bishops in the manner which the Pope did from Rome. Indeed, their bishops were not seen as a smoothly-running hierarchy – the religious counterpart of the Late Roman civil bureaucracy, on which the Roman Church had been modelled – under the discipline of their archbishops, who were in turn under the orders of Rome. In the Christianised lands of the former Western Empire the bishops were supposed to be resident in the capital cities of each province, as an essentially urban office – as neatly set out at the Church Council of Nicaea in 325. Ireland had not been a Roman province, had no towns, and had not been Christianised under Roman influence but by post-Roman Britons (and Gauls?) led by Patrick in the second third of the fifth century. Its bishops tended to reside at royal courts and/or great provincial monasteries, administering the sacraments rather than imposing legalistic discipline, and arguably the leading abbots (often of noble birth) had more prestige. Columba, for example, was an Irish prince of the line of the Ui Niall 'High Kings'and ran his conversion of Dalriada and less successful missions to the Picts from the monastery of Iona as its abbot; his role as a bishop was less vital. The bishop's role was to celebrate the sacraments and preside at the royal court as its resident senior cleric, not to run a Church bureaucracy as in urbanised Roman bishoprics (e.g. in Gaul and Italy).It was the monasteries which were the 'power-houses' of learning, art, and missionary activity – and eager peripatetic missionaries led the way in converting new peoples, not Rome-directed bishops. This extended to 'Celtic' Britain too, as South Welsh monastic trainees such as St Samson and St Paul Aurelian moved into Brittany to set up rural monasteries and convert the locals. Their 'home areas' were, like Ireland, not urbanised – and their monasteries were centred in the 'desert' away from centres of secular power, as in Ireland. If there were any fifth-century monasteries in pre-conquest 'England' they would have been similar, but the only one we have any – problematic – evidence for is the enigmatic Glastonbury in Somerset, allegedly founded in the first century AD. The British Church did not 'civilize' incoming Germanic leaders, as the Gallic one did to Clovis in France. Indeed, Bede fulminated about the British Church for not bothering to convert the Anglo-Saxons, and recounted an unsuccessful first encounter between St Augustine and the Welsh bishops (traditionally held at Aust near Bristol) around 600 where the possibility of them co-operating in conversions was ruined by mutual 'communication problems'. (Supposedly the Welsh bishops felt insulted that Augustine did not stand up politely to greet them as they arrived but kept sitting as if he was their superior.)[28]

The Iona traditions were imported to Northumbria by Oswald's ally Aedan, abbot of Lindisfarne – which was clearly modelled on Iona – as well as bishop of the kingdom.[29] The tradition of the leaders of the 'Celtic' Church in Northumbria being abbots as well as bishops continued with men like Eata, abbot of Melrose in Lothian, and Cuthbert, an austere hermit on the Farne Islands who was reluctant to leave his solitary life to preach or tour, and was alien to usual Roman practice – the new monastery of St Augustine's that the eponymous Saint set up at Canterbury, capital of Rome-converted Kent, had no such missionary role. Questions of doctrine and practices in 'Celtic' Church lands were dealt with by occasional religious councils, and the Abbot of Iona did not seek administrative authority over churches established by his missionaries.

Oswald's successful reconquest of Northumbria from the plundering Cadwallon of Gwynedd in 634 thus had a crucial effect on Northumbria's development. He brought in 'Celtic Church' missionaries from Dalriada and Ireland, most notably St Aedan the first bishop/abbot of Lindisfarne, and the Northumbrian Church thereafter showed signs of Irish influence. Paulinus had based his mission in the city of York, former second episcopal see of Roman Britain, according to a Papal plan to revive the Late Roman ecclesiastical hierarchy; Aedan, like Celtic bishops in Ireland, was based at the royal court and 'doubled up' as abbot of the new monastery on the island of Lindisfarne. This trend for a greater missionary role for monasteries – and for adventurous monks wandering Britain and Europe converting the pagans – now made itself felt in those areas of northern Britain converted by monks from Iona, and Northumbrian missionaries moved down into southern Britain including Mercia (Peada's kingdom under Oswy's protection in 653–6 and after 658 all of the main kingdom), Essex and East Anglia. Arguably the Iona-derived tradition of wandering missionaries, not directed by Rome but spontaneous, played a major role in European conversions later – as the Irish monks had ventured as far as southern Gaul/Francia and the Alps, so now English missionaries after c.690 headed off to Frisia (St Willebald) and Germany (St Boniface, martyred in 754, originally a West Saxon from near Exeter). Within Northumbria, even decades later the venerated Cuthbert, later as a saint the occupant of the famous regional shrine at Durham Cathedral after his body was taken on many wanderings in the 870s to escape the Vikings, provided a picture of Iona-style austere and 'anti-social' retreat to the wilderness for the faithful to emulate. Living in a 'cell' on a remote island and praying and fasting with only the seabirds for company,[30] Cuthbert was the regional inspiration for his form of Christianity right through the medieval period – and was far from the sort of urban-based, worldly courtier bishops preferred by the Papacy.

Oswald's responsibility for the distinctive and British/Irish tone of Northumbrian Christianity was thus decisive and a contrast with the plans of Edwin and Paulinus. Bede treated him as one of the Christian hero-kings of his book, and also reckoned him as fifth 'Bretwalda', i.e. the leader if not direct overlord of (most of) his fellow-kings[31] – but in reality this status is dubious given the survival of Cadwallon's ally Penda. It is likely that an alliance against Penda lay behind Oswald's involvement with Cynegils of Wessex, to whose kingdom he journeyed (traditionally in 635). Oswald married Cynegils' daughter Cyneburh to seal the alliance, and the West Saxon king converted. Oswald was present at Cynegils' baptism by Bishop Birinus, at Dorchester-on-Thames. The site of the ceremony, in the north of Wessex, probably indicates that Oswald travelled overland across Mercia, but he may also have visited Dorset (leaving or arriving by sea?) if the link between him and 'St Oswald's Bay' near Lulworth is authentic.[32] If he ever held military supremacy in southern Britain in the mid-late 630s, this did not involve or result from a direct clash with Penda and it is unclear if the latter recognized him as overlord or just avoided antagonising him. However, as seen in the previous chapter, in 642 the two powers finally confronted each other, and the site of their conflict indicates that Oswald attacked South-West into Shropshire. Whether he was ravaging to bring Penda and his local ally Cyndylan of Powys to battle, to catch one of them alone before he joined his army with the other, or seeking to link up with local (British?) allies is unknown. Oswald was defeated and killed on 5 August at 'Maserfelth', later known as Oswestry ('Oswald's Tree'), or in the Welsh record 'Maes Cogwy'. The 'tree' name referred to his fate: Penda dismembered his body, allegedly in a pagan ritual, and hung the pieces up in a tree. Given Penda's military pre-eminence at this point, any Northumbrian military overlordship must have lapsed – did Bede avoid mentioning this as embarrassing to his 'narrative' of Christian success? A year later his younger brother and heir Oswy was able to recover the remains; Oswald's head was taken to Lindisfarne and the body was buried at Bardney in Lincolnshire. Oswald was probably aged in his late thirties (thirty-seven according to Bede); his heroic death for the Faith was made the most of by Bede and other writers as an example to Christian kings[33]

With Oswald's brother Oswy, a further strain of British and Irish influence on the kingdom of Northumbria emerged – though the uniqueness and non-Roman practices of the Northumbrian Church were eventually to be reined in, probably for a mixture of international prestige plus administrative convenience. The third son of Aethelfrith, and his younger son by queen Acha of Deira (sister of Edwin), Oswy was probably born in 611–12. He fled into exile in Dal Riada with his family after Aethelfrith was killed in 617 and was brought up at the monastery of Iona and converted to Christianity. Either before or after his brother's restoration in 634/5 he took part in campaigning in Ireland and formed a relationship (? marriage) with the princess Fina, daughter of 'High King' Colman 'Rimid' (d. 604), by whom he had his eldest son Aldfrith (king of Northumbria from 685 to 704). He returned to Northumbria with Oswald after Edwin's death at the hands of Cadwallon in 633/4, possibly in the reign of their half-brother Eanfrith in Bernicia (633/4 – 634/5) but certainly when Oswald led a Dal Riadan-backed army to drive out the Gwynedd army in 634/5. He was Oswald's principal supporter and married the British princess Rianmelt/Riemmelth, daughter of the (former?) king of Rheged, c.636 – presumably a dynastic alliance to secure the loyalty of her people, former foes but probably a vassal-kingdom with truncated territory by this stage.[34] Any remaining male kinsfolk seem to have lost political power and Oswy may have been intended as Oswald's local viceroy. If he was married to Fina he had to repudiate her for this diplomatic alliance, but Rhianmelt either died or was divorced within a decade or so. In August 642 Oswald was killed by Penda invading Mercia at Oswestry and Oswy succeeded. Bede names him as next 'bretwalda' after Oswald, implying an unbroken line of Northumbrian military/ political overlordship, but it is probable that his bias towards the militantly Christian kings of his homeland led him to play down Penda's military dominance south of the Trent in 642–55. Oswy could not maintain his brother's close links with Wessex, whose king was driven out by Penda in ?645–8, or intervene to save his Christian ally King Anna of East Anglia from destruction c.653. He also had to accept the continuing autonomy of Deira under its own sub-kings, with Osric's son Oswine succeeding him in 634/5; Oswy married their cousin Enfleda, daughter of Edwin, c.644 to bolster their ties and his own claim to Deira. In 651 Oswy invaded Deira, and the outnumbered Oswine disbanded his army sooner than fight. He was hunted down and executed, and Deira was handed over to Oswald's son Aelfwald. Unfortunately the plan backfired – Oswine was regarded as a saint by indignant Deirans and became the centre of a cult (the first of several 'martyr kings' who were regarded as political victims). Queen Enfleda insisted that her husband build a monastery to atone for killing her cousin, and Aelfwald was to desert to Oswy's enemy Penda in 655.[35]

The threat of Mercia continued to loom over Northumbria from 642–55, and Penda had the better of most encounters. He was able to ravage Deira after his victory at Oswestry and in c.644 he raided into Bernicia – a long march from the border – to attempt to sack the dynastic centre, Bamburgh, in an evident attempt to humiliate Oswy; a change in the wind-direction put the fire out in time.[36] The two powers eventually agreed an alliance in or around 653 with a double marriage, whereby Oswy and Enfleda's son Alchfrith (probably his father's heir, which suggests that Aldfrith was seen as illegitimate) married Penda's daughter Cyneburh and her brother Peada, new sub-king of the 'Middle Angles', married Oswy's daughter Aelfleda (Elfleda).[37] This led to an influx of missionaries from Northumbria into Peada's territory to convert him and his people. Oswy may also have been involved in the election of his late half-brother Eanfrith's son Talorcan as king of the Picts c.653, which probably brought a possibility of Pictish aid against Penda and a secure northern border. This family link and probable politico-military alliance suggests cross-border and cross-ethnic politics, rather than any 'inevitable' and long-lasting struggles between the two peoples; we shall see that it has been suggested that the internecine rivalries of Pictish noble dynasties in the seventh century made an 'outside candidate' as king a compromise that could avert civil warfare. In 655 Penda felt threatened enough to resume the offensive, with a huge army including thirty 'duces' (sub-rulers). Oswy relied on geography for defence and avoided battle, retreating far into Bernicia, and Penda eventually accepted a treaty with Oswy's younger son Ecgfrith as his hostage. During his return march across Deira Oswy was emboldened to attack him, possibly by heavy rain bogging down the Mercians. In the battle of the river 'Winwaed', probably near Leeds, on 15 November 655 Oswy won a complete victory and Penda and many of his men, including King Aethelhere of East Anglia, were cut down or drowned in the river.[38]

Oswy was now the most powerful military leader in England, and could more fairly be called 'bretwalda' (if this title was used then rather than being applied retrospectively). He was able to break Mercia up temporarily, repaying the compliment of his enemies' breaking up Northumbria in 633/4 by annexing Mercia's Northern territories (probably as far as the Trent). Peada, his son-in-law and vassal, remained as king of the 'Middle Angles' untl he was assassinated in obscure circumstances in spring 656. Oswy may have connived at this to remove a rival as his daughter, Peada's wife, was blamed for complicity in the murder in later decades within Mercia,[39] and from Bede's account he kept Mercia kingless for three years (i.e. until autumn 658?) when Penda's younger son Wulfhere, who he had been trying to hunt down, was used as the focus of a Mercian revolt by disgruntled nobles. His ruthless policy of eliminating rivals failed in Mercia as it had done in Deira (now ruled by the loyal Alchfrith) in 651, and Wulfhere was able to operate as senior warlord of the Southern English without further interference.

The main internal problem in the kingdom in the 660s was the difference in practices observed by the two 'wings' of the Church in Northumbria, those taking their lead from Rome and those following the Irish Church and Iona. Oswy's queen Enfleda, brought up in the Roman practices by her father's bishop Paulinus, celebrated Easter at a different date from himself and the Iona-trained clerics at Court (led by Bishop Colman, an Irishman). The Roman practices were also followed by Oswy's son Alchfrith who was ruling as sub-king in Deira, and his appointment of a local but Rome-trained candidate, the vigorous and confrontational (St) Wilfrid, to take over the Deiran bishopric from Oswy's nominee Eata led to the zealous Wilfrid imposing Roman practices across Deira. Personal rivalries, especially involving the quarrelsome Wilfrid, and disputes over office were added to the problems over matters such as Easter and the correct form of monastic tonsure and in 664 Oswy summoned a religious council at Whitby/Streoneshalch to reach a definitive solution. His kinswoman, abbess (St) Hilda (King Edwin's great-niece), who headed a 'double monastery' there of monks and nuns, acted as hostess, Oswy presided, and representatives were summoned from Canterbury and Iona to put their rival cases. The ultimate decision lay with Oswy; although the proceedings and outcome may have been distorted by Bede's account to make it seem inevitable, it probably preserves the essentials of what happened. The supposedly winning argument that the Roman case was backed by St Peter the Apostle, who had been given the keys of Heaven by Christ, was an expression of the reasoning that the Papacy was a powerful ally, major foreign kingdoms like that of the Franks were its supporters, and its remote 'rival' Iona was backed only by Dal Riada and the northern Irish kingdoms. In choosing the Roman case Oswy was allying himself with a powerful international institution and most of Europe. As a result of his choice a number of personnel who would not accept it, led by Bishop Colman, left his kingdom; Rome's principal spokesman at the synod, Wilfrid, won royal favour and in 669 succeeded (St) Chad, Colman's successor, to become bishop of all Northumbria.[40] The kingdom was now religiously aligned to Europe, but despite the decision its Church retained a distinctly 'Celtic' cultural if not political tone (as seen by its famous illustrated Gospels).

Chapter Six

Known Unknowns? Some Missing
Or Garbled Royal Details

The early and final years of East Anglia: a series of kings lost in the Fenland mists?

The rulers of minor Anglo-Saxon kingdoms are often no more than names, even in the pre-735 period for which we have scattered historical data from Bede as well as (later) Welsh sources, and as seen the *Anglo-Saxon Chronicle* – which technically covers all the kingdoms from the 'conquests' onwards – is heavily biased towards Wessex and ignores many events in larger as well as smaller kingdoms that were hostile or not important to Wessex. The data available in (often medieval copies of non-extant) early monastic and urban charters often consists of no more than names of the royal grantees or witnesses, though this gives us extra names which we would not otherwise possess for minor kingdoms such as Hwicce and Magonsaeten (almost certainly Mercian vassals throughout their history) in the Midlands and Sussex and Essex in the south-east. We do not know the names of any kings of the 'south Saxons' of Sussex between the alleged 'founder' Aelle (who the *Chronicle* records as landing at 'Cymensora' in 477, defeating the British at 'Mearcredesburn' in 485, and conquering the fortified Roman town of Anderida/Pevensey in 491)[1] and Aescwine who reigned in the 660s-70s. So were there even reigning kings in this period, or did the completion of the 'conquest' and establishment of a small but secure kingdom by Aelle and his 'sons' lead to a lapse in the need for one (mainly military?) leader until the struggle between Wessex and Mercia for regional control or internal consolidation impelled the emergence of a new king in the 660s? We do not even know the names of the alleged 'Jutish' kings of Wight between the supposed leadership that 'conquered' the island in the 530s (see Chapter Three) and the disaster of c.686 when the aggressive and expansionist new Wessex king Caedwalla conquered the island, killed its king Arwald and several princes in a presumed act of dynastic extermination, and forcibly Christianised the pagan inhabitants.[2] Similarly, although we know the names of assorted minor kings of Sussex in the eighth-century, when it was firstly a Wessex and later a Mercian vassal, as late as the 770s we do not know their relationships to each other or more than their basic strategic alignment to their neighbours. Who was 'pro-Wessex', who was 'pro-Mercia', and whether any kings were removed by their overlords as disloyal is unclear, although it has long been reckoned that as their Mercian overlords were referring to them as 'earldormen' (i.e. provincial governors not of royal rank) by the 770s we can assume that centralizing Mercia was seeking to reduce Sussex from a kingdom to an integral province of Mercia. The use of the rank of 'king' for their rulers duly vanished, as it had in Magonsaetan from c.700 and in Hwicce a few decades later. Similarly we have no recorded heirs to Frithuwold in the kingdom of Surrey after c.690, and in East Anglia – a much larger state and originally as powerful as Mercia c. 620 – the coins of independent kings vanish to be replaced by Mercian coinage after Mercian king Offa 'the Great' executed its ruler (St) Aethelbert in 794. The East Anglian coinage only reappears than a short time around 825, at the time that the *Chronicle* (sketchily) records the collapse of Mercian power and reassertion of East Anglian independence.[3] The case of the neighbouring kingdom of Essex (the East Saxons), as old and originally independent a state as East Anglia, is similar though it seems to have retained 'kings' of its original royal line through to the 830s – however much the Mercians regarded them as its dependent governors. In Kent, the kingship may have lapsed under Mercian pressure in the mid-780s – or the evidence may just be missing. It may also be significant that some mid-late eighth-century kings had their overlord Offa to witness charters with them and others, for example, Egbert (ruled c.764 to 780) did not – did the latter do this as defiance, and was this why Offa removed Egbert? Certainly a major revolt occurred against Mercian rule when Offa died in 796, led by a renegade ex-monk called Eadberht 'Praen' (presumably of royal blood) sponsored by the Frankish kingdom overseas, and was brutally suppressed. Kent was then ruled by a Mercian 'collaborator' king from the Mercian royal family, and never regained its independence;[4] in 825 it passed into the hands of Mercia's successor as regional 'strongman', King Egbert of Wessex, who made his son (Aethelwulf, later king of

Wessex and father of King Alfred) its king. Thus, the absence of evidence – worse for some kingdoms than others – means that there are major mysteries over who ruled when and their pedigrees in most of the smaller kingdoms, and where evidence has survived (e.g. charters and references in major works like the *Chronicle*) it may be as much due to luck as to the importance of the rulers in question. Even in Wessex, we do not know whether the 'official' pedigree of King Egbert (ruled 802 to 839), the first of his kingdom to be reckoned as 'Bretwalda', was accurate in tracing his ancestry back to King Ceawlin (ruled c. 560 to 592)[5] or was a piece of 'spin' – or whether the similarity of his father Ealhmund's name to that of a king of Kent in the 770s-780s means that the latter was that ruler and so Egbert had a claim to Kent as a descendant of its royal house.

What we know of the kings of East Anglia is remarkably limited considering its size and importance by the seventh century – as seen above, in ?617 its king Raedwald managed to defeat and kill the greatest contemporary warlord in England, Aethelfrith of Northumbria, and install his exiled rival Edwin of Deira as king. Raedwald was reckoned by Bede as the current overlord of the English, i.e. probably the 'Bretwalda', from c.617 to his death around 625 (the date of which is unknown). He was also the probable candidate as the evidently rich and prestigious ruler buried in the 'ship-burial' grave at Sutton Hoo which was excavated in 1939, the largest and most impressive hoard of royal Anglo-Saxon treasure found in England.[6] But for all his political dominance Raedwald remains a shadowy figure about whom little is known, and the same applies to most of his dynasty – whose pedigree shows that they must have come to power well after the arrival of the first 'Germanic' settlers in East Anglia, whose distinctive Anglian 'grave-goods' and other valuables can be dated well back into the fifth century.[7] As with Mercia (see Chapter Four), it appears that a unified kingdom was only created several generations after the initial settlement occurred, and that wide-ranging groups of settlers – traders or warriors? – were moving into the region on their own initiative for many decades before royal leadership emerged. So why did the latter occur, and indeed was there more peaceful immigration – or even an adoption of new Germanic 'fashions' by extant Brittonic residents from only a limited group of incomers? – as the long-assumed 'invasions? The question of whether the evident continuity from 'post-Roman' to 'Anglo-Saxon' settlements in rural areas, with no reversion of 'abandoned' land to scrub but continous useage of farmland, implies an absence of 'invasion' applies to East Anglia as much as to other kingdoms, and as of the fifth-century and sixth-century East Anglia was indeed 'on the front line' – if there was one. The 'Anglo-Saxon' styles of wood-built rural halls in 'new' settlements in the region may indeed be post-Roman rather than 'Germanic', and there is a mixture of 'post-Roman' and 'Anglo-Saxon' goods at crucial local sites such as West Heslerton and (in nearby Essex) Mucking suggesting co-existence, not expulsion.

There is also some modern dispute between archaeologists over whether the changing distinctive styles of 'Anglian' brooches and other metalwork dated to the fifth-century found in graves in the region reflects a rejection of 'Late Roman era' Germanic styles, presumably those used by Germanic mercenaries imported by the Romans, as post-Roman immigrants arrived 'under their own steam'. Is there a definitely earlier adoption of these post-Roman styles in East Anglia as opposed to Lincolnshire, Essex and Kent, as suggested by H. W. Bohme in the early 1980s,[8] and does this imply that 'independent' post-Roman settlers first arrived in East Anglia not Kent? Or does the apparent similarity of the styles of brooches dated to the fifth century in East Anglia to those in use in Jutland, southern Sweden and Schleswig-Holstein suggest close 'contact' with those regions, and hence a 'Danish' cultural alignment that may have continued via later trade and made the area a natural target for invading Danes to settle in after 865? (For this, see J. Hines, *The Scandinavian Character of Anglian England in the Pre-Viking Period*, BAR British Series, 1984). Does the rising number of socially stratified 'elite' burials (as seen from their more elaborate grave-goods) in the sixth century as opposed to the fifth century, and the emergence of a separate and 'richer' burial area at the site at Sutton Hoo near Rendlesham, suggest the emergence of a 'nobility' and in due course of a royal family to head this stratified society? The ethnic identities of the region's inhabitants in c.400 and c.600 may have changed less than was long supposed, but the dominant language certainly became Germanic and any continuation of the old Roman tribal district of the 'Iceni', the one-time tribe of the great Queen Boudicca in the 50s CE, became that of the 'North Folk' (i.e. Norfolk) and the 'South Folk' (i.e. Suffolk) and then seems to have merged as the land of the 'East Angles'. How many of the new arrivals were ethnically or culturally 'Danish' as opposed to 'North German' or

'Frisian' is another matter, and people may have adopted new social and cultural identities.

Traditionally the dynastic founder of the ruling house, the 'Wuffingas', was Wuffa son of Wehha.[9] The grandfather of king Raedwald, who died in the 620s, his date is too late for him to have been involved in the first, fifth-century Germanic 'settlements' of East Anglia. (Historians now disagree how violent and military-led this was; possibly most settlement was relatively unopposed, or else the records of warfare have been lost.) We can only guess that from the local nomenclature – which becomes entirely Germanic in this period – the smaller-scale groupings of the 'North Folk' and 'South Folk' were united into one kingdom by Wuffa and/or his contemporaries. The later centre of royal power was in Suffolk around Rendlesham – was this the family's original home-area? Assuming that he called his son Tytila after the military Gothic hero Totila who ruled the 'Ostrogoths' in Italy in the 540s, he presumably had Continental contacts (trading or military?) and was aware of the wars in Italy and wished to name his son after their Germanic war-leader.

Notably even at the time of its greatest military success in the early seventh century we have minimal information on East Anglia compared to its neighbours, and very few fixed dates for its rulers. For a minor kingdom this would not be unusual, as seen above; for a kingdom that dominated the region for several decades and had a ruler who could 'take out' one of the greatest warlords of Northumbria it is surprising. Again, it is a result of location, politico-religious alignment, and the chance survival or not of records; one main source, Bede, is only interested in East Anglia as its history impinges on that of Northumbria, as when Raedwald enabled his Christianising hero Edwin to secure his family heritage as king of Northumbria in ?617 and when Edwin and later on Oswald and Oswy sent missionaries to the kingdom. One king, Sigebert son of Raedwald, was banished by his father, and was converted to Christianity by missionaries sent from Northumbria and launched an abortive conversion of his kingdom (involving both the Burgundian bishop Felix and the Irish monk Fursa) which resulted in his murder and a relapse to paganism[10] – but we do not have the dates for this beyond 'the mid-late 620s'. Nor is it clear if he was banished by his resolutely pagan father as a Christian, or if his conversion was coincidental to his exile. He then abdicated to become a monk, was recalled by his successor

Egric to help in the East Anglian resistance to an invasion by their pagan neighbour Penda of Mercia, refused to carry a sword in the resulting battle as he had foresworn violence, and was killed along with the king in their defeat by Penda[11] – but we do not have the date of that either, unlike the similar 'martyrdom' of Oswald of Northumbria by Penda a few years later in 642. The second wave of Christian conversion that followed under their devoutly Christian cousin King Anna was led by Northumbrian monks sent down from Lindisfarne so it was of interest to Bede, but its dates (and that of Anna being killed in battle by Penda) are imprecise too.[12] While Bede is vague as to East Anglian dates and ignores them completely after Anna's brother and successor Aethelhere, a vassal of Penda's, was killed fighting in his army at Winwaed in November 655, the *Anglo-Saxon Chronicle* ignores them altogether except for their own king Cenwalh's exile in East Anglia after an attack by Penda in the mid-640s.[13] There were major monasteries in East Anglia, for example, that at the isolated Broadland Burgh Castle outside Great Yarmouth (the ex-Roman fortress of 'Gariannonum') and at Dunmow/Dunwich, so chronicles may have been written – but if so they did not survive. So is our lack of clarity about East Anglian dates and dynasts largely due to the bad luck of invading Scandinavians ravaging and conquering East Anglia in 869–70 and then settling it as part of the 'Danelaw', destroying all its monasteries?

Raedwald is the most obscure of those rulers reckoned as a national overlord or 'bretwalda' by Bede and the *Chronicle*, and his dates of accession or death remain a mystery. He was probably the first king to extend the dynasty's power beyond the isolated settlements of the 'North Folk' and 'South Folk' in the East Anglian peninsula, and logically if he had a large and experienced enough army to destroy the veteran warrior Aethelfrith and his battle-hardened troops in battle in ?617 they must have had a considerable degree of military experience in unrecorded wars. Given that the confrontation of ?617 with Northumbria involved the East Anglians crossing the Trent, presumably the border between the two states,[14] at this point they were presumably contending for control of the small regional state of Lindsey and Raedwald had secured it before he attacked Aethelfrith – one reason for the war? Their pre-617 history is not recorded and is usually assumed to have been largely peaceful. This may be inaccurate and if Raedwald's father Tytila was called after the era's most prestigious and (initially) successful Germanic warlord his parents presumably hoped for a similar 'profile' for him. Essex to the south, incorporating the declining but still commercially important town of London, had been a vassal of Kent under the latter's great king and 'Bretwalda' Aethelbert (ruled c. 560 to 616/17) and was ruled by his brother-in-law Sledda and nephew Seabert, but probably the death of Aethelbert led to it slipping away from his family's control as its new Christian bishopric then lapsed in a pagan revival. Was this connected to East Anglia influence, and were the settlements of the Fenland and on the Icknield Way to its south part of Raedwald's kingdom? As with so much of seventh-century history, we can only guess but somehow Raedwald acquired the resources and reputation to become as powerful a regional leader as Aethelbert had been before him and as Edwin's ex-patron and restorer he may have overshadowed Northumbria too until Edwin extended his realm across the north-west of Britain to reach Gwynedd and the Isle of Man. The amount of sixth-century Germanic archaeological 'finds' in East Anglia shows that the area was settled early and relatively thickly, though as we have seen questions are now arising how much of this was residual Romano-British in origin; the good agricultural land would have added to prosperity. Raedwald, a pagan so disapproved of by Bede, probably had international trading-links too given the appearance of Eastern Roman ('Byzantine') objects in the ship-burial at Sutton Hoo which has been suggested as being his and which was certainly around his time of rule. He exiled his second son Sigebert (a Frankish name testifying to overseas links) who had become a Christian, not definitively for that reason,[15] and died some time around 625, probably after a reign of several decades given the way he had built up his kingdom's power, and was succeeded by his elder son Eorpwald. The amount of treasure at the Sutton Hoo burial (some of it foreign) would indicate a powerful and wealthy ruler, and as Christian rulers were normally buried in churches the occupant of the burial-mound ('how') was probably a pagan; the tradition of ship-burials for great pagan kings appears in the Anglo-Saxon epic *Beowulf.*

Raedwald's elder son and successor, Eorpwald, was unable to hold onto his father's role as a regional overlord, in the same manner as Aethelbert of Kent's son and successor Eadbald. In this case the role of regional leader and/or 'Bretwalda' (if this latter was a contemporary term) was taken

. Great Doward Hill, near Monmouth. In legend, where Ambrosius trapped his foe Vortigern and the .tter was killed when his fortress caught fire. (© *Pauline E/Creative Commons*)

. Segontium Roman fortress at Caernarfon, Wales. The legendary and possibly actual residence of the .ate Roman commander turned emperor, Magnus Maximus – alleged ancestor of many of the Welsh .ynasties. (© *Richard Croft/Creative Commons*)

3. Bridge at Amberley, Arun valley, West Sussex. A crucial strategic site defending the Arun valley from Saxon attacks from the coast – was it named after Ambrosius because he stationed troops here? (© *Tim Venning*)

4. The traditional landing-site of 'Hengest' and the first Anglo-Saxon mercenaries/settlers in Britain at Ebbsfleet near Sandwich in Kent. (© *Bill Boaden/Creative Commons*)

5. Calshot near Ower on Southampton Water, Hampshire – a possible landing-site for 'Cerdic', founder of the kingdom of the West Saxons or 'Gewissae'. (© *Phil Champion/Creative Commons*)

6. Charford, on the River Avon near Ringwood – possibly 'Cerdicsford', where Cerdic fought the Brtiish of Dorset around 518. (© *Barry Deakin/Creative Commons*)

7. The Wrekin hillfort, Shropshire. A major strategic site in the British kingdom of Powys as the Anglians of Mercia expanded West – was it king Cyndylan's headquarters of 'Pengwern'? (© *Jeremy Bolwell/Creative Commons*)

8. Oswestry in Shropshire, aka 'Maes Cogwy', where king Penda of Mercia killed St.Oswald of Northumbrbia in battle in 642. The church dedicated to Oswald. (© *Colin Parks/Creative Commons*)

9. Heavenfield, near Hexham. The site of Oswald's epic defeat of Cadwallon of Gwynedd to save Northumbria in 633/4. (© *Oliver Dixon/Creative Commons*)

10. Lindisfarne. The main 'Celtic Church' monastery and missionary centre in Northumbria, set up with monks from Dalriada by Oswald's ally St Aedan. (© *Richard Webb/Creative Commons*)

11. Traprain Law hillfort, Lothian. The main fortress of the North British kingdom of Bryniach, taken over as a royal headquarters by the Anglians of Northumbria. (© *Richard Webb/Creative Commons*)

12. Bratton Down, Salisbury Plain, Wiltshire. Probable site of King Alfred's epic defeat of Guthrum' Scandinavian invaders at 'Ethandun' in 878. (© *Rick Crowley/Creative Commons*)

13. Hyde Abbey, Winchester. Burial-site of King Alfred after the Reformation-era demolition of the royal mausoleum, the New Minster. (© *David Tyers/Creative Commons*)

14. Church of King Edward 'the Martyr' at Corfe Castle, Dorset. The only church in England dedicated to one of its kings as a saint. (© *Tim Venning*)

15. The probable site of King Edward's assassination at 'Corfe gate', Corfe Castle, in March 978. But was his stepmother Elfrida implicated? (© *Tim Venning*)

16. Battlefield of Hastings, 1066. In fact at the nearby town now known as Battle; the abbey hill is the traditional and likeliest location, then possibly known as 'Senlac'. (© *Philip Halling/Creative Commons*)

17. Site of the Battle of Hastings. (© *Philip Halling/Creative Commons*)

by Raedwald's client Edwin; Eorpwald tried to convert his kingdom to Christianity under Edwin's influence but ended up murdered in a pagan 'backlash'. Bede mentions this but not its date; the *Chronicle* ignores it. A usurper king (?Ricgbert, Eorpwald's murderer) was then overthrown after a three-year reign, probably around 630, and Raedwald's younger brother Sigebert returned as king and set about the conversion of his people.[16] He had more success than Eorpwald had done, and was sent a Frankish missonary bishop called Felix by Archbishop Honorius of Canterbury who set up his see and monastery at 'Dumnoc' (either Dunmow or the coastal town of Dunwich, later lost to the sea). Possibly the alignment to Canterbury implies that Sigebert, who had gone into exile in Francia which had cultural links with Kent, was more comfortable with the Rome-aligned Kentish Church than with the Northumbrian Church, or that there was opposition to a Northumbrian link in his kingdom due to it implying subservience to the expansionist Edwin – but this can only be speculation. Sigebert also founded monastery schools to train the next generation of Christians. After a five-year reign he abdicated to enter a monastery, his kinsman Ecgric succeeding (c.636/7?). He was recalled by popular demand to lead the national army against the invading Penda of Mercia three years later, either as a saintly talisman who should win Divine backing or as a man with more military experience. Refusing to use a sword as he had rejected violence and carrying a staff, he was killed in the East Anglian defeat that followed, along with Ecgric.

A similar lack of precise dating is apparent with the reign of the next king, despite his clearly being even more influential in cultural and religious terms than Sigebert. This was Anna, who from the Anglian royal genealogies was the eldest son of Eni, younger brother of Raedwald. When his cousins Sigebert and Egric were killed in battle by Penda Anna succeeded, probably already a convert to Christianity under the influence of Sigebert and his new bishop, Felix.[17] Penda did not press his advantage, and Anna was able to survive his attentions for a decade (possibly due to Mercia regarding Wessex as a greater military threat). Anna continued Sigebert's favour to the Church and founded more schools and monasteries, but was more notable for his quartet of talented and determindly Christian daughters who proved major actors in Church patronage in coming decades and were all canonized. Their similar tastes and activities suggests early training at a missionary court by their father.

Athelthryth/Etheldreda (St Audrey), the most famous, founded and led Ely nunnery after ending her marriage to King Ecgfrith of Northumbria (ruled 670/1 to 685); Seaxburh married Earconbert of Kent (ruled 640 to 664), founded Minster-in-Sheppey, and then took over Ely as abbess;[18] and Aethelburh became abbess of Faremoutiers-en-Brie in Francia.[19] The tradition of active Christian patronesses was duly inherited by the daughters of those that had children, making Anna's influence by proxy long-lasting through the seventh century.

He gave refuge to Cenwalh of the West Saxons when he was driven out of his kingdom by Penda c.645, persuading him to convert to Christianity. Whether or not his interference in protecting Penda's victim led to Mercian punishment, a second serious Mercian attack followed c.649, a major monastery was sacked, and Anna was temporarily driven into exile. He was soon able to return, probably at the end of the campaigning season as Penda had to withdraw, but was killed in a third Mercian invasion around 625/3. Penda installed his younger brother Aethelhere as his vassal, and the latter was killed fighting for him at Winwaed near Leeds in November 655.[20] There has been speculation that Aethelhere might be the king to whom the main grave-mound at Sutton Hoo with its ship-burial was dedicated as no body was found there and he was drowned so his body might not have been recovered, but was he too minor a king for so sumptuous a memorial?

The darkness of political obscurity returns to East Anglia after the death of Aethelhere, and though its rulers' names and approximate dates are known for the next century or so nothing more is recorded in outside sources and we are largely reliant on archaeology and what can be inferred from it (e.g. the wealth and tax-revenues of this prosperous kingdom with its successful agriculture and trading settlements, the latter based on the major port of Ipswich). The genealogies record that the younger brother of kings Anna and Aethelhere of East Anglia, Aethelwold, succeeded the latter on his death in battle at Winwaed. The disaster temporarily destroyed the power of East Anglia's Mercian overlords so he was presumably independent from both Mercia and Northumbria and benefited from this greater freedom of action. He seems to have asserted a degree of influence over his neighbours in Essex and used it for the benefit of the Church, inducing King Swithhelm to accept baptism in the late 650s.[21] The reunification and reassertion of Mercia under Wulfhere from 658 may not have been an immediate threat. Aethelwold died in 663/4 and was succeeded by his nephew Ealdwulf; he was in his 17th year as ruler at the time of the synod of Hatfield in 680[22] so this dates his accession. He was probably quite young when he succeeded, given his lengthy reign of 50 years which is the longest recorded for Anglo-Saxon history. His mother Hereswith was sister of abbess (St) Hilda of Whitby and great-niece of Edwin of Northumbria,[23] her family having fled thence to Kent in 632/3 so his father had evidently acquired her via a family alliance to the royal house of Kent or the half-Kentish Northumbrian Queen Enfleda, daughter of Edwin and wife of Oswy. East Anglia was prosperous enough for the introduction of coinage in the later seventh century and presumably kept up its trading-links with the Continent. Ealdwulf appears to have died around 713, when he was probably at least in his sixties, and was succeeded by his son Alfwold.[24] Ealdwulf had reigned for around fifty years, so Alfwold was probably already in his thirties or forties. Little is known of his reign, during which East Anglia appears to have remained at peace as a junior ally of Mercia without the tension and border-wars which marked the latter's relationship with its other large Southern neighbour Wessex. He was the dedicatee chosen by Felix, author of the hagiography of the Fenland saint Guthlac of Crowland Abbey, and may thus have commissioned the book as an act of piety.[25] He sent a supportive letter to St Boniface, the Wessex missionary working to convert the Frisians close across the North Sea from his kingdom. Alfwald died around 749 after a reign of thirty-six years, probably elderly and it seems without heirs.[26]

It is at this point that the end of the royal genealogy of the Wuffingas pushes East Anglia into total obscurity despite its evident prosperity. Alfwald is the last known ruler to have been a member of the ancient royal house, the Wuffingas, and his successor Beonna's name would suggest an east Mercian origin. He and his co-rulers, Hun and Alberht (were they relatives or not?), were probably in a weak political position as lacking dynastic legitimacy; the appointment or election of three men may have been a resolution to rival claims within the nobility or a move by East Anglia's powerful neighbour and apparent overlord Aethelbald of Mercia (ruled 716 to 757) to keep the kingdom weak. As Aethelbald had lived in hiding in the Fens before his accession, under the reign of the alleged tyrant king Ceolred of Mercia who had apparently wanted to kill him, he may well have known the region better than his predecessors from personal experience, and as he claimed to be 'king of the Anglians' (English?) in his charters he clearly regarded himself as the region's overlord. Beonna soon emerged as sole ruler as not many of his fellow-kings' coins or charters survive, and the increased silver content of his coinage suggests a time of agricultural and mercantile prosperity. He seems to have survived into the 760s, but the absence of later coinage may obscure a longer reign.[27] The next king, Aethelred, had a dissimilar name and was probably not related – and in his case we do not know when he succeeded and how this occurred, rare for a supposedly major kingdom. He is indeed known only through his saintly son Aethelbert's greater fame. He succeeded the equally obscure Beonna at an unknown date, and the current power of Mercia under Aethelbald's cousin Offa 'the Great' (ruled 757 to 796) would make it probable that East Anglia was his vassal-state at this time. The best that can be said of its kings is that they avoided the declining status into 'ducal' or 'ealdorman' rank '(i.e. as governors not of royal rank) that afflicted smaller kingdoms within Mercia (Hwicce) or allied to it (Sussex) or the constant warfare which marked Mercian struggles with Kent. Logically Aethelred was at least acceptable to Offa who may have been a relative; his name may indicate that he was called after the holy King Aethelred of Mercia. At some date prior to 794 (possibly 779)[28] he was succeeded by his son Aethelbert. The fact that in 794 the latter was seeking a (first?) bride, Offa's daughter, can be interpreted as making him reasonably young – in which case he would have been born in the 760s or 770s and his father would be around 20 years older.

As will be seen, the venerated Aethelbert achieved a posthumous fame far beyond his borders as one of the select group of 'martyr' kings murdered by their enemies and subsequently sanctified – in his case, he was assassinated by either Offa 'the Great' or his wife in Herefordshire in 794, apparently during an official visit to Mercia. Whether he was really seeking a Mercian royal bride at the time and whether he was targeted by a paranoid Offa as a potential rebel in order to 'make an example' to others, the lack of any East Anglian coinage for a few years after his killing would probably imply that the kingdom was suppressed and incorporated into Mercia by the expansionist Offa. If so, it followed in the path of the suppressed kingdoms of Hwicce and Magonsaetan (and

Surrey?) within Mercia and Sussex and – temporarily – Kent outside it. Were its kings as local governors banned from claiming royal rank or coining their own coins? Similarly, it is only speculation that as in Kent it was able to reclaim its independence after Offa's death by rebellion but this was suppressed by brute force by the new Mercian king Coenwulf (ruled from 796 to 821). Does the emergence of new East Anglian coins for a king 'Eadwald' around 800[29] reflects a similar but short-lived attempt to resume autonomy? Was this defeated or did the East Anglians submit to renewed Mercian rule more peacefully as the (West Saxon) *Chronicle* does not record any known rebellion or its suppression? Did the fate of Kent then put the East Anglian elite off revolting until Mercia's power declined after Coenwulf's death? East Anglian history in the early ninth century is largely blank, and no rulers are recorded between Eadwald c.800 and Athelstan who was reigning around 825. The strong overlordship of Mercian kings Coenwulf and Ceolwulf from 796 to 823 meant that no new ruler could succeed except with their permission. Possibly the absence of royal coinage from East Anglia in these years indicates a requirement to use Mercian coins and refusal to grant royal rank to their governors of the kingdom, whether of royal blood or not.

The resumption of East Anglian coinage and presumed independence after 825 poses its own problems, the evidence in the *Chronicle* being sketchy. Just who was Athelstan, who emerged as the man issuing the new royal coins?[30] Was he of East Anglian noble or royal blood, was he a former Mercian governor, or given his apparent Wessex links was he from Wessex? He was probably the unnamed king who turned to Wessex for aid in throwing off Mercian control in 825, taking advantage of Egbert's defeat of Mercia at Ellandun. The new king Beornwulf of Mercia (ruled from 823 to 825/6) invaded in retaliation but was killed, thus saving East Anglian independence; it suggests a major degree of determination and competence on the part of the outnumbered East Anglians and their king. The next Mercian king, Ludecan, met a similar fate a year or so later (827?). The *Chronicle* probably downplayed his role in favour of its own king's ancestor Egbert, who overran Kent and Essex in 825 and was now the new regional overlord – and by 829 was claiming the rank of 'Bretwalda', the first such overlord from Wessex since his presumed ancestor Ceawlin in the later sixth century. King Athelstan of

East Anglia seems to have acquiesced in the overlordship of Egbert, now the greatest military power in southern England, after 825.[31]

Athelstan disappears from the meagre records after 837, with Aethelweard (from his alliterative name probably close kin) succeeding him. He may have ruled for up to thirty years, albeit as a Mercian governor for Coenwulf who happened to hold royal rank until 825. As an Athelstan ruled Kent as king from c.839, it has been suggested that they were the same man and he was transferred there by the rulers of Wessex.[32] In this case Athelstan would have been a younger son or grandson of Egbert as the King Athelstan of Kent had that pedigree, and this would put his rule in East Anglia in a new light. He would thus have been appointed in c. 825 to rule East Anglia as a supporter of the king of Wessex, and would have succeeded Egbert's elder son Aethelwulf, his brother or father, as sub-king of Kent on Egbert's death. But this remains speculation, as does the genealogical links of the next king – Beorhtric, predecessor but not necessarily a relative of the presumed last king (St) Edmund, who was succeeded by the latter in 854.

Misconceptions that are not taken into account: one king per kingdom, or one 'High King' plus other junior kings? The case of sixth and seventh century Wessex.

As we have seen, there was more than one king in Northumbria at the time of its greatest success in the later sixth and seventh centuries – and the same may apply to Mercia too. In Northumbria, the union of Bernicia and Deira was enforced by war by Aethelfrith of the former state in c.604, and was kept up after his defeat and death in ?617 by his replacement Edwin of Deira. After Edwin was killed by Cadwallon of Gwynedd in 633/4, the kingdom broke into two again under Gwynedd/Mercian pressure, and though Oswald (Aethelfrith's second son) restored its independence at the battle of 'Heavenfield' he kept on – or had to keep on for reasons of local particularism? – a junior co-ruler for Deira throughout his reign in 634/5 to 642. This was maintained by his brother and successor Oswy (another Bernician but in this case married to Edwin's daughter so with a greater claim on the loyalty of Deirans), but he was clearly chafing at this restriction as in 651 he overthrew his junior king in Deira, Oswine, by unprovoked invasion. Oswine generously avoided fighting to avert a massacre of his smaller army and fled, but was killed anyway.This backfired, as he was seen as a martyr and Oswy had to agree to erect a shrine to him; Oswy installed his nephew Aelfwald as his new junior king in Deira but the latter deserted him and defected to the invading Penda of Mercia in 655. After this setback Oswy made sure to keep the throne of Deira in the hands of his own sons, i.e. his eldest legitimate (?) son and heir Alchfrith in 655 to ?664 and then his younger son Ecgfrith in 664? to 670. When Ecgfrith succeeded to Northumbria in 670/1 he passed Deira on to his own brother Aelfwine, logically as his 'puppet', and when the latter was killed in battle with Mercia in 679[33] Ecgfrith finally annexed Deira. But until this point Northumbria had usually had at least two kings, one senior, and in equally successful Mercia we have seen that even the great centralizing warlord Penda (ruled c. 625 to 655) had his brother Eowa as co-ruler to 642 and his eldest son Peada as co-ruler, i.e. king of the 'Middle Angles', in 653 to 655.

By this reckoning, the notion of 'one kingdom, one king' for each Anglo-Saxon kingdom in the sixth century and seventh century is something of a mistake, even for the largest and most aggressive states; and it also appears in smaller states where the argument that dividing power to a 'local level' was easier for reasons of political 'reach' was not valid. In small and compact Essex, for example, we see that when king Saebert (first Christian king so backed by the centralising Church in Canterbury, and nephew and presumed vassal of Aethelbert of Kent) died in 616 he was succeeded by three sons – Saeward, Sexred and Saexbald. These then decided to reject the Church and return to paganism, apparently after a quarrel with the bishop of London over one or more of them attending pagan religious ceremonies as well as church services – presumably to appeal to disgruntled subjects who preferred the 'old ways' and might revolt if not appeased.[34] The date of these rulers' deaths is unclear, so this data clearly did not matter to either whatever record the West Saxons were keeping of regional events (whch later became the basis for their *Chronicle*) or to the Church in Canterbury (which Bede consulted for his account of southern events and from which he presumably acquired the story that the 616 reversion to paganism in Essex nearly caused the bishop of London to give up and leave until an angry angel rebuked him in a dream).The East Saxon kingship then reverted to one man, i.e. Sigebert 'the Little' (son of one of the brother kings, but which one is unclear), but in c.653 it passed to two brothers, i.e. Swithhelm and Swithfrith, and after them in c.663 to two cousins, i.e. Sigehere and Saebbi. On the later occasion, one (Saebbi) was a devout Christian and one apostasised back to being pagan, so partisans of both religions were satisfied.[35] There were more double kingships in the early eighth century, and the coincidence of this with the large extent of the ruling dynasty brings in the possibility that sharing the kingship was one way of satisfying rival contenders and averting civil war. Any geographical division within Essex is unclear, and the same applies to the occasions in the later seventh century and early-mid eighth-century when the kingship of equally small Kent was divided. In the cases of Essex, Kent, and Wessex, we have a large royal family and regular 'indirect' transmission of the kingship between cousins, not father-son or brother, sometimes by remote connection as with Caedwalla's accession in Wessex in 685/6 – but we have no idea how many of these successions were peaceful and by agreement as opposed to being by effective coups (as Caedwalla's was).

Nor do we know if there was a concept of cousins 'taking it in turns' to claim the succession in a planned system (the same problem as with the Picts), though this is possible in small and coherent Essex where civil wars are not recorded. In the case of Kent, a geographical division has been suggested when one king witnessed charters mainly in the east and one did so in the west in the early 690s, as the regional division between east and west Kent was extant by this period with each having a separate bishopric. The latter's rule was held by Swaefred, son of the king of nearby Essex, so thus suggests an East Saxon incursion at a time of disputes.[36] There was also one case in Kent of a clear 'political' co-kingship created to avert civil war, when in 673 king Egbert (acceded 664) died young and his under-age son Eadric, under his Mercian mother's regency, and his younger brother Hlothere/Lothar (a Frankish name) shared the kingship. Hlothere seems to have been raised up by a 'separatist' faction to oppose Mercian influence, so the double kingship averted a civil war.[37] He was overthrown and possibly mortally wounded by Eadric once the latter was adult, c.685.[38] Later, after Eadric's defeat and death or expulsion by the invading West Saxon warlord Caedwalla in 686, the latter's defeat of the Kentish rebels after they had murdered his brother and puppet-king Mul,[39] and the abdication and death in Rome of Caedwalla,[40] the reassertion of Kentish independence in 689 led to a double kingship in Kent again for a couple of years, with one contender (Sigeherd) an intruding East Saxon prince. In all these cases it would appear that rival branches of the royal houses of Essex and Kent were at odds and sharing the throne was the result, and the possibility arises from the number of these cases that the notion of one king per kingdom was not a 'given' at this point in Anglo-Saxon political culture. As we shall see when dealing with the Pictish kingdom to the North, that had either one 'High King' and a number of junior kings or else several co-rulers – and in Ireland, whence various influential Christian missionaries came, one 'High King' ruling over five autonomous provincial kings plus their own juniors in local territories was the post-fifth-century norm. Indeed, in Ireland each small regional territory or 'tuath' was entitled to its own hereditary king, and the number of kings – that is, men accorded royal rank as 'ri' – in the island was substantial. Beyond the indirect influence of Gaelic custom on Northumbria via Dal Riada and its Iona missionaries, any notion of Irish political customs being reflected in 'Germanic' Britain is usally discounted. But the multiplicity of kings in a number of large and small English states in the sixth century and seventh century does raise questions as to whether at this early stage of development this was common, or even the norm – and did any system of 'one High King plus assorted junior kings' emerge in an English kingdom?

The greatest possibility of the latter existing is in the West Saxon kingdom, which indeed is usually referred to in the extant records in the sixth century and seventh century as that of the 'Gewissae' – a word possibly meaning 'confederates' – not of the West Saxons. In the central South of Britain a mixture of Saxon and Jutish settlements and neighbouring British kingdoms were combined into the 'West Saxon' kingdom by the warlord Ceawlin in the 570s and 580s; the archaeology does not suggest any substantial Saxon presence in Hampshire, the supposed base of his dynasty's power from his 'grandfather' Cerdic's time. (See Chapter Three.) He may have ruled from the upper Thames valley, where there was more Saxon settlement including an early 'nucleus' around Sutton Courtenay, or have come from a mainly British and Jutish realm in the south to take over the area. The conquest of Wiltshire is supposed to have occurred in the 550s, moving from South (the fall of 'Searobyrig', i.e. Old Sarum, in 552) to North (Barbury Castle, 556), which suggests an advance from Hampshire. Ceawlin's power extended at least to the Cotswolds and possibly to the Severn valley after his defeat of three Britsh kings at 'Deorham' (?Dyrham near Bath) and conquest of Bath, Cirencester and Gloucester in a battle identified by the *Chronicle* as occurring in 577.[41] Supposedly acting in alliance with the Saxons who had moved into Buckinghamshire (from the Fens?) via the Icknield Way under 'Cutha' or 'Cuthwulf', he was probably lord of the Thames valley as well as the Central Southern counties of England but suffered some sort of military reverse at 'Fethanleag', probably in Oxfordshire, c.584. (As seen, this campaign has also been linked to one in the lower Wye valley.) He was defeated in a major battle at 'Wodensbyrig', ie probably 'Adam's Grave' near Swindon, and driven out of his kingdom by his rebel nephews Ceol and Ceolwulf in 592, and was killed in 593.[42] Given that his nephew and successor Ceol was supposed to have reigned for six years to 597 according to the Peterbrough version of the *Chronicle*,[43] the latter either became Ceawlin's accepted co-ruler or seized power in 591. (The Winchester version, to confuse matters, gives him a five-year reign, i.e. from 592.). Was this a sign of impatience by the younger generation with a power-hoarding warlord? If the two princes' father Cutha (as named in the *Chronicle*) was the 'Cutha' recorded by the *Chronicle* as being killed in the battle of 'Fethan Leag' in 584, i.e. Ceawlin's brother, the man who the *Chronicle* presents as defeating the British at 'Bedcanford' (Bedford??) and overunning the Aylesbury area in 571,[44] this raises the possibility that he was Ceawlin's co-ruler in this region. The Aylesbury area is to the northeast of the later West Saxon state and a local presence by Ceawlin's brother seems to imply that it was his (sub-?) kingdom and a part of Wessex in the 570s; so did this pass on from him to Ceol and Ceolwulf? Did they use it as a base for their overthrow of their uncle in 592 – and when did Wessex lose control of this region? Or is the statement that 'Cutha' the conqueror of the Chiltern region was Ceawlin's brother a later guess or 'political' invention aimed at stressing West Saxon claims to this region? Another mystery is the apparent death of Ceawlin's 'son' Cuthwulf, not a king as recorded by the *Chronicle* genealogies but co-commander with his father at the victory of 'Deorham' in ?577,[45] before his father. Did he die in battle, and did this indicate an unexpected dynastic setback for Ceawlin? Did this open the way for Ceol and Ceolwulf to make a play for the throne? What if Ceawlin's son had lived to succeed him and avert a rebellion in 592 – would Wessex have survived into the seventh century as a major power or broken up in a reaction to Ceawlin's exhaustive use of its manpower on warfare?

The kingdom of the 'Gewissae' then declined under a multiplicity of rulers in the seventh century, with king Cynegils (ruled c.611 to 643) leading in war with a co-ruler called Cwichelm who did not succeed him. Indeed, we are not even clear whose son Cynegils was – Ceol and Ceolwulf are both named in different sources (Ceol by the Winchester version of the *Chronicle*). It had many men of royal rank, possibly ruling the later 'counties', in the mid-seventh century, and some of these do not appear in the large – and later in date – royal genealogy. It appears from what Bede states to have had no formal 'king' but rule by sub-kings for ten years to c.683/4,[46] which presumably dates from the death of Cynegils' son Cenwalh (ruled from 643? to either 673 or 674/5). In contrast to the claims of this distant Northumbrian, the local charter evidence does continue a line of kings after Cenwalh – starting, indeed,with the era's only sovereign queen regnant, Cenwalh's widow Seaxburh. She ruled for either a few months or a year, the latter according to the West Saxon regnal list, and was succeeded by a man not listed in the royal genealogies, Aescwine. He was in turn succeeded by a man of more direct but confused royal lineage, Centwine, who ruled from c.676 to 685 – who is in one version of events called the brother of Cenwalh but in that case was for some reason excluded from the throne in ?674 when he was the obvious candidate to succeed the latter.[47] Why was Seaxburh chosen as ruler then, did Bede leave her out of the reckoning as this legalist Churchman could not accept a woman ruler, did the West Saxons allow female succession unlike their neighbours, and was she superseded as ruler because the state needed a man to command its armies? Why would Bede claim the kingship had lapsed if there was a man still recognised in charters and genealogies as king of Wessex, or did he mean that the 'central kingship' or a 'High Kingship' acceptable to the regional sub-kings lapsed? Was Centwine not recognised as king by some of his sub-rulers? For that matter, the 'ten years gap' claim as dating from the death of Cenwalh does not reach to the accession of the centralising warlord Caedwalla to the throne of Wessex in 685/6, as Cenwalh ruled for thirty-one or thirty-two years from c.611. This would imply that it was in fact Centwine who restored the central kingship, earlier than 685, and the probable occasion for him to do this would have been the major campaign of 682 when the *Chronicle* records him as defeating the western British of Dumnonia (Cornwall and parts of Devon) at an unknown site and chasing them as far as 'the sea'. Given that the kingdom of Wessex had acquired central Devon around Exeter by the mid-660s as future missionary St Boniface was born there then, this would suggest a victory somewhere around Dartmoor and a pursuit of the Britons down the Tamar valley into eastern Cornwall, or a victory around Okehampton and a pursuit as far as around Bude or Barnstaple. This success would either result from or lead to a reunion of the kingdom of Wessex under its victorious war-leader.[48] By definition, until this point the state would have been governed by autonomous local dynasts, presumably of kingly rank like the father of later ruler Caedwalla, and we have scattered evidence in charters of such men controlling local areas in the 660s and 670s, for example, Cenfus, apparently father of the later (c. 674/5) king Aescwine. Given that Cynegils' son Cwichelm, who ruled with him in the 620s but failed to succeed him and so presumably died young, was buried at 'Cuckhamsley Knob' on the Wiltshire downs, did he rule this region? What region did Caedwalla's father Ceonberht, attested to as a king by the hagiography of Caedwalla's ally St Wilfrid, rule and why was his son a landless roaming warlord by 685? Similarly, as far back as 626 the *Chronicle* account of Edwin's invasion of Wessex after king Cynegils' attempt to assassinate him has Edwin killing a number of (unnamed) kings but not Cynegils or his son Cwichelm.[49] Were these regional rulers ruling hereditary sub-states, who owed loyalty to the supreme 'High King' of Wessex – and was there a distinct and acknowledged system of sub-rulers, as in an Irish kingdom or probably Mercia?

Chapter Seven

The Odd Ones Out?

The Kingdom of the Picts: A Unique Survival of Matrilinear Descent? Why Was the Succession so Complicated?

Sources: very sketchy in detail and later in date. Mainly the *Pictish Chronicle*, a list of legendary and historical (post-fifth-century) kings of Picts and post-843 Scots; dated to the reign of the last ruler mentioned, Kenneth II (d. 995) but only survives in a fourteenth century copy in the *Popplewell Manuscript*. There are also sporadic dates in two Irish chronicles – the *Annals of Ulster* (covering 431–1489), compiled in the later fifteenth century at Lough Erne in Ulster using earlier data, and the *Annals of Tigernach* (only data for 489–766 survives), compiled in the eleventh century at Clonmacnois, central Ireland. Some post-766 details may survive within the later *Chronicon Scottorum* (extant copy dating to c.1640).

The monarchy of the Picts is particularly problematic, and suffers from a paucity of early sources for the fifth century and sixth century even compared to the British/Welsh and Anglo-Saxon realms. In addition it is the subject of major divergences of opinion by historians on its very nature and method of succession, as in contrast to its neighbours there was no relatively straightforward line of succession from father to son (or from time to time between brothers and cousins). The British and Anglo-Saxon royal genealogies may be agreed as of dubious authenticity for their earlier centuries and they suffer from gaps in the record even for the eighth century and ninth century, as the earlier chapters have made apparent. But at least we have an approximate idea of who succeeded whom, what their family links were, and when this happened in the major kingdoms, plus some details for the lesser ones. The lines of succession there are complicated at times, but usually reasonably close relationships between the successive kings can be traced even if some transfers were clearly 'forced' by revolt or murder. In the case of the Picts, the surviving royal lists do not record more than a couple of instances of a brother succeeding his brother, and none of fathers being succeeded by their sons. Some later kings are clearly the sons of men identifiable as earlier kings, so the latter did leave sons – and not all of the latter can have been too young to rule when their fathers died. In most cases, the family relationship of each king and his successor is unclear, they often do not appear to come from the same group of close kin, and the best that can be suggested is that an uncle was succeeded by his nephew or one person by his cousin. Uniquely for either 'British/Welsh' or 'Anglo-Saxon' kingdoms, some if not most of the relationships between successive rulers appear to be via females, and women are far more prominent in royal lineages. No sons of royal princesses appear to have traced their right to the throne of other British mainland kingdoms via female descent, except on rare occasions where the male line appears to be extinct – e.g. king Oswy of Northumbria's last wife Riemmelth/Rhianmelt of Rheged as its heiress when Northumbria conquered or annexed it. This ties in with the statement in Bede that the Pictish succession passed through the female line – not when there was no male line available, but as a matter of course and the legal norm. This is cited by Bede as being due to an old legal agreement dating back to the time that the Picts were a migratory people who had not yet settled in what became Scotland; they went to Ireland to gain military help for their seizure of a land to settle in and were given access to Irish womenfolk to marry in return for a promise that their kingship would descend through the female, i.e. Irish, line. (The word used for 'descent' as in royal lineage here is 'prosapia' which is Bede's usual term for royal succession to a kingship, so this is clearly meant though it can refer to either male or female descent.)[1] This is clearly an unhistorical 'foundation myth' which Bede had heard somewhere in northern Northumbria (adjacent to the Pictish kingdom), possibly connected to the Northumbrian-Pictish political links under kings Eanfrith (ruled Bernicia 633/4) and Oswy (ruled all Northumbria 642 to 670/1) who had Pictish kin. Alfred Smyth has suggested an Irish or Dal Riadan origin for it, as the version told by Bede refers to the latter region as seen over the sea by the storyteller (i.e. the latter is in Ireland). It would thus be an 'origin myth' told of the Picts in Dal Riada and would seek to place the Picts as part of the Irish world, as 'incomers' beholden to the Irish for their help in taking over their mainland kingdom.[2] It appears elsewhere in twelfth-century Scots sources too, and was evidently widely believed.

Its divergence from the norms of British succession added to the mystique of the defunct Pictish kingdom as a unique and peculiar state with its own ancient culture, which was bolstered by the lack of a translatable Pictish written language and the unique nature of Pictish art (e.g. on surviving memorial stones across Scotland). The intricate decorations in Pictish artistic symbols on these stones could be seen as related to their habit of decorating their bodies reported by the Romans.[3] This notion of a distinct and 'odd' Pictish kingdom and culture which 'vanished' as it merged with the Scots kingdom of Dal Riada in the 840s duly passed into folklore and affected the opinions of later historians, who had little evidence to go on so myth tended to take over. The nineteenth century and early twentieth century enthusiasm of antiquarians and anthropologists for the survival of ancient and 'primitive' cultures across the world fed into this, and the idea of royal succession by female descent in the kingdom caused speculation that the Pictish state was an ancient 'matriarchy' where women had a special status and power. This was mixed up with the anthropological notion of an ancient worldwide religion of the 'Mother Goddess' plus her subordinate male consorts, which was later replaced by a patriarchal cult of male gods, for example, the replacement of the cult of the goddess Cybele or the 'Earth Mother' Gaia by the 'Twelve Olympians', headed by Zeus, in Ancient Greece and Crete. (Zeus was originally a minor consort of a dominant goddess in Crete.) The matriarchal rule of the Mother Goddess and the subordinate rule – and ritual sacrifice to ensure good harvests? – in the ancient religion of mankind was popularised by the Late Victorian anthropologist Sir James Frazer in his study of ancient myth, *The Golden Bough*, and influenced major early twentieth-century poets such as Robert Graves. In this vein the Pictish kingdom was excitedly suggested as an 'ancient survival' where the original rule of a matriarchy was reflected in its succession passing through the female line, and this fed into ideas that the Picts as a 'race' and a culture were 'non-British' and probably a very ancient people of Neolithic origin continuing to use Neolithic religion and cultural practices.

The northward spread of the use of iron and the social stratification of a 'peaceful and egalitarian' Neolithic British culture into the hillfort-living, war-mongering peoples of the Iron Age was suggested as the work of an 'incoming' people from the Continent, logically the 'Celts'. They had pushed the original peoples of Britain northwards into the barren lands of northern Scotland, and these had survived on the margins of Britain as the 'Picts'. If any of these people survived in lands further south, it was as a 'hidden' or a subordinate people, living in hiding – and they could have inspired the early British and Anglo-Saxon legends of the hidden and diminutive 'fairy folk'. There was a similarity to the situation in Ireland, where the established medieval 'history' had it that the warlike patrilineal people who became identified with the 'Iron Age' warrior tribes led by the ancestors of the 'High Kings' i.e. the 'Sons of Mil', invaded and superseded the earlier people of the 'Tuatha De Danaan' around 1000 BC and the latter then retreated into hiding in the 'Otherworld' as the magical 'Fairy Folk'. This notion of a distinct ancient Pictish people being displaced into hiding or to the margins of Scotland has long since been disproved. Nowadays the idea of 'invasion' of the British mainland around 500 BC by a distinct 'Celtic Iron Age people' from Europe, an ethnic grouping with new cultural practices symbolised by their useage of iron not bronze for their weapons, is thought much less likely than peaceful cultural change and the adoption of new fashions. As with the question of Anglo-Saxon 'mass invasions' mentioned earlier, the two cultures seem to have cohabited for decades at some archaeological sites and their 'distinctive' possessions mingle in discoveries; the 'new' was adapted slowly, not brought in suddenly by invaders. The 'DNA' of modern Britain shows substantial survival from Neolithic times and no major difference between the genetics of the Welsh (i.e. post-Roman Britons) and the residents of 'Pictish' areas of Scotland. But it had a long history in British culture and long clouded perceptions of the Picts as some strange sort of Neolithic ethnic survivals – and the idea of remote and hostile pagan 'Picts' surviving in the wilds of upland Scotland was referenced by novelists such as John Buchan in the 1890s (in an atmospheric story in *The Watcher By The Threshold*) and Rosemary Sutcliff in the 1960s (where King Arthur, aka the Brittonic warlord 'Artos the Bear', is aided against the Saxons by the 'Little Dark People' in the Ettrick region in *Sword At Sunset*). Children's novelist Arthur Ransome referenced the theory in *The Picts and the Martyrs* (1940), where Dick and Dorothea Callum, an academic's children, hide out in the Lake District woods like 'Picts'.

Nowadays, however, the Picts are seen as a relatively 'normal' Brittonic people who were part of the tribal groupings of mainland Britain at the time of the Roman occupation, and any cultural distinctness (e.g. in the unique use of fortified round towers, 'brochs', not unfortified farms in the Hebrides and the absence of any hillforts) can be traced to the poor soil, difficulties in land-based travel, and atomised social structures of the remoter regions. The vagaries of Pictish succession can be traced to political problems, such as the need to accomodate a multitude of competing noble lineages by 'rotating' the kingship – and earlier analysts tended to neglect the crucial question of the (seven?) Pictish sub-kingdoms under the rule of the 'High Kings'. Logically, it can be argued that the complex succession arrangements and many different lines of royal descent reflect a constantly competing group of sub-kingdoms with their own claims on the High Kingship', and if one line of men had tried to secure the latter permanently their rivals would have joined forces to evict them so the kingship could not descend 'father – son – grandson' anyway. This is the theory put forward by Alfred Smyth in his study of early Scotland, *Warlords and Holy Men* (1984), and supported by Alex Woolf and Alasdair Ross.[4] The sub-kingdoms may well have descended from father to son in the normal way as seen in Wales or northern Britain, but we do not have these lineages. But as we shall see, their kingdom and its structure and practices of government and succession clearly had its own features even if these are not traceable to any separate ethnicity or culture. (The normal British practice of patrilinear succession may have taken over in the seventh century as the number of 'outside' successions by princesses' foreign-born sons ended, as Woolf suggests.) Nor is it yet agreed how exactly the High Kingship's succession rules worked, though several logical plans for this have been suggested and there are parallels with Ireland where the rival lines of the 'Ui Niall' dynasty (descendants of the semi-mythical early fifth-century ruler Niall 'of the Nine Hostages') in western Midhe and Ulster alternated the kingship between them. Also, the descent of the Pictish 'High Kingship' did clearly involve the sons of Pictish princesses as well as princes, some of them non-Pictish rulers imported from other states, so this factor was unusual and indeed unique, as David Sellar points out. It may be due to a complex political 'trade-off' between rival dynasties which was then rationalised in myth as a 'venerable tradition,' not some ancient anthropological custom.

The sense of a 'people apart' with their own culture of the name and identification of the 'Picts' commences with their kingdom's names. This is somewhat problematic, the name meaning 'Painted Men' and probably being a nickname given by themselves or their enemies. Logically it refers to their use of woad or tattoos to decorate themselves. The name is first recorded around AD 300, in the Roman historian Eumenius' account of the reconquest of the province of Britain from a rebel regime in 296 by 'Caesar' (deputy emperor) Constantius 'Chlorus' ('the Pale'), father of Constantine the Great. Constantius proceeded to restore the northern frontier – Hadrian's Wall – by a war with the 'Picti' who had been attacking across it, suggesting that they were the people directly to its North in the Southern Uplands of Scotland as well as further North. The 'Picti' name, i.e. 'Painted People', probably refers to the locals' habit of decorating themselves with woad and having tattoos, which the Romans looked down on as 'uncivilised'. The peoples of the region north of what became Hadrian's Wall in the 120s were earlier known to Roman historians as the 'Caledonians' when Roman governor Cnaeus Julius Agricola first conquered it around 81–2, a name probably related to the Brittonic word 'caled' – 'hard' or 'tough' and meaning 'the tough people'. There is no indication of whether they were what would nowadays be called a 'tribal confederation' rather than one distinct polity; they were conquered by Agricola in a lengthy five-year campaign which took him north from Yorkshire to the eastern Highlands and saw Roman military bases established up the east coast of Scotland from Lothian (eg. Newstead/'Trimontium' in the Eildon Hills) to the Inverness region. The Caledonians under their leader Calgacus (probably meaning 'The Swordsman') had been heavily defeated around 84 at the battle of Mons Graupius, probably in Aberdeenshire or Atholl and linguistically linked to the Grampian Mountains. Eventually the Romans, constantly harassed by tribal uprisings which were possibly assisted by the tribes further south such as the Brigantes in Yorkshire, pulled back to a permanent stone frontier from the Solway Firth to the mouth of the Tyne – Hadrian's Wall – in 120–1 under Emperor Hadrian. The Caledonians thus remained independent and had sporadically raided South of the Wall in times of Roman weakness, such as after the death of Marcus Aurelius in 180–1 and during the civil war between governor Clodius Albinus of Britain and Emperor Septimius Severus in 193–7. Severus subsequently tried to conquer them in 208–10 and re-established Agricola's bases in eastern Scotland as far north as the legionary camp of Carpow, on the Tay near Perth, but the war was abandoned by his heir Caracalla after he died (at York) in February 211.

But were the Caledonians, who Agricola's son-in-law the historian Tactitus regarded as a 'normal' tribal British people not any separate culture, the same as (or the direct forerunner) of the Picts? They were not 'Celts', but nor were the pre- or post-Roman Britons – the latter referred to themselves as the 'Britanni', and at this time the 'Celts' were merely a part of the tribal peoples of Gaul as named by Julius Caesar. The term 'Celts' for the whole of Ancient British culture before and after Rome, plus the culturally and socially similar peoples of Gaul ,was only invented by the anthropologist Edward Lhuyd in the 1690s. Was there any difference in culture or ethnicity between the peoples of what is now England and those of Scotland – and if so where was the 'dividing-line'? The earliest post-Roman 'Celtic' – Welsh – reference to the peoples of Scotland was in the largely fabulous work of the 1130s 'historian' Geoffrey of Monmouth, whose mythical account of Britain had the kings of Scotland descended from 'Albanactus', a legendary figure of around 1000–900 bc who was supposed to be a son of the founding British king Brutus – an exiled prince of the royal Trojan dynasty living in Italy and connected to the ancestors of Romulus, founder of Rome.[5] Quite apart from the name of this king clearly being invented to create a connection to the ancient name of Scotland, 'Alba' (as Wales, or 'Cambria', was first ruled over by his brother 'Camber'), the story was evidently a literary fabrication devised to give a prestigious British royal link to the Ancient Roman story of its Trojan founders, Vergil's *Aeneid*. The Scottish sources were later and were no more trustworthy than Geoffrey of Monmouth, but at least they spoke of a distinct 'Pictish' kingdom of supposedly ancient lineage with a long line of monarchs back before Roman times. Their alleged 'king-list' dated back through sixty monarchs ending in the ninth century, but did not agree on the personnel in question. There were two separate literary accounts – the *Series Brevior*, a Scots or northern English fourteenth century list deriving from one apparently written in the reign of King Alexander II (ruled 1214 to 1249), from which the list of the 1370s historian John of Fordun was derived, and the *Series Longior*. The latter had two different versions, both derived from an original probably dateable to the reign of King Malcolm III (ruled 1057/8 to 1093) – the 'Series Longior 2', preserved in the Irish *Lebor Bretnach* (a copy of Nennius' *Historia Brittonum*), and the 'Series Longior 3', in the eleventh-century Irish *Lebor Gabala Ereinn* or 'Book of Invasions of Ireland'. The 'SL 3' also survives in the 1360s *Popplewell Manuscript*, written in Northern England. The original source for these manuscripts has been suggested as being a lost document written in the 860s or 870s, soon after the merger of the kingdoms of the Picts and Dal Riada by joint King Cinaed/Kenneth mac Alpin (ruled ?842 to ?858), presumably designed to advertise his links to and rightful descent from the two kingdoms' royal families.[6] As seen in the contemporary Welsh and Anglo-Saxon genealogies, it reflects what was believed to have happened and had a political purpose so some of its claims may well have shaky or have reflected myths recounted by heroic poets rather than transcribed from ancient chronologies. Scribal mistakes are possible – and it is not clear if the list is one of a series of 'High Kings' ruling over all of the Pictish realm or if it includes a dynastic list from one or more sub-kingdoms before any 'High Kingdom' was created. Nor is the date of the latter's creation clear, though it was a known habit of medieval writers to glorify their realms' leaders by seeking to push back the creation of their kingdoms as far as possible.

These men might be a dim literary memory – via centuries of oral record? – of the kings who had led the Caledonians and 'Picts' against Rome, although the number of generations referred to in these 'records' implies a kingdom stretching back beyond any need to combine against the Romans to around 400 BC. But had there ever been one ancient kingdom as opposed to a myriad of independent local tribes – barring temporary coalitions to fight off invading Romans, such as that led by Calgacus? And did stories of one Scottish kingdom just reflect an anachronistic desire to create a 'back-story' for the early medieval Pictish kingdom back beyond the time of Christ? Given the identification of early parts of the king-list to a lost 'original' source of the eighth century as suggested by Marjorie Anderson[7] and the 'updating' of this around 860–70 when the Pictish and Dalriadan kingdoms had recently unified, the inspiration for any literary/propaganda attempt to create an 'ancient' dynasty would be too old to be the fictional British 'High Kingship' postulated by Geoffrey of Monmouth in the twelfth century. The 'Trojan origin' myth of a supposed prince 'Brutus' invading and settling Britain which Geoffrey used was however referred to vaguely by 'Nennius', writing c.829, so it was evidently early Welsh and might have given Pictish 'spin-doctors' an idea for their mythologizing. There was also probably inspiration from the parallel case of Ireland – from which the 'Scottish' settlers of Argyll in the early centuries AD came – as medieval literary myths spoke of one Irish 'High Kingdom', centred at Tara/Temhair near the Boyne, dating back to around 1000 BC. So had this precedent been used to create a similar 'history' for an ancient Pictish kingdom, placing it as ruling a far larger area and more coherently than in reality?

Regarding cultural evidence, language certainly showed that the inhabitants of 'Pictish' central and north-eastern Scotland in the first centuries AD had spoken a dialect of Brittonic akin to that of ancient Welsh and Cornish (and Bretons) – 'P-Celtic' as defined by early modern linguistic historians. By contrast, the Irish and the Irish immigrants to Argyll from c. AD 500, the Dal Riadans, spoke the alternative 'Q-Celtic' dialect. Most of the 'Pictish' names for geographical features in their kingdom are in fact more closely related to early Brittonic/Welsh than was once thought, though there were elements of a non-Brittonic language too which might be a Neolithic survival.[8] So were the Caledonians and 'Picts' closer ethnic and/or cultural kin to the southern British than to the Irish? In cultural terms, in the hillier areas of south-central England and the north as far as Fife and Perthshire 'Brittonic' Iron Age culture was distinguished in archaeological remains by a greater difference between social 'classes' than in Neolithic Britain, with concentrations of people in larger rural settlements and in defensible hill-forts (which became larger and more elaborate from c. 500 BC to c. 100 BC). Famous southern British hillforts which the Romans had to storm, such as Maiden Castle in Dorset, were seen by twentieth-century historians as 'tribal capitals' and proto-towns – or at least places chosen for the concentration of the people and their valuables (mostly livestock) in time of war. As they were defensible, there was obviously warfare – presumably struggles for status and possession of resources within and between tribes and smaller local groupings. This culture extended into what became southern Scotland, with tribes such as the Votadini in Lothian, the Damnonii in the Clyde valley, and the Novantae and Selgovae in Galloway (as named by the second-century AD Alexandrian geographer Ptolemy) in 'Pictish areas' north of Hadrian's Wall who were culturally and thus presumably ethnically kin to their southern neighbours. Great hillforts in Southern Scotland, such as Traprain Law in Lothian, were part of 'Iron Age' British culture – but although 'tribal' names, with normal Brittonic wording, were recorded north of the Firth of Forth by Ptolemy (e.g. the Epidaii in Argyll and the Taexaci, probably in Buchan) there were fewer hillforts in this region. In Roman times the use of hillforts indeed declined even in the South, being replaced by smaller, but still fortified, farmsteads. North of the Great Glen they were virtually non-existent, and society appeared to be atomised into smaller local communities. Was this a sign of a different culture from the 'Iron Age British' culture of the south – or even of an entirely different ethnic civilization? Or was it just due to poorer resources in a less fertile area which could not support large farming communities – there were less material possessions worth seizing in raids by predatory warriors so less need for defensible settlements? The existence of small, scattered and often undefended farming settlements in northern Scotland resembled the Neolithic pattern for southern Britain – but was this just due to the poorer soil and atomised social structure in a remote area, not a different ethnic grouping?[9]

There is also the confusing question of whether there was one Pictish kingdom or two, which duly fed into the disputes among historians over what exactly the king-lists in the *'Series Brevior'* and *'Series Longior'* commemorated – the rulers of one kingdom rather than two, and if so which, or those rulers who came from one but had titular command of both? It was guessed that the 'Verturiones' tribe referred to by late Roman historians as being active around the lands between Forth and Tay and/or in Atholl were linguistically linked to the later regional name for this area, 'Fortriu', but did this imply a separate regional kingdom of this district from that of the Caledonians? And did the sporadic Irish chronicle references to various Pictish rulers as 'rex Fortrenn' (i.e. king of Fortrenn/ Fortriu) as opposed to 'rex Pictorum' mean that these were two separate titles, for the rulers of two separate kingdoms, or just interchangeable titles for one man? If there were two kingdoms not one, then logically the 'Fortriu'/Fortrenn title referred to a regional kingdom, probably south of the Mounth in Atholl and thus the kingdom of the Southern Picts; the king of the north would be 'king of Moray'. Ammianus Marcellinus in the 370s refers to the Picts as consisting of two tribal divisions – the *'Dicalydones'*, evidently the Caledonians, and the *'Verturiones'*, apparently the men of the area between Tay and Forth that came to be known as 'Fortriu'.[10] These would seem to be the Northern and Southern kingdoms of the 'Picts' respectively. The later Irish king-lists and references to the accessions and deaths of kings of the Picts are a dubious source for early history, and seem to rely on legend and to be hazy about dates and details of rulers until the first half of the fifth-century – suggesting that not much was remembered about the earlier period of the Pictish 'kingdom' if it existed as an identifiable unit at this period. But from the mid-fifth century they provide an extra 'handle' to the dates of what happened when and who was reigning at a particular point.

In addition, there was the question of the supposed 'seven sub-kingdoms' of the Picts which in the *Series Longior* were ruled by the families descended from the seven sons of the first Pictish 'High King', 'Cruithne' (whose name means 'Pict' so he was clearly an eponymous hero-ancestor like 'Brutus' for the Welsh myths of ancient Britain). All but one of these were definable geographical regions within the Pictish kingdom, headed by Caithness as the most senior and so presumably the most prestigious – with the exception of 'Fotla', 'Foltlaig', or 'Fidach', which has been suggested as meaning 'New Ireland' and so probably Atholl. Were these seven kingdoms historical, and if so how old? And was the neat linkage of all their dynasties to one family, with each sub-kingdom's first ruler as a son of the founder Cruithne, an echo of (or the inspiration for) the legendary Welsh division of the regions of Gwynedd among the sons of founder Cunedda? Which 'High Kings' came, or were supposed to come from, which sub-kingdoms and was there a regular system of rotation to give all a fair chance of the succession? And if so, was this the mythological 'projection' back into ancient history of a real rotation of the 'High Kingship' among the inter-related provincial kings in the historical period of the kingship from c. AD 400?

More recent historians doubt if 'Fortriu' refers exclusively to the southern region, and it has even been suggested as being the area of Moray further North. This is the argument of Alex Woolf.[11] There are references to King Macbeth of Scots, who ruled the whole former Pictish kingdom from 1040 to 1057 and was a member of the then royal house of Moray in the north as son of its 'mormaer' Findlaech, as king of Fortrenn. Also referred to as king of Fortrenn in a Moray context is the great eighth-century warlord Oengus or Angus, king of the Picts from c. 728 to 761, who ruled the south too and fought the Strathclyde Britons on their common frontier North of the Firth of Clyde. There is also the question of the mysterious 'Maetae' tribe who assisted the Caledonians in fighting Emperor Septimius Severus around the Tay valley in AD 209–11. Were they the men of Fortriu by another name, or the 'Pictish' people of Fife or Atholl? Was there one Pictish kingdom centred south of the Mounth, in Fortrenn and Fife, and another to the north in Moray, as in early medieval times? Or was this 'back-dating' guesswork done on unreliable evidence? The unusual nature of their transmission of the 'Pictish' kingship, which did not pass once from father to son from its known origin around the early fifth century until the 780s in the preserved 'king-lists', and only rare and late succession from brother to brother can be taken as proving a divergence from normal patrilinear British practice, but explaining it and pinning it down as due to a defined legally-binding 'system' is another matter.

Ascribing this to custom or a more practical political 'trade-off' to avoid civil war is difficult, though it can be argued that as some non-Pictish (in the male line) rulers from other states were able to become 'High Kings' of the Picts at times when their homelands did not have military supremacy over the Picts they 'must' have been invited in. This would be on account of their being useful 'neutral' candidates whose accession would not spark off a civil war. In that case, the question arises of 'who was eligible for the High Kingship and on what grounds', and as their fathers were non-Pictish their descent from Pictish rulers must have been via their mothers. This as will be seen, is likely in the case of the half-Northumbrian mid-seventh century king Talorcan mac Eanfrith, son of the Bernician ruler of 633/4 – his father was the son of the great Aethelfrith but only reigned precariously for around a year in Bernicia, never ruled in Deira, and was under constant threat from the invading Gwynedd warlord Cadwallon who eventually killed him. The Bernician dynasty's control of all Northumbria was soon restored by Talorcan's uncle Oswald and he and his next brother Oswy were the pre-eminent warlords of northern Britain from 635 to 671 so they may have had the military and political 'clout' to impose their nephew as king on a divided Pictish realm, but there is no record of either of them doing so by force apart from a vague reference by Bede to Oswy subduing most of the Picts (direct subjection as opposed to installing a puppet-king?). A degree of consensus and a Pictish-Northumbrain alliance against their mutual foe Dal Riada is likely. Similarly, the name of the great Pictish warlord and 'High King' Brude or Bridei mac Beli of the 670s to 690s, the man who defeated the final Northumbrian attempt to conquer their kingdom in 685 at the epochal battle of 'Nechtansmere' and killed the invading King Ecgfrith (ruled 670/1 to 685), son of Oswy, sounds British and linked to Beli, the earlier seventh-century king of Strathclyde and he is referred to by St Columba's biographer Abbot Adomnan of Iona as son of the king of Dumbarton ('capital' of Strathclyde). Was he the son of this Beli, brother of King Owen of Strathclyde who killed the king of Dal Riada in battle in 642, and thus a 'Strathclyde candidate' for the throne representing an anti-Northumbrian alignment?[12] Bede refers to Brude/Bridei as the cousin of Ecgfrith, so this implies that either he was closely related to Talorcan mac Eanfrith, who was Ecgfrith's first cousin (as Molly Miller reckoned), or he had another family connection to him, possibly via the Northumbrian King Edwin (Alex Woolf's idea).[13] Some kings may even have ruled both the Pictish and Strathclyde kingdoms, though not necessarily at the same time – e.g. the obscure early seventh-century 'Nechtan nepos Uerp' whose uncle/ancestor Uerp could be the Strathclyde royal-related noble 'Uid'. Uid's sons Gartnait, Talorcan, and Bridei were all kings of the Picts too.[14] Also possibly of foreign origin was the late 650s king Gartnait 'mac Donuel', but it is unclear if his father was a 'Domnhall' of Dal Riada – the name seems Irish/Dal Riadan – and if so whether this was the King Domnhall who ruled Dal Riada in the 630s. Another 'non-Pictish by male descent' candidate, as will be seen, is the case of the first king Bridei or Brude, recorded as 'mac Maelchon', who ruled from c.558 to 586. His father has been suggested (e.g. by John Morris) as king Maelgwyn of Gwynedd, who is said to have had a Pictish wife, and in this case he would have been a symbol of a Pictish-Gwynedd alliance against the northern Anglians of Bernicia and his 'brother' would have been King Rhun of Gwynedd who marched up the Pennines to the Hadrian's Wall and Lothian area around the 560s.[15] But this is less certain, given the lack of clarity over whether 'Maelchon' could be a Pictish name after all.

Other arguments among recent analysts have concerned the question of whether the enigmatic Pictish succession rules allowed succession as 'High King' to the sons or grandsons of any Pictish princess, or only specific ones. Could the names (some 'royal' i.e. those of past Pictish kings) given to assorted future kings at their birth imply whether they were eligible or not? Did the grant of a specific name imply that the child was high up the succession list, or alternately to be barred from the throne? This is Isabel Henderson's theory.[16] N Evans (in 'Royal succession and kingship among the Picts', in *The Innes Review*, vol 59, no. 1, pp. 1–48) agrees that more men with 'royal' names tended to succeed to the throne, implying that such an honour improved their chances even if it did not make it automatic and force was also important. Other ideas include that kings could be renamed at their accession to give them an appropriate 'royal' name, or that accession via the female line was specified as being of a deceased king's sister's son rather than his own son (though this relies on a somewhat shaky interpretation of the Pictish royal lineage that is not universally accepted). Alternatively, the succession of any grandchildren of a previous ruler was legal but not that of children (at least directly). But in either case the useage of specific and presumably 'royal' names for those who did succeed seems to drop off after the quick successions and probable civil wars of the 720s, and the successions of the period from c.760 to 790 are equally muddled so a breakdown of any existing 'system' is logical. It has been argued by Dauvit Broun that these periods of muddle and apparent feuding over the throne led to 'normal' patrilinear succession emerging, at least among the lineage of the brothers Constantine/Custennin and Angus who held the throne from c.790 to 834, and also that as the latter two also ruled the kingdom of Dal Riada the latter's royal family were now mixed up with and influenced the Pictish succession.[17]

The mythology of the 'founding king' Cruithne and his sons may also have been created in this period to stabilise the official 'narrative' of the 'High Kingship' as being always within one dynasty and so worthy of obedience on hereditary grounds.

A turbulent history of non-direct family successions: but what 'evidence' is only guesswork?

Cruithne and his seven sons, dated to several centuries before the era of Christ, are cited as the first rulers of the Pictish kingdom by one tradition, having come over from Ireland. The name of 'Cruithne' is in fact that given by ancient scholars to the Pictish people as a whole, and probably originates from the 'Q-Celtic' word for 'Britons'; he was thus an eponymous founder for the kingdom, seen in later memory or myth as being Irish-speaking and/or of Irish descent. He was stated in the early legends as the son of an exiled Irish king, Gub. The traditional length of the supposed reigns of his descendants is subject to the caveat that it was a common mistake of early recorders of dynastic lists to line up all the names in their possession as a neat 'father-son' descent whereas it was probably more complicated than that. Some kings may have ruled concurrently. The seven sub-principalities of the kingdom – later ruled by the seven 'Mormaers' and in the twelfth century by the Normanised seven 'Earls' – were supposedly traceable to Cruithne's sons. These mini-states were listed in *De Situ Albanie*, a document in its surviving form part of the early fourteenth-century *Poppleton Manuscript* in the Bibliotheque Nationale, Paris. The first of its two lists gives: Angus/ Mearns ('Enegus cum Moerne'), Atholl/Gowrie ('Adthole et Gouerin'), Menteith/Strathearn ('Sradeern cum Meneted'), Fife/Fortriu, Mar/ Buchan, Moray ('Muref')/Ross, and Caithness. The second list is more difficult to interpret, being geographical in dividing the seven states up by their boundary features (rivers and mountains) one of which ('Hilef') is unknown, but includes Argyll.[18] The line of the Pictish 'High Kings' in Pictish and Irish sources was descended from the eponymous Cat, ruler of Caithness – which suggests a political tradition, used by later genealogists, that Caithness was the most powerful sub-kingdom. An alternative first ruler was Cathluan, son of Irish king Gub. Cat or Catluan was succeeded by his son Gede, and he in turn by his son Taran who allegedly ruled for a hundred years. 'Taran' was the name of a Brittonic god of thunder, and there is a parallel between his possible mythical origin and those of the legendary early British kings Bran 'the Blessed' and Beli.

The first definitively historical king recorded in non-Pictish evidence was Drust mac Erp, whose death is placed at AD 449 by the Irish *Annals of Clonmacnoise* (possibly a few years out). He reigned for allegedly twenty-nine years (100 years according to the *Pictish Chronicle*), and St Patrick's mission to Ireland in c. 435 is supposed to have been in his nineteenth year as king. Either him or a near-contemporary must have had notable success in raiding south against the British if the Saxon traditions are correct that the British over-king 'Vortigern' had to send a Saxon force north to fight him. Logically the end of Roman rule in Britain in 410 led to some if not all of the garrisons of Hadrian's Wall leaving, possibly in the army of the rebel emperor Constantine III to fight in Gaul in 407 – though archaeology shows settlement by farmer-soldiers on this frontier continuing into the mid-fifth century. Someone – seaborne Picts? – burnt down the Roman signal-stations on the Yorkshire coast around 400, and there was a fifth century Germanic settlement on the lower Humber which may have been the mercenaries who British/Welsh legend says King 'Vortigern' employed.

Little apart from approximate regnal dates is known even of the longest and/or most successful Pictish rulers of the fifth century and early sixth century, assumed to include the long-ruling Drust and his brother, the mid-fifth century Nechtan 'Morbet' ('of the Speckled Sea'). Nechtan was apparently exiled to Ireland by his brother, who was succeeded by an obscure king called Talorcan, but returned to take the throne later and ruled for twenty-four years. His sobriquet might indicate a naval dimension to his rule, possibly as a raider of southern Britain, or just refer to his coming from overseas to rule. According to legend he founded a Christian monastery at Abernethy to give thanks for his safe return, having promised this to St Brigid in Ireland when she prophesied his rule. He was succeeded by an equally obscure king called Drest, who ruled for around thirty years, then by Galam/Galan (fl. 500) who ruled for fifteen years, then by co-rulers Drest mac Drust (or mac Uudrost) and Drust mac Girom. Then came Gartnait for six or seven years, his brother Cailtram for one or six years, Talorcan mac Muircholach for eleven, Drest mac Munait for one year, and Galam for two or four years. What is notable about this obscure period is that even a long-reigning and so presumably secure ruler, such as Nechtan and the two Drests, was not usually (if ever) succeeded by his son – clearly they could not over-rule the expectation of their great provincial lords that the succession would alternate between families.

The choice of an outsider, Bridei/Brude mac Maelchon, around 557 suggests an inability to find a suitable local candidate. Given that his predecessor Galam reigned with him for at least a year and may have died as late as 580, it is possible that discontented nobles staged a revolt in Bridei's favour and forced Galam to accept him as co-ruler and later to step down – or that Galam was seen as an inadequate ruler for the contemporary wars with the Irish settlers of Dal Riada. Maelchon is an unusual name and has been claimed to be King Maelgwyn of Gwynedd in North Wales, notably by John Morris in the 1970s, though this remains unproven. There is no tradition of Maelgwyn – the strongest ruler in Wales – using an army to force the choice of his son on this distant kingdom, so if he was 'Maelchon' he presumably married a Pictish princess and the Pictish nobles called on his son as a 'neutral' candidate who did not attract local enmity. Or did Bridei bring useful Gwynedd troops to a kingdom under threat from the recent Irish settlements in Argyll?[19] But some historians regard the similarity of names as coincidence. Whoever he was, Bridei/Brude was recorded by the Irish *Annals of Ulster* as routing the Dal Riadans early in his reign, in 558 or 560, so he may have brought new military vigour or reorganised the Pictish army. Bridei/Brude mc Maelchon was succeeded by another presumed son of a Pictish princess and a foreign ruler (as suggested by John Bannerman), Gartnait son of Aedan of Dal Riada.[20] The *Life of St Columba* makes it clear that when the saint went to Bridei's court around 565 he was reigning over a pagan, Druid-led establishment based at a hillfort on a rock near Inverness, probably Craig Padraig near the Beauly Firth. A prince of the ruling Irish 'High Kings' dynasty of the Ui Niall in Midhe, the formidable Columba/Columbcille, founding abbot of Derry ('The Oaks') in Ulster's Irish origin probably meant that his lack of a warm Pictish welcome (or many converts at first) resulted from him being seen as a Dal Riadan ally. King Bridei shut the gates of his main residence near Inverness as Columba arrived, but they miraculously flew open to admit the saint. After assorted trials of miraculous powers between Columba and the Druids, the king was duly impressed and he and his followers are supposed to have been baptised en masse in Loch Ness. A sixth-century monastic community has recently been discovered near Portmahomack in Easter Ross, not far from Bridei's 'capital', so this may be a monastery placed there by Columba to help convert the Court and nobility.

Gartnait mac Domelch, Bridei's successor, may have been the Gartnait who was son of the Picts' neighbour, King Aedan of Dalriada. If so his choice implies a radical change in inter-state relations to alliance with the former foe, logically against a mutual enemy – the southern Pictish (sub-) state of the 'Maetae' in Fortrenn who are recorded as fighting Aedan around 590? Aedan, greatest ruler in southern Scotland, was the first known local sovereign to convert to and promote Christianity and was also the first to receive Church anointing, from St Columba. Did the elderly Columba, who died in 597, promote this Pictish-Dal Riadan alliance? Gartnait died around 599 according to the Irish *Annals of Tigernach*. Another Nechtan ('nepos'/?grandson of Erp/Urb), this time with no definite foreign connection, then succeeded and reigned for twenty or twenty-one years; one theory has it that he was also ruler of the neighbouring kingdom of Strathclyde and so had a British father but this is only a guess.[21] He was definitely a Christian and promoted the religion in his dominions; Bridei mac Maelchon may have eventually converted but if so was not known as a Christian enthusiast. Nechtan gave sanctuary to Eanfrith, son of his predatory neighbour Aethelfrith of Northumbria, after the latter was killed by his challenger Edwin near Doncaster in ?617. Aethelfrith had united the north-eastern Anglian settler kingdoms of his own Bernicia (the Northumbrian coastlands) and Deira (Yorkshire) around 604, and Edwin was the exiled heir to overrun Deira but had no ancestral claim to Bernicia and was installed in power by an East Anglian army. The resulting new state soon became the greatest 'power' in central-northern Britain, Aethelfrith having defeated the Northern British at the famous battle of 'Catraeth' (Catterick?) and then the Dal Riadans at 'Degsastan' (Dawston in Liddesdale?) around 600. It now controlled Lothian and the Firth of Forth region, formerly the kingdom of Din Eidyn (Edinburgh). Thus its kings were a threat to the Picts as well as to their surviving British neighbours in Strathclyde, and it was logical for the Picts to take in a useful pretender with a 'rightful' claim on its throne. Eanfrith was to marry a Pictish princess, probably daughter of Nechtan's sister and a lord called Gwid or Uid (who may have been the Gwid or Uid of Strathclyde who fought for the British against Bernicia in the 590s). When Edwin was killed by his Welsh foe Cadwallon of Gwynedd in 633/4 Eanfrith took over Bernicia briefly only to be killed by Cadwallon as well within a year. His younger brothers Oswald and Oswy then returned to Bernicia from Dal Riada, to expel the Welsh.

Eanfrith's son Talorcan succeeded Talorc mac Gwid/Uid, possibly his uncle and thus Nechtan's brother-in-law or son-in-law, to the Pictish throne around 653. ('Uid' may be the north British, probably Strathclyde noble Gwid referred to in the *Gododdin* poem c.600, but this could be coincidence; much speculation has been built precariously on similar-sounding names.)[22] It is not known if this represented an alliance between Talorcan's uncle Oswy of Northumbria and the Picts. Oswy was threatened by the Angles of Mercia under Penda, ruler from c. 626 to 655, who had killed Oswald in 642, and their Welsh allies to his south and needed allies. Talorcan's chief claim to fame was killing the king of Dal Riada, Dunnchad, in battle at Strath Ethairt in 654. Gartnait mac Donuel (Domnall?), who succeeded Talorcan around 657 and reigned for six or six-and-a-half years, may also have been a Northumbrian vassal or nominee. Again, his father's name gives cause for speculation as Domnall 'Brecc', 'the Freckled' (killed 642), had been king of Dal Riada in the 630s; was Gartnait's selection a sign of an alliance to Dal Riada, or was 'Donuel' unconnected to Domnall of Dal Riada?[23] His brother Drust succeeded him in 663, a rare example of the throne staying in the same family and possibly enforced by Oswy; Dal Riada was currently pushing northwards to overrun the Inner Hebrides as far as Skye so the Pictish kingdom may have been under serious military strain and needed Northumbrian help. Oswy's death in 670 led to a Pictish revolt which may have unseated Drust. He was deposed in 671, logically during this revolt, and died in 677. The Picts suffered a severe reverse and massacre by Oswy's son and successor Ecgfrith in c.672, but their loss of Skye was reversed around 680 by a new king, Bridei/Brude mac Beli. His mother was probably a daughter of Eanfrith and his father may have been the Strathclyde ruler Beli mac Nechtan from his name – or was this coincidence? His selection may indicate an alliance with Strathclyde against Northumbria. He is said to have defeated the Scots heavily and besieged their principal fortress, Dunadd in Lorne. A war with Ecgfrith followed with the threat of conquest by Northumbria from the 670s; Northumbria even imposed its own bishop in Fife. This was reversed after King Brude defeated and killed Ecgfrith in 685 at Nechtansmere in the Mearns. The siting of the battle suggests a large-scale Northumbrian offensive up the east coast of Scotland north of the Tay, possibly the most ambitious war by a ruler of northern England since Roman times. The aggressive Ecgfrith, a hot-tempered ruler who was famous for his defiance of the Roman Church over St Wilfrid's exile, presumably hoped to crush the Picts decisively; instead he lost his life and crippled Northumbria's northern expansionism.[24] A Pictish military revival followed, logically incorporating the manpower of reconquered Fife and the Firth of Forth region. Brude died in 693 and was the first Pictish king to be buried on the holy island of Iona with the Christian kings of Dal Riada, by Abbot Adomnan (St Columba's biographer) who was clearly a personal and political ally. His successor Taran was deposed within four years by a rival, Brude mac Derile, who resumed the state's military success; 'Derile' has been suggested as a female name and his father is unknown.[25] The number of possibly female names for kings' defining parents declines sharply after 730, so this has been suggested as indicating the end of any tradition of inheritance via the female line. Possibly this was just a reflection of the successive seizures of the kingship by a smaller number of lineages, especially that connected to the great 730s-50s warlord Oengus/Angus.

A century or so of quiescence by the monarchy concerning the – potentially invaluable – Christian Church was ended as king Nechtan mac Derile (who succeeded his brother Brude in 706) was converted to Christianity by Curetan, a missionary bishop despatched from Iona. Nechtan had been in Ireland for an important synod at Birr in 697 with Adomnan, and evidently saw the advantage of aligning his kingdom with the Church, a policy which the Dalriadan monarchy had been far quicker to take up; possibly the siting of Iona in Dalriadan territory had meant Pictish suspicion of its missionaries' motives. Now there was a new wave of conversions under the eighth century religious movement of the 'Celi De' (Culdees), the 'Friends of God', who were to set up monasteries in Pictish lands such as that at Dunkeld. The Iona Church also finally adopted the 'Roman' date for celebrating Easter and other practices in 716, so the Pictish Church was brought into line with European practice. But political stability did not follow the alliance of church and state, unusual for a British monarchy. Pictish power suffered from some sort of internal strife in the 720s, when Nechtan retired or was deposed. Possibly the fact that he had succeeded his own brother gave rise to resentment among ambitious 'mormaers' that his family was monopolising the throne. Nechtan's successor (724) Drust faced revolt from him in 726, defeated and imprisoned him, but was then driven out by Alpin mac Eochaid, a Dal Riadan prince (great-grandson of 630s King Domnall Brecc but son of a Pictish princess). Order was restored by King Oengus or Angus (ruled 729–61), who defeated Drust in three battles, drove out Alpin, and resumed a period of Pictish military predominance. Around 736 he became king of the Dalriadans too – the first union of 'Scotland' north of the Forth. Details are so obscure that we cannot tell if this was partly by by consent or entirely by conquest, but it was principally due to a practical need to evict his old foe Alpin, now king of Dal Riada; the Picts were clearly the senior partner in the alliance. The union apparently ended after Angus' brother Talorcan was defeated by the army of Strathclyde under king Teudeber at Mugdock in 750, thus weakening his military power and emboldening a Dal Riadan revolt led by Aed 'Find' ('the Fair'). Angus held onto the Pictish kingdom until 761, and was succeeded by his brother Brude. Then c.763 the throne passed to Ciniod mac Feredach of Loarn (Lorne), from a different branch of the dynasty which had been fighting Angus. He suffered a decisive defeat by Aed 'Find' in 768, and the two kingdoms seem to have been on a more equal footing for the obscure final decades of the eighth century. Around 775 Ciniod was succeeded by Alpin mac Feret, who was replaced in turn by Talorcan mac Drust (possibly 'Dubthalorc', 'Black Talorc', king of the Southern Picts, who died in 781). It is unclear if these two obscure rulers shared the throne for a time, voluntarily or due to being unable to evict each other, or if the next king – Talorcan mac Angus, ruled c. 782–5 – was the son of the great mid-century king Angus and so presumably heir to his warband. In any event, the kingdom was clearly unstable again.[26]

In 789 the Dal Riada prince Constantine, presumably with a Pictish mother, drove out king Conall mac Tadhg and probably seized the Pictish throne; sources disagree on the length of his reign (over thirty years?). He was to ascend the Dal Riadan throne too in 811, and was clearly the most powerful and secure Pictish ruler for a generation as he ruled for over thirty years. He built a new fortress at Forteviot in western Fife and a church at Dunkeld, and was probably driven to relocate Pictish power to the east of Scotland by heavy Scandinavian settlement in the North-West. From the genetic and place-name evidence, it would seem that the brunt of settlement fell on the northern Pictish lands of Moray, threatened by Vikings in the Hebrides; but Dal Riada was closer and was more immediately threatened. Constantine's brother Angus II succeeded him in both kingdoms in 820–34, possibly aided by the need for them to act together against the Viking threat; the union was unlikely to have lasted if they had not faced such a foe and had to pool their resources. But Cinaed/Kenneth Mac Alpin, who succeeded to the Pictish throne after their army was destroyed by the Vikings at Forteviot in 839, was the first to make such a union last. This was no doubt due to loss of Pictish manpower during Viking ravages which was most apparent after the defeat and death of King Eoganan and his nobles in battle in 839. The later patriotic Scots assumption that Kenneth conquered the Picts by force (and a legend that he murdered their last, disputed king Drust by treachery) are now thought to be less likely than an agreement by (most but not all?) of the latter to merge their realms to combat the Vikings; cultural similarities appear to have been growing for some time. More likely, the self-made warlord Kenneth was a 'new man' from the Gaelic west of Scotland (Galloway?) who had a Pictish mother so he was eligible for their kingship, and he merged two kingdoms into one new unit with the backing of (most of) both older kingdoms' elites on account of the crisis of Scandinavian conquest that both faced.[27] Notably, the title of 'king of the Picts' continued to be used for Kenneth and his brother Donald and son Constantine I; the latter was later reckoned in the Pictish royal chronicle to be their seventieth and last ruler. Was there a 'personal' not institutional union of the kingdoms which only later turned to a permanent union, as with Wessex and Mercia in England in the 910s?

Chapter Eight

Was the Creation of One Kingdom of England a Dynastic Accident?

The 'Great Army' invasion of 865: how and why? Subject to 'myths' as with the Anglo-Saxon 'invasions'?

In the winter of 865–6 what was subsequently referred to as the 'Great Army' of Scandinavians landed in the western part of East Anglia, apparently in the Fenland, and started a process of piecemeal conquest of the Anglo-Saxon kingdoms. Previously from the first attack in 793 the 'Vikings' – a name of uncertain origin but probably meaning 'men of the fjords', though this would technically mean Norwegians and many if not most of the invaders/settlers of southern England were ethnically Danes as shown by their DNA – had concentrated on raiding in the form of 'hit and runs' by the crews of individual or small groups of ships, and there had been only rare incursions by anything that could be described as an 'army' let alone one intent on settling. Nor did the Anglo-Saxon records, mainly the *Chronicle* (written up later in the century so not that remote from events), usually refer to individual leaders – this time there were three named brothers plus a group of high-status 'kings' and 'jarls' who are named as fighting Wessex at the battle of Ashdown in Berkshire in January 871.[1] In fact, there had been at least one large-scale earlier invasion, in 851 when the attackers had sailed up the Thames with '350 ships' to invade Mercia, taken London, and defeated King Beorhtwulf but when they moved on into Wessex had been defeated heavily at 'Aclea' (possibly Ockley in Surrey, in which case they had probably been moving south-west along Stane Street towards Chichester) by King Aethelwulf and his son Aethelbald.[2] If there had been twenty to thirty men per ship this army must have consisted of several thousand men and so been organised by a coalition of raiding groups, but the 866–71 invasion not the 851 one was known as the 'Great Army' so the later attack was probably larger. Whether the 851 attack was intended just to loot towns and monasteries as usual or to settle lands if things had gone better is unclear, and by the winter of 854–5 the Vikings were bold enough to stay for a winter on the island of Sheppey off the Kent coast so they were becoming more ambitious.[3] Year-round raiding of a wide area from an 'occupied zone' on the coast had been the practice for some decades in the similarly afflicted Ireland which also had a group of smaller states not one large state able to provide a large army, so a permanent coastal presence may have been considered by ambitious captains for the 850s. In Ireland the Vikings had set up coastal bases and trading-towns at Dublin, Waterford and Limerick – could London have gone the same way in 851? In the event, the process of conquest and settlement only commenced in 866. The 'brothers' who led it are attested by the contemporary sources as Halfdan, Ivarr 'the Boneless', and Ubbe/Hubba and the first two of these would go on to rule another kingdom of Scandinavian settlers in Dublin, where it seems that Ivarr was already active in the 840s; and both would die in eastern Ireland too, Ivarr in 873 and Halfdan in battle in Strangford Lough in 877. But the naming of their father as Ragnar 'Lothbrok', i.e. 'Leather-Breeches', is problematic given that the pirate warlord and ruler of that name attracted all sorts of unlikely and generic stories, rather like the Jutish 'invader' of Britain, Hengest, in the fifth-century. He was placed in different time-scales by different stories and genealogies, though usually in the early-mid-ninth-century, was linked to assorted acts of heroic bravery and cunning, and in the context of the invasion of England in 865–6 the latter was said to have been in vengeance for his violent death. Specifically, it was claimed that he had been captured raiding Northumbria a few years earlier by king Aelle – a historical personage reigning there by 862 – and had been thrown into a pit of snakes and bitten to death. His sons then duly declared vengeance and decided to conquer not only Northumbria but all England.[4] But this story of treachery, violence and oaths of vengeance was the normal procedure for Viking Age 'sagas' and was somewhat generic, and being thrown in a pit of snakes was also suffered by other heroes, for example, King Harald 'Hardradi' of Norway, ruled 1047 to 1066, who was supposedly punished in this fashion by the Eastern Roman/Byzantine authorities while serving in their 'Varangian Guard' in c.1042 but managed to kill the snakes and escape. It and the whole question of invasion as vengeance for Ragnar by his sons do not appear in Anglo-Saxon sources, and making a political or military decision part of a personal vendetta was normal for contemporary tales. The actual reasons for the invasion may have been more practical, e.g. the division of the land of England into a number of smallish states with none of their kings having a distinguished military reputation, making them seem easy prey to bored warriors in search of loot or poor peasant-farmers in search of better land.

The Vikings systematically tackled the Anglo-Saxon kingdoms, starting with the weaker ones – but this had been standard practice for some decades for their roaming bands of warriors on the Continent, who tended to hone in on weaker states. The West Frankish kingdom of Charles 'the Bald' after 840 was their main target there, with its many long and wide rivers providing easy access plus useful civil wars between Charles and his brothers ruling the Low Countries, Germany and Italy (and later his disinherited nephew Pepin in Aquitaine). As with Wessex in the 870s and early 890s, a determined long-term resistance led to the Vikings leaving – kings Louis III and Carloman drove the local Vikings out of modern south-west Belgium and Arnulf drove them out of north Belgium and the Netherlands in the 880s. The size of the Frankish army was larger than that available to either English or Irish provincial kings, which may explain why the latter were more vulnerable to crushing defeat and settlement. Nor was retreating 'out of range' of an attack practical in England. In small East Anglia in 869–70, the local resistance could not retreat out of reach of the Vikings after a major defeat and regroup – and in Northumbria and Wessex the resistance would have to retreat to a remote, infertile area like Bernicia or Cornwall.

Military logistics as much as personal vendettas may have brought a major Scandinavian force to England in 865. The later Norse sagas, naturally, found the 'revenge' factor – the tale of the warlord Ragnar Lothbrok thrown into a snake-pit by the king of Northumbria and his three sons swearing vengeance – more exciting. It was easier to hold down conquered territory in England, and harder for their foes to regroup inland and fight back; even Mercia was smaller than the West Francian kingdom of Charles 'the Bald'. Shrewd incoming warlords could easily assess the size of their enemies' military resources and so select an easy target. Obtaining the maximum amount of land seems to have been the main lure for the participants in the invasions as they did not satisfy themselves with one fertile Anglo-Saxon kingdom; in

Ireland the resistance had been just as (usually) badly co-ordinated and piecemeal but the Vikings preferred to settle on the coasts and did not do so permanently inland in the 'midlands' (unlike in central Mercia in England). The question of 'land-hunger' and a population explosion in the Norwegian fjords or the peninsula of Jutland is usually taken as one cause, with opportunistic would-be settlers testing out the kingdoms of western Europe to see which would provide least resistance. There were already large-scale armies, the 'White Foreigners' (Danes) and 'Black Foreigners' (Norwegians), in fertile and divided Ireland, dating from the 840s, and tradition speaks of major Viking warfare with the Picts and Scots in the newly united kingdom of Scotland; probably by the later ninth century the invaders had settled the Hebrides. The recent DNA research shows that the population there has a mainly Norwegian origin. None of the current English kings as of 865 had a prestigious military reputation, although Burghred of Mercia (ruled from c.852 to 874) had overrun Powys in 853, and this may well have been a factor in deciding on the attack. Northumbria was in the middle of a civil war between kings Osbert and Aelle, Edmund of East Anglia was young and had few resources. Wessex's co-victor over the Vikings in 851, the young king Aethelbald had died in 860 – his early death, when he cannot have been much over thirty (if that) as he had not witnessed charters until the later 840s and had fought his first battle in 851, is one of the royal mysteries of the era. So is the early death of his younger brother Aethelbert in midwinter 865–6;[5] why exactly did so many royals in Wessex die young in the mid-ninth century (and the tenth century) and was there poor health in their family? As a result the major military power of southern England was in a weak position; the remaining Cerdicing princes Aethelred (probably born around 844/5) and Alfred (born 848/9) were young and untried in war. Is it significant that the Vikings had attacked Wessex in king Egbert's old age (to assist the Cornish in rebellion) in 838, when his son Aethelwulf was new to the throne in 840, and after Aethelbald's death in 860?

A narrow margin of survival for Wessex.

The invasion was clearly carefully planned – the attackers landed in East Anglia, too small a state to resist them, and blackmailed King Edmund into giving them horses and supplies so they could attack Northumbria. Probably hoping for immunity from conquest in return for encouraging them to leave, he co-operated – and did not assist either Northumbria or (in 868) nearer Mercia to resist. The invaders then conquered Deira while Osebrt and Aelle were fighting each other and occupied York as a walled base to withstand counter-attack, defeated and killed the two kings when the latter attacked them, and moved on into eastern Mercia to sail up the River Trent and occupy Nottingham. As with York, the entrenched Vikings sat it out with their supplies and loot in a fortified town with river-access for their ships and dared the locals to attack them; the Mercians called in help from Wessex but were unable to storm Nottingham. Eventually king Burghred had to come to terms with the invaders. Having disposed of both kingdoms, the Vikings then returned and conquered East Anglia at leisure in 869, destroying its smaller army (at Hoxne?) and capturing and killing its King Edmund, before moving on south-west to Wessex which alone had bothered to come to its neighbours' aid.[6] The numbers of the invaders are unknown, and may have been exaggerated by later myth – nor is it clear if all the Vikings who attacked Wessex in 870 had been with the invasion from 865 or if the latter's success encouraged more land-hungry aspirants to arrive from Scandinavia to join in the later campaigns.

The Viking division of conquered Northumbria and Mercia (each left with an Anglian puppet-king ruling part of it) and conquest of East Anglia, all fertile lands able to sustain many settlers, did not satiate the invaders. In 875 Mercia was divided, with the lands west of Watling Street being left to a 'puppet' king (Ceolwulf II) and the east being settled as the 'Danelaw' i.e. the lands where Danish customs and law came to prevail. Deira was divided for settlement among the conquerors with a line of 'collaborator' Anglian kings ended, and less fertile Bernicia was left to the Angles under the autonomous 'earldormen' of the dynasty based at Bamburgh. East Anglia had already been settled after the death in battle of King Edmund late in 869 – with a possibility that an obscure local king, Oswald, was set up to rule the Anglian inhabitants for a few years as his coinage appears though no record mentions him. Like the 'collaborator' king Ceolwulf II who was allowed to keep western Mercia as a Viking ally and was dismissed by the *Chronicle* as an 'unwise king's thegn', all such magnates who worked with the new settlers appear to have been marginalised from the official records and where possible written out of history. The dominant 'narrative' imposed by the surviving and eventually triumphant kingship of Wessex was one of necessary and divinely-blessed resistance by the Christian English people to the 'heathen', as seen in the *Anglo-Saxon Chronicle* with its central storyline of Alfred's wars. This deliberately left out those prepared to work with or for the Scandinavians as 'traitors' to their people and their faith, although the destruction of the monasteries and bishops' sees in the Scandinavian-ruled regions of the north and east decimated literacy and ended a major source of written records and the end of royal lines atomised administration so the lack of surviving written details from there was inevitable. As in the post-Roman period, information about events and ordinary lives in a transformed society with new settlers is scanty, much of what has survived is literature not chronicles, and the written records come from 'official' sources; distortion may have crept into what we 'know'. Only scattered written references and coinage gives any idea of who ruled the new Scandinavian 'zone'; and (as with the incoming Anglo-Saxons in the fifth century and sixth century) we cannot be certain of the number of incomers and where they settled. There are many 'Danish'-influenced place-names in the 'Danelaw', especially in Norfolk, Lincolnshire, the East Midlands, and Yorkshire, e.g. the suffixes 'by' and 'thorpe'. But, as with the 'Anglo-Saxon' place-names across England, this does not tell us how many remaining inhabitants from the previous society adopted the new names – and indeed both Anglo-Saxon as a language and 'Anglo-Saxon' DNA is too close to that of Scandinavia (Denmark in particular) to be able to separate them.

There was enough fertile land involved in the lands settled in the 'Danelaw' to provide homes for thousands of land-hungry Scandinavians, and the incomers had clear military supremacy over the locals whose leaders had been defeated in battle and killed or (like Burghred of Mercia) had given up and fled the country. There was no urgent need for the 'Great Army' to tackle Wessex either, but it did so twice – firstly in 870, when the other kingdoms had been defeated and partly occupied but not yet settled, and secondly in 875–6 after settlement. Wessex was fought to a standstill in the 'battle-winter' of 870–1 and probably forced to pay tribute (Alfred's propagandists seem to have covered this up), but it was still in existence with an intact if mauled army and a capable war-leader in

Alfred. The sites of the major battles indicate that the invaders, initially based at Reading on the middle Thames to give their ships access to the sea, had been moving west into Berkshire – to be checked at 'Ashdown'. What we know about this crucial battle is less than was once thought, as Margaret Gelling has argued convincingly that the name was a generic one for the entire ridge of the Berkshire downs west of Reading so any attempt to place the site (once assumed to be near the Uffington 'White Horse' which G. K. Chesterton and others assumed to have been carved to commemorate it) and reconstruct the battle is dubious. Cholsey nearer the Thames, on a lower ridge than Uffington Down, has also been suggested – and the identity of the person who won the battle (King Aethelred or his brother and lieutenant Alfred?) was clearly argued over at the time as the latter's biographer Asser pointed out that the invaders were caught off guard before they were ready to fight by Alfred pre-empting his brother's planned advance. The Vikings suffered heavy losses, but the practical impact was small; they drove a West Saxon attack off Reading and then pursued them south across Hampshire and Wiltshire. After the surprise defeat for the invaders and major losses at Ashdown in January 871, the main battles were at Basing in northern Hampshire, 'Meretun' (Merton or Marten?) in the Winchester area or western Hampshire, and Wilton in eastern Wiltshire. The death of king Aethelred at Wimborne Minster in eastern Dorset after Easter 871 may imply that he had had to move his headquarters there, in retreat westwards – though he apparently owned the local estates as it was inherited by his son Aethelwold.

Despite the major West Saxon victory at Ashdown and a number of drawn battles, the defenders seem to have been forced into terms when a second Viking force arrived to assist the invaders in the summer.[7] The Wessex war of 870–1 was reckoned as having nine national battles and countless skirmishes, with nine jarls and one king killed;[8] it seems to have occupied a similar heroic status in subsequent memory in Wessex to 1940 in modern Britain, with the embattled and outnumbered defenders surviving impossible odds under an indomitable leader. But this leaves one major question. The kingdom of Wessex had been fought to a standstill though not overwhelmed and was no threat to Viking control of eastern England as of 875, so why attack again? But Guthrum, not the sons of Ragnar, took on Wessex. This new offensive to take over the last surviving Saxon kingdom is perhaps surprising, considering the limited objectives of earlier attacks on England and of the Viking tactics in Ireland – where no attempt was made to conquer the entire island and large-scale raids across the surviving kingdoms from the occupied coast plus occasional interventions in local civil wars were not followed by much inland settlement. In Ireland the new Scandinavian settlements at major harbours on the coast – Dublin, Waterford, and Limerick – ruled their hinterlands and the fertile central plain was ravaged, but there was no grandiose division of each province among settlers. Nor was destroying Wessex in 875–6 a case of a 'master-plan' by the sons of Ragnar, who appear to have led the first attack on Wessex in the 'battle-winter' of 870–1 and so had experience of the terrain and a stalemate to avenge. By this time Ivarr had left for Ireland to re-establish himself as King of Dublin, where he was to die in 873, and Halfdan's rule seems to have been centred on York with an eye on events in Ireland where he intervened to back up his nephews' rule of Dublin in the mid-870s then contended for a kingdom himself. The obscure Ubbe/Hubba was probably in South Wales, and at this time Dyfed in south-west Wales had no recorded kings so it was probably anarchic and partly occupied by Scandinavians on the coasts. None of the sons of Ragnar took part in the attacks on Wessex in 875–8, and probably Halfdan, as ruler of York, had already satiated his closest lieutenants with lands there. The settlement of Deira and eastern Mercia in 874–5, plus East Anglia, provided the Vikings who were in the 'Great Army' at those dates with plenty of land. But some opportunistic attackers were clearly intent on carrying on the war until they received a check, as they did in Francia. Given the nature of Scandinavian – as with Germanic – leadership, success depended on a warlord having loot and land to give his followers and thus attracting support over a long period. Possibly each division of a kingdom left some warriors – recent arrivals who had not taken part in the major campaigns of conquest? – without land and they gathered round an ambitious captain who could offer them a new target. Guthrum, never heard of in the war of 865–71, suddenly emerges as the leader of the attack on Wessex in 875 and would fit this concept of an 'excluded' minor war-leader keen to carve out his own kingdom.

Guthrum's choice of Wareham in southern Dorset, a peninsula between two major rivers a few miles inland from the coast and adjacent to the huge Poole Harbour, for his base shows his grasp of strategy – as with

York in 866, Nottingham in 868, and Reading in 870, the Vikings took a defensible town with river-access to the sea and proceeded to plunder the hinterland and dare the enemy to attack them. Nor had southern Dorset been involved in the war in 870–1, so there was plenty of fresh loot to seize there. Wessex stood on a 'knife-edge' again from 876 to 878, and the large Viking armies on the Continent felt it worth returning for another attack in 892. In 876 their eventual evacuation of their base at Wareham (in the centre of previously unravaged territory, and close to the sea so easy to supply) was probably due to the fortuitous loss of their fleet in a storm off Swanage, a few miles down the coast with rocky headlands and strong tides that clearly caught out the non-local invaders. This piece of luck probably then aided Alfred in forcing the land-based Viking expedition, now transferred west to another riverine base at Exeter in unravaged Devon, to agree to terms and promise to leave Wessex in 877. He had been able to blockade the Vikings at Wareham into an eventual agreement to leave, and their leader was ordered to swear to keep the agreement on his sacred arm-ring of the god Thor as the pagan equivalent of holy relics. But Guthrum broke his word, and the Viking army's swift transfer to Exeter by land via an unexpected night-time breakout and march without being intercepted implies that they expected to be able to repeat their defiance at Wareham there, with supplies arriving up the Exe from the sea. However the catastrophic loss of '130' ships off the nearby coast at Swanage in a sudden storm as they headed by sea towards Exeter, and the non-arrival of replacements from other Viking groups, prevented the invaders from bringing in adequate supplies once they reached Exeter. They were forced to negotiate sooner than expected, and had to agree to leave Wessex for good. The unexpected storm off Swanage was thus the crucial blow that stopped Guthrum from holding out at Exeter as long as he had done at Wareham, and it enabled Alfred to recover his position after Guthrum had seemingly made a fool of him for naivity by nonchalantly breaking his oath. Guthrum was forced to swear again on his sacred arm-rings to leave Wessex alone and give many hostages, and he took his army back to Mercia – but broke his word again as soon as a chance for attack arose.[9]

Guthrum returned to the attack at midwinter 877–8, probably encouraged by the prospect of catching Alfred unawares at Chippenham close to the Viking bases in south-west Mercia. Attack by land was also less vulnerable to the disruption of supplies than attack by sea, as Guthrum had found – and the fact that Alfred was finally to confront him within a few miles of Chippenham in spring 878 indicates that however much of Wessex had submitted Guthrum had based his army around that town in its north, close to his supply route to Mercia. It is possible that West Saxon 'spin-doctors' covered up the extent of local submission to him and most of Wessex may have surrendered; if there was any 'collaborating' among the elite their identities have been forgotten (or blotted out deliberately?) apart from one later reference to an 'ealdorman' called Wulfhere who had committed treason around this date, presumably as a Viking collaborator. Alfred was caught out as he had been at Wareham and had to hide in the impenetrable Somerset marshes, seeming to have abandoned his people and evidently lacking the ability to fight Guthrum for several months in midwinter. Probably most of Wiltshire, Dorset, and Hampshire were lost though he soon managed to build up a small and mobile guerrilla force.[10] It is to this period that the legend of 'King Alfred and the cakes' belongs; in fact it is first recorded in a life of St Neot over a hundred years later and there is no contemporary authority for it.[11] The moral stories of the Saint prophesying that the king would lose his throne and be reduced to a fugitive, and being proved right as Alfred humbly accepted, and the King submitting to a scolding from his hostess after he forgot to make sure a cottager's wife's cooking did not get burnt were typical 'morality tales'. The most that can be said is that the heroic nature of the struggle and the 'miraculous' recovery of the King's patrimony thanks to evident Divine backing in 878 attracted stories in subsequent generations, as in the more secular story of Alfred infiltrating the Viking camp before the battle of Ethandun disguised as a harper and finding out their battle-plans from their drunken gossip which first appears in William of Malmesbury's account c. 1125.[12]

The subsequent landing in north Devon by Hubba implies that that area was holding out, though the uncertain details of the campaign and location of his defeat may imply that 'ealdorman' Odda retreated to a well-defended hillfort (Cynwit/Countisbury?) and so was nervous of open battle. The '23 shiploads' of Vikings were routed, Hubba and many of his men (1,200 according to the *Chronicle*, 800 according to the tenth-century chronicle of Aethelweard) were killed, and a sacred 'raven banner' was captured.[13] Within a few months Alfred was able to summon enough men to a rendezvous on the Somerset-Dorset border at 'Egbert's Stone' (?near Longleat) to fight a battle, thus having approximately equal numbers at Ethandun. He then had the time to move up onto the ridge of Salisbury Plain for a battle in the open country there, probably unhindered; the resultant battle at 'Thandun', the 'place of slaughter', was probably on the edge of the ridge at Bratton Down above Westbury. The Vikings were heavily defeated and fled back to Chippenham, where they were besieged. Crucially, after this defeat at 'Ethandun' Guthrum could not sit it out in Chippenham as the sons of Ragnar had done in Reading after defeat at Ashdown in 871 – probably due to not having enough men left to man the walls. Alfred could starve him out as at Exeter in 877, and this time Guthrum was demoralised enough to keep his word to leave and live in peace with Wessex in the subsequent Treaty of Wedmore permanently – and to take his Christian baptism at Aller as Alfred's godson seriously.[14]

From survival to reconquest.

Military victory was followed by Alfred's famous administrative reforms, which reorganized Wessex for defence – with the caveat that he may have begun some of them before 878. Wessex had been divided into a network of counties run by royal officials (led by the ealdormen) not by semi-autonomous sub-kings since Ine's time, with the local levies for the army led by the ealdormen. Now Alfred arranged for a Wessex-wide network of fortified towns, the 'burhs', which served to gather troops and supplies and deny these vital positions to invaders; the Scandinavians could no longer attack suddenly, seize a major town, and build a fortification there to sit out a siege and plunder the countryside. The advantage of a safe defensive position in any confrontation from now on belonged to the West Saxons; and the presence of the defenders in a strong position dominating the invaded countryside would force attackers to spare many men from plundering to watch them. If they gave up and moved on, it diminished the amount of territory they could plunder; if they stayed to besiege the 'burh' it gave Alfred time to arrive with the main army. The 'burhs' thus ended several Scandinavian advantages used in 870–8, and can illustrate Alfred's strategic thinking, pragmatism, and administrative ability – though the flexible and durable state of the existing Wessex administration by c.860 (e.g. the local division into shires run by royal appointee 'ealdormen') may well have given him a 'head start'.[15] Who created this useful system of local government is one of the mysteries of West Saxon development, but the most likely candidate is king Ine (ruled 688 to 726), Caedwalla's cousin and successor and allegedly the brother of Alfred's direct ancestor. Next time a raiding fleet tested Wessex, at Rochester in 884, the locals held out in the fortified town; the invaders had to build their town camp outside, could not storm the town, and were duly starved out and forced to leave by Alfred (885).[16] In 886 he took over the vital position of London, which guarded the lower Thames from invasion, and handed it over to his new ally Aethelred, the ealdorman of Mercia who had taken over from the late 'collaborator' Ceolwulf II. Mercia had legal claim to the place and Alfred avoided antagonism by not using his military supremacy to secure it; Aethelred, now or recently married to Alfred's daughter Aethelfleda, proved a staunch ally for Wessex. Working with, rather than insisting on dominating, Mercia and using the greater military 'muscle' available to Wessex sparingly with respect for Mercian sensibilities shows Alfred's subtle and 'inclusive' strategies to use his leadership of the unconquered English wisely, thus reducing the chances of resentment, and it appears that he had worked (quietly?) with the despised Ceolwulf too until his death or deposition c.882 as in 2015 coins bearing their names together were found in the 'Watlington Hoard' in Oxfordshire (near their border).[17] Ceolwulf – the date and circumstances of whose end are unknown, reflecting our lack of knowledge of later ninth century Mercia – was probably deliberately written out of history by the 'narrative thrust' of the *Chronicle*, as directed by Alfred, but in fact he had enough resources and sense of initiative to invade Gwynedd in 878–9 and his troops were not evicted until a Welsh victory on the river Conwy in 881 (known from Welsh sources). Did Mercia attempt to restore its morale and resources by attacking Gwynedd after the death of its great king Rhodri 'Mawr' in battle with the Vikings in 878?

Alfred also rebuilt a powerful navy, able to challenge raiders at sea, and in 884 raided the Stour estuary in East Anglia to defeat a local fleet and sink 16 ships. Victory at sea was not always secured, and Alfred was not the 'founder of the English navy'; his father Aethelwulf (ruled 839 to 858) had also had a fleet and this (apparently based in his sub-kingdom

Kent) had had occasional victories against Viking fleets in the early 850s so logically he had had experienced sailors.[18] But it put raiders on the defensive, adding to his kingdom's defensibility. The main Scandinavian 'raiding-army' was occupied in northern Francia through the late 880s, but in 892 it returned to Kent after being fought to a standstill by the Franks in Flanders. Denied their usual fortified towns as bases by the West Saxon 'burhs', the invaders were forced into amended tactics by Alfred. They had to build their own camps but varied tactics with one invasion and camp in northern Kent (Milton) under Haesten and a second in the south (Appledore). Alfred positioned himself between them, and outsmarted the invaders when they sat it out waiting for the West Saxons levies' term of military service to expire so their army would have to disperse or else leave their agricultural work at home neglected. Alfred instituted a rota whereby only half the army was in service at any time and when one half had to be discharged the second took over – one of many inspired and logical improvisations. The second major Viking war turned into a mixture of prolonged sieges and occasional breakouts for plundering expeditions across country. Alfred's son Edward won his first victory at Farnham in 893 as the blockaded Southern army at Appledore broke out to plunder across Sussex into Hampshire; the defeated raiders had to flee to the Thames valley in a failed attempt to get to the northern army, which Haesten had evacuated to a new camp at Benfleet in Essex. A diversionary attack on north Devon and Exeter by an allied fleet drew Alfred off, but on his return Benfleet was blockaded and (in Haesten's absence) stormed. The Scandinavians in Essex, reinforced from the north, moved off to western Mercia, but West Saxons and Welsh came to the Mercians' aid and the invaders were besieged at Buttington, starved out, and defeated in battle. The remnants escaped back to Essex. 894 saw Scandinavian defeat in north Wales and a second campaign in Essex, this time based on a camp on Mersea Island, while more raiders attacked Exeter and the Chichester region, and in 895 the West Saxons besieged the invaders' camp on the river Lea upstream from London. Alfred protected the harvest so the raiders could not damage it and built fortified bridges across the river so they could not bring supplies in by river (a tactic which might have helped earlier Anglo-Saxon sieges had it been adopted then, e.g. at Nottingham in 868) and they broke out to try their luck in western Mercia only to be cornered and besieged again (this time at Bridgnorth). The Scandinavian army managed to break out in spring 896, but this time they did not return. Alfred also had some success at sea against continuing 'hit-and-run' raids on the South coast in 896 with a new type of longship superior to enemy vessels. Beyond this military success, he also seems to have been recognized as overlord by the rulers of Wales; he was sought out as their senior ally against raiding Vikings and his alliance with Wales prevented attacks by Aethelred's Mercians. The autonomous Anglian enclave of Bernicia established a relationship with him, which the West Saxon propagandists interpreted as vassalage. All the English not under Danish rule recognized his authority, although any such terms were only honorary.[19]

In military matters Alfred had managed to drive back two prolonged and serious attacks, and this was the last serious invasion for three generations. The successful defence of Wessex (and Mercia, where his daughter and son-in-law adopted the 'burh' system and received military aid during invasions) was centred on his planning, and this was duly adapted for reconquest of all England in the 910s. But he also did his best to revive learning for the future of Christian English culture, allegedly lamenting the fact that there was not one man able to read Latin books left in his war-ravaged kingdom, bringing in foreign scholars, and establishing his own palace school to educate the sons of the nobility. His circle of scholars, copying out vital or useful literary works, included Asser from Dyfed, John the 'Old Saxon' from Germany, and Grimbald of St Bertin, a Frank. The stories in Asser may be influenced by Einhard's life of Charlemagne, but this need not mean they were invented; Alfred had visited Francia and Rome at an impressionable age and modelled himself on Charlemagne. Keen on maximising literacy, he learnt to read and write Latin himself and undertook translations – historians differ if he was illiterate or just unable to use Latin until Asser taught him. His significant choices for translations showed his concept of Christian rule, justice, and ethics as well as personal spirituality and interest in Rome – Pope Gregory 'the Great's *Pastoral Care*, Boethius' *Consolation of Philosophy* and St Augustine's *Soliloquies*. Presumably influenced by the current Carolingian Francian ideal of a king as the spiritual and cultural as well as military-political leader of his people, he did his best to revive monasticism as well as learning, founding one monastery (which needed a foreign abbot) at Athelney and (probably) a nunnery at Shaftesbury.[20]

He played up his own and his elite's role as just and inspiring Christian leaders, educating the next generation to follow suit, and his interest in the past of his own people is seen in his commissioning of the *Anglo-Saxon Chronicle*, which glorified (and sanitized?) the record of the West Saxon monarchy.[21] It played up Wessex's right to lead the English, and set down the record of the heroic wars against heathen conquest for future generations; past defeats in the early history of the Anglo-Saxons plus the history of Wessex's foes seem to have been editorially sidelined.

Personal mysteries of Alfred: his health and his remains.

Probably the most significant and outstanding ruler of Ango-Saxon England, Alfred died on 26 October 899, aged probably fifty or fifty one. Even his health is a subject of legend and controversy and remains a mystery, though it is very rare for any Anglo-Saxon king to have his health discussed in an apparently contemporary source at all so it was presumably thought worthy of inclusion as an important factor in his career. But was this a straightforward tribute to how the king overcame his own frailty as well as the Vikings, or a piece of religious propaganda about the devout and holy king defeating his afflictions (and the temptations of sin) with Divine help? The fact that it was 'recorded' by a cleric and treated in somewhat muddled and cliché-ridden terms similar to those used in hagiographies has added to the controversy over its accuracy. Can we trust his biographer, a Dyfed cleric resident at his court called Asser (d 909)? Asser's stories about his chronic sickness and repeated physical collapses are dismissed by some as written into his biography to make him seem like a saintly sufferer chastised by God, or even as one clue that this 'contemporary first-hand account' of his career is full of stock clichés and muddle and so Asser's 'eye-witness' role must be doubted. Did Asser collect gossip from a time before he came to Alfred's court, was he really the king's intimate, is his use of stories similar to those of other kings (e.g. Einhard's stories of Charlemagne's interest in learning and his 'palace school') and bishops suspicious, or was the biography actually compiled from assorted accounts by a Fenland scholar, Byrtferth of Ramsey, c.1000 and just attributed to Asser to make it look authentic? The latter is Alfred Smyth's theory, using evidence of formulaic stories in the book and its apparent late tenth-century linguistic terminology.[22] Alfred was supposed to have prayed for relief from one illness (or lust?) and promised to accept any infliction which God imposed on him without complaint. He was then struck by a new illness at his wedding in 868, and had sporadic attacks thereafter – though these were not enough to seriously hinder his active career including several winter months 'on the run' as a fugitive. The confusing account of his illness defies accurate analysis, though Crohn's disease has been suggested,[23] and in political terms it probably added to his iron self-control, patience, and moral imperatives. The large number of early deaths among the males of his house, including his great-grandson King Eadred in his early-mid thirties, the latter's nephew Edgar at around thirty-two, and the latter's grandson Athelstan in his twenties, suggest some hereditary ailments. Edward 'the Confessor' (ruled 1042 to 1066) was the first male of his family to reach the age of sixty since (probably) Egbert in 839; the royals of the Carolingian house in Francia and some of those of Wales and Scotland often lasted into their sixties and seventies. To add to the mystery about Alfred the search for his remains has now become as intricate as that for King Richard III, due to the destruction of Hyde Abbey outside Winchester (where his body was removed from the 'New Minster' adjacent to the cathedral when the Minster was pulled down to make way for the new Norman cathedral c.1110) at the Reformation. Assorted (royal?) bones were apparently dug up at the site in 1788 and some were re-buried at the local church of St Bartholomew but have since been dispersed; however some of these have recently been re-discovered. Only one thigh-bone was dateable to the ninth or tenth century rather than the time after c.1200 when the site was used as a medieval cemetery; but its owner seems to have died at the age of around fifty so this could be a last relic of Alfred (or his son King Edward 'the Elder'?). A similar mystery – at the moment – surrounds the identity of the 'royal bones' from the pre-Norman Winchester cathedral which would have had to be moved when it was replaced by a new building in the 1090s. They were dispersed by pillaging iconoclastic Parliamentarian soldiers during the Civil War. Some of these – and some royal bones taken from Hyde Abbey – were apparently placed in a chest now on display there, which was reported by Thomas Hughes in his *King Alfred the Great* (1901) as having been done by Bishop Stephen Fox (d 1528). But this was clearly done before the Reformation in the 1530s, and he does not quote his source or say if they included Alfred's bones; and it is not clear if the cathedral remains scattered in the 1640s were restored to the chest intact or mixed up with others. Were these mixed with non-royals, and how many are tenth century and eleventh century? Some have been examined though DNA tests still await, and female remains might be those of Aethelred II's and Cnut's wife Queen Emma (d. 1052).

Reconquest: the founding of England?

At Alfred's death on 26 October 899 Edward, probably in his late twenties, was an experienced commander used to the army, and seems to have been his father's choice to succeed him. He had already commanded part of the royal army at a major victory over a raiding Viking army at Farnham in 892, so he had proved his ability.[24] The choice of him passed over his cousin Aethelwold, elder son of his father's brother King Aethelred, who was a little older and probably lacked his experience; the aggrieved 'atheling' (a term meaning 'throne-worthy' used for Anglo-Saxon princes) seized Wimborne Minster (probably his own manor) and Twynham (Christchurch) in eastern Dorset in revolt. Edward moved swiftly and advanced to the nearby hillfort of Badbury Rings to cut him off from the hinterland. Besieged in Wimborne, Aethelwold boasted that he would die rather than surrender but fled by night to the Scandinavians in Northumbria, apparently with a nun who the king had forbidden him to marry (which dispute may have sparked off the confrontation). Aethelwold was accepted by the Scandinavians in York as their king, though his position was soon disputed, and in 902 he moved south to win the adherence of the settlers in East Anglia. In 903 Aethelwold launched a major raid across the Thames at Cricklade, probably as a 'probe' to gain loot and assess his support; he shied away from battle and retreated into East Anglia before Edward could catch him. Edward eventually called off the chase in the Fens, probably because of extended communications in enemy territory and because his men's term of service was expiring, but during the West Saxon return march the contingents became separated and the disobedient Kentish troops were caught alone and attacked. A battle followed with many senior casualties on both sides, and though the Scandinavians held the battlefield Aethelwold and the East Anglian Danish King Eorhic/Eric were killed. This ended the challenge to Edward's throne,[25] though the threat may have been more serious than implied in the way that Edward competently tackled it given the willingness of a senior prince to start a civil war and of (bored or land-hungry?) Scandinavian settlers to back him. A Wessex civil war was the best hope of the warlords of the 'Danelaw' in defeating the threat posed by the unity of Edward's Wessex and his equally able sister Aethelfelda's Mercia, and because this break-up of English power did not happen we tend to forget that to contemporaries used to inter-royal feuds it would have been a real threat. Edward and his son Athelstan managed the 'narrative' of royal unity successfully, however, and challenges to it (e.g. the revolt or not of the atheling Edwin in 933) tend to be – deliberately – downplayed in the *Chronicle*.

Some years of peace followed, apart from opportunistic raids away from the West Saxon heartland. In 906 Edward confirmed peace with the Scandinavians of East Anglia and Northumbria. In 910 a large army of raiders from the 'Danelaw' invaded Mercia, and Edward sent an army to assist the defence; the raiders retired from the Severn valley and were caught and heavily defeated at Tettenhall (Staffordshire).[26] Ealdorman Aethelred died, probably early in 911, after ruling western Mercia since around 883 in harmony with Alfred and Edward; the role of Alfred's eldest daughter Aethelfleda, 'lady of the Mercians', as Aethelred's wife and the close ally of her father and brother is only now appreciated and she was clearly as capable a leader and administrator as both of them. Edward now succeeded to the crucial border fortified towns of London and Oxford; close co-operation with his sister Aethelfleda, now sole ruler of Mercia, followed and it appears that they co-ordinated building new fortified 'burhs' to defend old (and soon new) territory. In spring 913, while Aethelfleda was creating new strongholds in the west and central Midlands, the West Saxon advance began with Edward building his first new 'burh' beyond the earlier English/Danish border of Watling Street, at Hertford. This protected the area north of London and threatened the Danish settlers in Essex. Next summer he invaded Essex to build a fortification at Witham, dominating the county's main riverine landing-places that Viking reinforcements could use and so securing full Wessex control of the Thames estuary, and the locals submitted. A major raid by the Danes in Northampton and Leicester on Bedfordshire was driven off, and in 914 Edward had to deal with the arrival of a large raiding-force from Brittany (led by Ohtar and Hroald) in the Bristol Channel. The small south-east Welsh kingdoms were plundered, but when the invaders moved into Ergyng/Archenfield (English south-western Herefordshire) they were defeated and Hroald was killed; the survivors had to promise to leave Edward's lands, and his fortified positions along the Southern side of the Channel kept their resulting raids to a minimum. Attacks on Watchet and Porlock were driven off and Edward ransomed captured Welsh clergy, building up a good reputation with their kingdoms.

Having secured the west, Edward then proceeded to Buckingham to build strongholds both sides of the river there, and with his army threatening the East Midlands Jarl Thurcytel and the men of Bedford and Northampton submitted. In 915 he built a new stronghold at Bedford to control this annexed area, and in 916 returned to Essex to fortify Witham. Thurcytel and some of his men left for Francia with the king's agreement; the Danish settler elite, clearly divided among the leadership of small local nuclei, now had a choice between co-operating and joining the king's grand 'project' or leaving England. By definition, most of the potentially anti-Wessex leaders would leave and so the remaining 'men of status' would be less likely to challenge the king. All this time Mercia was also building new 'burhs' as far north as Cheshire, evidently in co-ordination with Edward. The year 917 saw the process of annexation moved on to a new phase, preceded and possibly instigated by a retaliatory Scandinavian attack from Northampton and Leicester in breach of a treaty; the settlers by now must have realized that Edward was intent on swallowing up their groups one by one so it was a case of 'now or never'. But they were at a disadvantage compared to similar Scandinavian settler groupings in Yorkshire (based on the major commercial town of York, 'Yorvik') and eastern Ireland (based on Dublin and Waterford) who also came under attack from the hinterland in this decade; the settlement and administration of the southern 'Danelaw' appears to have been decentralized into local units and these were outnumbered by the invading armies of Wessex and Mercia. In York and Dublin there was usually one war-leader to rally the settlers and lead an army to resist in this period; the East Midlands and East Anglia seem to have lacked this advantage. The raiding-army of Northampton and Leicester (two of the regional Scandinavian 'Five Boroughs') attacked Edward's recently-built 'burh' at Towcester but were held back by the townsmen until help arrived. Another raid around Aylesbury (i.e. south-west into

Buckinghamshire) followed, and the East Anglian and Huntingdon (i.e. Fenland) Danes moved west to build their own fortification at Tempsford (on the upper Ouse) and raided Bedfordshire. An East Anglian attack on the English stronghold at 'Wigingamere' also failed, and the English stormed the enemy stronghold at Tempsford and killed the local Danish king and several jarls. Next the Danes invaded Essex to besiege Maldon after the harvest but were driven back, and Edward launched an autumn campaign which protected the building of a new 'burh' at Towcester and led to the submission of Jarl Thurferth, Northampton, and all the Danes south of the Welland. The takeover and refortification of Huntingdon and Colchester followed, and the settlers and the raiding-army in East Anglia and Essex submitted. The settlers and their army in Cambridge then chose Edward as their lord, and he secured full control of East Anglia.[27]

The joint advance of Wessex and Mercia came to a successful conclusion in 918, though it also faced a potential threat in the sudden death of Aethelfleda (aged in her late forties, probably forty-nine) which could have caused her army to revolt from following her brother's leadership. In late May/early June 918 Edward marched to Stamford and built a new stronghold, upon which the local Danes submitted so he now had control of southern Lincolnshire and access as far as the lower river Trent. Leicester meanwhile submitted to Aethelfleda, securing the central-eastern Midlands south of the middle Trent. The two armies were moving north in concert, but the campaign was halted as Aethelfleda died just before midsummer, leaving only a daughter, Egwynn – who could not command armies and was unmarried so she had no husband to challenge her uncle. Edward marched immediately to Tamworth to secure control of Mercia. He was already undertaking military leadership within Mercia and had probably secured control of their armies with his sister's agreement (no Mercian commanders in the recent campaigns being recorded). His niece could not lead armies and there is no evidence of any threat to his domination of Mercia, but he preferred to annex it outright and deny Egwynn the right to succeed; there was no known resistance except a Chester mutiny in 924. It is possible that he had promised the Mercian leadership that his eldest son Athelstan, born c. 894 and brought up at Aethelfleda's court, would succeed him as their king.[28] In effect, his coup was the first stage in the creation of the kingdom of England, coinciding with the takeover of the 'Danelaw'; he may have intended at this point to divide the kingdom again among his sons rather than a permanent creation of one kingdom. As of this date, he had at least two sons by his second (or first legitimate?) wife, Aelffleda – who he had married after fathering Athelstan and a daughter on Ecgwynn. These boys were Aelfweard, who was to succeed him at least in Wessex in 924, and Edwin. As we shall see, there is a major mystery about Athelstan's mother and if she was legally married to Edward or was cast aside as 'low status' when he remarried someone better-connected, with romantic – and contradictory – stories recounted 200 years later by William of Malmesbury about this.

As full ruler of Mercia as well as Wessex, Edward now completed his military/political takeover of the 'Danelaw'. The division of the land among the separate authorities of the Danes settled in different areas, principally the 'Five Boroughs', and recent Danish losses in the unsuccessful raids on English territory plus the departure of some irreconcilable settlers for overseas would have aided his advance. The Mercians' western neighbours, kings Idwal of Gwynedd/Powys (ruled 916 to 942) and Hywel and Clydog of Dyfed, sought his alliance and according to the *Chronicle* recognized him as overlord. The historicity of this claim, which appears in the Anglo-Saxon not the Welsh sources, has been doubted – possibly the Welsh regarded it as an alliance of equals and it must be remembered that they were also under military pressure from the reviving and plundering Scandinavian kingdom of Dublin, whose current ruler Ragnall was expanding his control over the new Norse settlers of Cumbria and annexing York in this period so they might need Edward's help against him. Later in 918 he marched to Nottingham, improved an earlier fortification, and received the submission of the locals, which gave him control to the Humber; in 919 he moved on to Cheshire to secure the line of the Mersey with a new 'burh' at Thelwall. Manchester was then rebuilt. He moved back to Nottingham in summer 920, and then fortified Bakewell to control the Peak District. He had now methodically secured control of all of England south of the Mersey-Humber line and his joint Wessex/Mercia/Danish army had military supremacy over the North; the rulers of the region duly recognized his power. Later that year Ragnall of York (grandson of Ivarr 'the Boneless', 'Viking' king of Dublin, one of the three brothers who had led the main Scandinavian invasion of England in 865–71) and the kings of the Scots (Constantine mac Domnhall, ruled 900–42) and Strathclyde (Donald) submitted to Edward; the mutual antagonism of Ragnall and Constantine and Ragnall's other concerns as overlord of Dublin probably aided the peaceful resolution of the Northern confrontations. With the Anglian line of Bernicia also accepting Edward as their lord he was effectively, if nominally, the first king of all England. But as with the Welsh kings in 918, the nature, extent, and acceptance of a claim to overlordship by Edward must be doubted[29] – possibly his new allies did not see it in that light.

The succession question in 924: was one successor rather than two intended or just accidental? Or the result of a coup?

The dominant position of the kingdom over its newly annexed territories in the 'Danelaw' and East Anglia and its northern vassals was a result of Edward's military and administrative success, and was a personal triumph. The loyalty of Danes in particular was not irreversible, and a Danish military challenge from York was to break up the new kingdom temporarily in 940–1. York had only nominally submitted to Edward and Ragnall died in 921 with his successor Sihtric not recognizing Edward as his lord. But Edward remained unchallenged until his death on 17 July 924, at Farndon-on-Dee in north-western Mercia (a location which shows that he was still spending much of his time in his new lands to secure personal loyalty). He was probably aged around 52–3.[30] He left an unprecedently large family by three wives (or one mistress, Egwynn, and two wives, Elfleda and Edgiva) – one surviving son by his first 'wife', two by his second, and two by his third, plus at least ten daughters. One daughter had married Charles of Francia c.919.

It is a moot point if Edward had actually married Egwynn, which might have affected how the elite (in Wessex in particular) saw the acceptability of their son Athelstan; 200 years later William of Malmesbury recounted the contradictory stories that he had either married and later divorced her or that she was a humble shepherdess who he had had a 'one-night stand' with. The claim that Athelstan's mother was a lowly concubine was apparently made by one of the leading opponents of Athelstan's succession to Wessex in 925, or so William claimed.[31] The latter also recounted the enigmatic story that at some point in Alfred's lifetime, when his grandson must have been five or six at the oldest, he had Athelstan dressed up in a purple (i.e. royal) cloak and decorated belt and 'knighted' (an anachronistic term for the tenth century) him at a public ceremony.[32] This was taken as presaging the boy's later royal rule, and implies that Alfred intended this sort of role for him – and that in Athelstan's adult years this was probably used as a justification or sign of Divine support via portents of his glorious future. This may have been exaggerated after his accession in 924/5 by his supporters, and conversely the 'concubine' story could have been played up or invented by his foes – the truth is hidden by layers of political 'spin'. Given that Athelstan's removal to his son-less aunt Aethelfleda's court may have occurred in his father Alfred's lifetime and this may have coincided with Edward's (re)marriage to a more highly-born bride, it is possible that Alfred and Edward feared a challenge to Athelstan's succession on account of his mother's birth or marital status and so chose to give him the heirship of Mercia instead.[33] This is logical but can only be guesswork – and did Aethelfleda intend Athelstan to marry her daughter and heiress Egwynn but Edward pulled out of this plan in 918?

Edward's intentions for the succession are unclear, except that his choice for Wessex was his elder son by his second (first legitimate) wife, Aelfweard, who died only a fortnight after him, around 2 August according to the *Chronicle*. A twelfth century list gives him a reign of four weeks, i.e. until around 14 August;[34] Athelstan derived his subsequent support from Mercia and may in fact have been intended as its king by Edward in 924 in a division of kingdoms. In that case, the death of Aelfweard en route from Cheshire to the Wessex capital at Winchester for his coronation may seem suspicious, as he could only have been in his early or mid-twenties; but no written source suggests any foul play.

Aelfweard seems to have died at Oxford, probably en route to coronation at Winchester or Kingston-upon-Thames. Notably Athelstan was not crowned as king until 925 and there seems to have been considerable opposition to his accession in Wessex, though the *Chronicle* does not mention this and probably covered up a tense 'stand-off'. It is only William of Malmesbury who refers to a serious confrontation among the elite and a plot to overthrow Athelstan, apparently led by one 'Alfred', which was detected and punished – presumably this group of plotters favoured Aelfweard's full brother, Edwin, as king.[35] Later stories spoke of a plot to blind Athelstan, i.e. make him ineligible to rule, at Winchester, capital of Wessex. Alfred was variously said to have been sent to Rome to swear his protested innocence before the Pope and to have died there (implying Divine judgement on him for trying to lie), or to have been executed.

Edwin presumably became Athelstan's heir in 925 as their half-brothers Edmund and Eadred were only toddlers, but was later to flee or be banished from England and die at sea in 933 in mysterious circumstances. The latter is an especially odd case, with the bald statement in the *Chronicle* that he drowned at sea (Peterborough version only, not the Winchester one) presumably a 'cover-up' of an embarrassing incident. William of Malmesbury, again repeating bizarre stories 200 years later, heard that he had been accused of a plot, denied it to no avail, taken to the coast, and cast off in an open boat by the king – evidently to get rid of him without Athelstan incurring divine wrath by actually killing him. Edwin was then discovered to be innocent after he had drowned, and the king executed the royal cupbearer for bearing false witness. The Anglo-Norman historians Henry of Huntingdon and Simeon of Durham also heard that he had been killed/drowned by royal order, and the abbey chronicle of St Bertin in Flanders (written in the 960s), where Edwin was buried after his body was washed up on the Flemish shore, heard he had been fleeing the country.[36] The latter is the earliest source, except the *Chronicle*, not subject to royal pressure, and most likely to be true, and it would seem that there were secret currents of princely rivalry or court intrigue going on – possibly due to resistance to one of the Cerdicing dynasty monopolizing the crown?

Athelstan's refraining from marriage is also unusual, and later it was said that he had promised to stay unwed when he was accepted as king of Wessex in 925 in order not to jeopardise the chances of his half-brothers (Edwin and the two sons of Edward's third marriage, Edmund and Eadred). The antiquity of this tradition is uncertain, but it would explain the mysterious 'stand-off' in Wessex in 924–5 before Athelstan's coronation – which the *Chronicle* carefully avoids mentioning. Had Aelfweard not died suddenly, would the unity of England have ended in 924 and the separate kingships of Wessex and Mercia resumed? This possibility is a warning against assuming that Edward deliberately created a long-term 'united kingdom' in 918. But it is only guesswork to suggest that there was something suspicious about Aelfweard's death, i.e. murder by Athelstan's partisans, as there is no contemporary evidence and that even later stories are confused. One version has it that Aelfweard was a hermit at Bridgnorth and did not even want the throne, being pressurised into taking it. If he had succeeded his father as king of Wessex in July 924 and Athelstan been recognised as king of Mercia, the co-operation but separate political leadership of the two states in 886–918 would have continued, and the warlike and politically ambitious Athelstan would have been likely to use the Mercian army to annex York and the Norse settlements of Cumbria in the late 920s. But if Aelfweard's early death indicates that the genetic weakness of the Cerdicing line affected him, it is possible that he would have died before either a son of his (born in the late 920s?) or his half-brother Edmund (born 920/1?) became adult. Would Athelstan then have claimed the throne of Wessex and eliminated Aelfweard's full brother Edwin? In any case, it should be remembered that in 957 the nobles of Mercia and Northumbria were to raise up 'tyrant' king Edwy's brother Edgar as their own king as soon as he was old enough to rule – the union of Wessex and the rest of England was not a 'given' from 924.

Chapter Nine

Three Major Royal Murders –
And Cover-Ups?

(1) St Aethelbert of East Anglia, 794

Aethelbert was the last but one ruler of East Anglia to make an impact outside his own kingdom in national memory – and like the last ruler, Edmund (d. 869), it was due to the manner of his violent death. Virtually nothing is known from contemporary sources except the date and basic facts of his death; as a result we are reliant on medieval hagiographies that may have included lost local written records or oral traditions or have invented most of their data. Unlike Edmund who was killed somewhere near the Norfolk/Suffolk county border (probably at Hoxne), his cult was not based in his own kingdom but in Herefordshire in the far west of the Midlands, the neighbouring kingdom of Mercia. This was ruled at the time of his death by the overlord of the southern English, Offa 'the Great' (ruled 757 to 796), who played a crucial role in his death and was carefully exonerated from personal involvement in it by medieval writers – so as not to damage his reputation as a patron of major monasteries and churches? – but was probably involved. He had apparently invited Aethelbert to Mercia where he was killed, and the killing took place at the village (a Mercian royal manor?) of Sutton Walls near Hereford – at the far side of Mercia from its then vassal-kingdom of East Anglia. Does this imply that Offa lured Aethelbert there, far from help, in a trap? As a result of the killing taking place there and Offa having the late king buried nearby at the town and episcopal see of Hereford, the cult of Aethelbert was centred there – the cults of Anglo-Saxon saints were centred at the shrines where they were buried as miracles were alleged to take place at their tombs and pilgrims flocked there. The local clerics duly made the most of having a saint in 'residence' and cultivated a 'tourist trade', commissioning lives of the saint and drawing in new visitors. There was also a notable element of royal saints often being celebrated as such for the violent and unjust circumstances of their deaths rather than their own virtues, though where possible (e.g. when the victim's moral achievements were well-known and undeniable) the saint was also portrayed as a moral exemplar. There could also be an element of implicit or explicit criticism of the person who had caused their deaths, without this being too harsh if the latter was a well-known and otherwise celebrated ruler whose kin and partisans might well object. The case of Aethelbert's death in 794 was like that of another vassal-king killed by the close associates of his overlord, (St) Oswine of Deira, whose overlord king Oswy of Northumbria had probably had to accept him as his local sub-ruler reluctantly, to satisfy local autonomist sentiments. Oswy duly invaded his realm with overwhelming force to depose him in 651; Oswine dispersed his army rather than have them massacred in a futile fight and hid himself away in a remote village but was betrayed by his host and hunted down and killed by Oswy's 'hit-men'. The shock and resentment at his killing was shared by his cousin, Oswy's wife Eanfled, and the Church (whose bishop Aidan had been a friend of Oswine's) and Oswy – otherwise known as a champion of the Church and a foe of the pagan Penda of Mercia – was forced to accept the creation of a shrine and monastery at the site.[1]

Aethelbert seems to have been removed in a similar manner by a power-hungry overlord who resented his surviving as king, albeit a vassal-ruler, of a region which was ripe for incorporation into his lord's kingdom. Offa had already reduced the kings of his vassal-kingdom of Sussex to the status of 'duces', i.e. governors, by the 770s as seen by his royal charters, and in neighbouring Kent he had at least ratified and probably imposed sub-rulers in the 760s and 770s, required his name to be listed as overlord on charters by its kings granting lands and rights, fought a presumably drawn battle with local rebels at Otford in 776, and from the mid-780s suppressed the local kings (and their coinage) altogether and granted charters on his sole authority. He was also launching major raids on the Welsh kingdoms of Powys and Dyfed beyond the massive new (?) border-marking ditch of 'Offa's Dyke' in the 780s, though it is unclear if he was aiming at conquest or just humiliating submission and tribute. Logically, East Anglia was next in line for similar treatment – and the small number of coins of Aethelbert that have been found compared to earlier eighth-century rulers may suggest that the kingdom was already required to use Offa's Mercian coins and not issue its own and was thus being treated more and more as a part of Mercia. Does the confused story of Aethelbert's killing hide a calculated 'power-grab' to remove the East Anglian kingship?

According to the medieval hagiographies Aethelbert ruled after his father Aethelred, but the dates and identity of the latter are unclear; so is any connection to previous East Anglian kings but their names do not suggest any links as these would normally be indicated by alliterative names. The first mediaeval life of him was by the Anglo-Welsh clerical historian Giraldus 'Cambrensis', who came from Pembrokeshire, c.1200 and the other has been linked by M. R. James in his 1917 *English Historical Review* article to the place where the cult was based, Hereford, not to East Anglia[2] – so neither later writers were interested in the East Anglian or political background. The martyrdom and miracles at the saint's shrine were what their readers wanted. The king's date of accession is unknown, but one mediaeval source refers to '779' without citing any documentary records. Nor is it clear when and how long his father Aethelred ruled, or if the latter was linked to earlier regional royals; few coins of him have been found and he was clearly a Mercian vassal, which may have required him to use Mercian coins.[3] Very little is known about Aethelbert except that he had the unusual distinction of being executed by his overlord Offa 'the Great' in 794 which was as far as known a unique fate for a Mercian vassal-king. The sub-kings of the regional kingdoms of Hwicce (based on Gloucestershire) and Magonsaetan (Herefordshire and Shropshire), who had been granting charters into the eighth-century, disappear after c.730 and 700 respectively so their kingdoms were presumably annexed, the kings of Sussex turn into 'duces' by c.770 but from their names seem to be part of the earlier royal family, and the kings of Mercia disappear from c.785 and reappear with the revolt of royally-connected ex-monk Eadbert 'Praen' as a rebel king in 796–8 after Offa's death. (He was duly defeated, captured, mutilated to make him ineligible for the throne, and imprisoned by new king Coenwulf of Mercia, but not killed.) But Aethelbert's fate was both more violent and not cited in his hagiography as being linked to his kingdom's conquest and incorporation by its overlord. The subsequent hagiographies of him state that he acceded to the throne aged fourteen and was a relative of Offa, who was at least the backer if not the installer of his line. In 794 he was summoned to the Mercian royal court, and somehow ended up being beheaded at the remote royal manor of Sutton Walls near Hereford; the location may mean that he was deliberately not invited to the main royal residences or Lichfield or Repton, where there would be plenty of courtiers and churchmen to witness events, or just that the warlike Offa was currently fighting (or inspecting his local estates) on the Welsh border and found Herefordshire more convenient. Aethelbert was beheaded by a royal officer called Grimbald, presumably on the orders of Offa who is named both by the *Anglo-Saxon Chronicle* and the twelfth-century histories of Wiliam of Malmesbury and Henry of Huntingdon as ordering the execution.[4] He was buried nearby in secret at Marden, presumably as Offa did not want his body returning home as an object of anti-Mercian veneration – a result of the cult of the similarly murdered sub-king Oswine at his shrine in Deira? But as with other cases of hidden or unceremoniously 'dumped' saintly murder-victims, miracles started occurring and the crime was thus publicised; the body had to be reburied with more honour in a public place in Hereford.[5] The *Chronicle* in the later ninth-century just refers to his being executed without elaborating on the facts, though its generally hostile tone to Mercia and the fact that the *Chronicle*'s commissioner King Alfred's grandfather Egbert had been exiled from his homeland to Francia thanks to Mercian pressure may imply that Alfred would not have covered up anything that would harm Offa's reputation. The St Albans version of Aethelbert's life puts the blame for the killing on Offa's queen Cynethryth, possibly from desire to exonerate their Mercian kingly patron by blaming his wife instead; she was accused of wanting to annex Aethelbert's kingdom and talking her husband into it.[6] Offa's womenfolk had a poor reputation, and Asser's life of Alfred records a West Saxon tradition that Offa's daughter Eadburh, who he had married off to his subordinate ally king Beorhtric of Wessex (ruled 786 to 802), was an evil serial killer who routinely poisoned her enemies and ended up accidentally poisoning her husband. She then had to flee to Francia, later becoming a prostitute in northern Italy which was clearly seen as an appropriate fate, and the title of 'Queen' was banned in Wessex due to her reputation. But did Cynethrith have a similar reputation for ruthlessness to her daughter, was the popular attitude to one transferred to the other, or was there truth behind the story? By contrast, Aethelred's intended Mercian fiancée apparently became a saintly nun.

A cult of Aethelbert grew up and he was subsequently sanctified as a 'martyr', showing that he was seen as having been unjustly victimized like Oswine of Deira. The date of death may have been the date on which he was commemorated, 20 March. His body was moved to Hereford, the nearby see, where a shrine was built at the cathedral with him as its patron saint. The cult does not imply any notable degree of holiness on the part of the recipient. A legend recorded in the twelfth-century stated that Aethelbert had journeyed to Mercia to negotiate a marriage-alliance with Offa, aiming for the latter's daughter Aelfthryth; it is possible that Offa, capable of ravaging insurgent Kent and imposing his own puppets on allied kingdoms, suspected Aethelbert of plotting to end East Anglia's vassal status and of inspecting Mercian defences for use in case of war. Alternatively, the recent (2014) discovery of a rare coin of Aethelbert in his native kingdom – i.e. coined in his own name, not that of his overlord Offa – has led to suggestions that this was an act of political defiance of Mercia and his execution was Offa's brutal retaliation.[7] In that case, or in case of a rumoured plan to revolt, Aethelbert could have been lured to Herefordshire and the queen oversaw his execution as her husband was busy elsewhere. The execution would have been intended as a warning to vassals of what awaited would-be traitors. It is possible that Offa sent his troops into and annexed East Anglia in 794, as the next king Eadwald is not known to have been established there before 798.

(2) King Edward 'the Martyr': King of England 975–8.

He was the son of King Edgar (ruled Mercia and Northumbria 957 to 975 and Wessex from 959 to 975), presumably by his first wife, Aethelfleda – though the number and legality of Edgar's marrages are among contemporary mysteries. He was probably born c.961, and was not a unanimous choice as his father's successor when Edgar died on 8 July 975 at the unusually young age of around thirty-two.[8] Edgar had left one survivor of two sons by his second or third wife, the reputedly ambitious Elfrida (Aethelthryth), Aethelred; the elder son, Edmund who appears witnessing charters from 966, had died in 971. Notably when Edmund first appeared as a witness he was styled (in a church document) 'legitimus prefati regis filius'; the older surviving son, Edward, was not. Aethelred was only aged around seven in 975, but was a serious candidate for the throne which raises questions about the perceived status of Edward's parents' marriage.[9] As with the first marriage of Edward 'the Elder' and ?Ecgwynn and the legitimacy of their son Athelstan, it is possible that Edgar – the subject of assorted (dubious) stories about his lechery and irregular sexual relationships in the medieval period – had conducted a first marriage that was not accepted by the Church, possibly as this was not carried out in a church as allowed by the Danish customs prevalent in the tenth-century 'Danelaw'. So was this marriage carried out while Edgar was ruling in Mercia and the North and not yet king of Wessex? The first post-1066 hagiography to refer to Edward, that of his archbishop and guardian (St) Dunstan by Osbern of Clare, referred to his mother as an ex-nun, but this was probably a mistake confusing her with the mother of his half-sister, (St) Edith of Wilton, Wulfthryth, who Goscelin of St Bertin's twelfth-century 'Life' of her daughter says ended up as abbess of Wilton. Edward's mother was named as Aethelthryth, daughter of 'ealdorman' Ordmaer, in a later life of Dunstan by the usually reliable Anglo-Norman historian Eadmer. Apparently Edgar married Edith's mother early in his reign over Wessex (c. 961/2?), but according to later hagiography by Eadmer and Goscelin she would rather have become a nun, wore a veil while being educated at a nunnery to avoid offers of marriage, and only accepted Edgar after his first choice, her kinswoman Wulfhild, turned him down. Later she left Edgar and became a nun.

Later allegations were made that Edgar had had an improper relationship with Elfrida during her first marriage, to the ' ealdorman' of East Anglia (son of his former guardian, Athelstan 'Half-King'), and had helped her to murder him so they could marry. No early source is known for this, and it first appears in William of Malmesbury's account c. 1125 where he says Edgar arranged an 'accident'; later Anglo-Norman romancer Gaimar wrote a lurid story of murder by Edgar and Elfrida which is unlikely as the king certainly made his 'victim's brother the new 'ealdorman' (which in case of murder would have exposed him to a revolt). It may be gossip based on the king's other alleged 'improper marriage' to a would-be or ex-nun and Elfrida's unsavoury reputation. It is possible that there was some question-mark over Edgar's first marriage, to Edward's mother, in the minds of the Wessex elite, with Aethelred also being preferred by some as 'born in the purple' (after his father's accession) in which case Edward may have been born before his father succeeded to Wessex late in 959.[10] Feuds between the kin of the late king's wives are also possible if they were of noble blood.

The current political dispute over the 'excessive' grants of land made by Edgar to the Church as he built up its power and wealth led to frustrated would-be secular grantees of land, keen to see this policy halted, opposing the Church (led by Archbishop Dunstan) and its candidate Edward. Notably, one major aspect of Edgar's Church policy had been to restore the landed wealth and local powers of the Church in the former lands of the 'Danelaw' where the Scandinavian settlements after 870 had led to a lapse in occupation of the regions' Church sees and assorted parishes, the closure of Viking-looted monasteries, and the granting out of former Church lands to new secular settlers – many pagan Scandinavians. As Edgar rebuilt the Church in the 'Danelaw' he sought to reverse this, and new monasteries (e.g. at Peterborough and Ramsey) were founded and granted large estates while the bishoprics were restored but were often reliant on also possessing estates in western Mercia or Wessex for much of their wealth. The archbishopric of York, in a region heavily settled by Danes in the 870s, was combined with the bishopric of Worcester under St Oswald (in office 971 to 992); the main bishopric of the East Midlands was based at Dorchester-upon-Thames, far from the region. Notably, ecclesiastical landholders could not pass on their lands to their heirs, unlike laymen; their estates reverted to the king on their deaths so this was useful for the sovereign in keeping up a source of patronage and control. The idea of using 'lifetime only' grants of estates to monasteries and clerics, who were then treated as effective royal agents in the localities, as a form of 'royal centralism' to avoid hereditary estates increasing probably came from Carolingian Francia; the monastic reform was inspired by that in Francia, e.g. at Fleury. By implication, this would have increased royal influence over a previously semi-autonomous region of the 'Danelaw' (where the narrative of conquest in the 910s shows that power was centred on local regions based on major towns) and caused resentment. Resistance to Edgar's land-grants was accordingly centred in Mercia. Led by Earl Aelfhere of Mercia, the protesters apparently sacked monasteries and rallied to Aethelred's cause.[11] Aethelred was young enough to be controlled by a regency; Edward was at least in his mid-teens and so less easily influenced. He was also to be accused of having a reputation for bad temper and hasty, violent action, even at this young age though West Saxon royal males reached maturity early. As this charge was made in the near-contemporary hagiography of his archbishop of York and supporter, St Oswald (d 992), it was probably remembered from his life by reports from witnesses, not a later legend, and it might partly account for why his half-brother's men were keen to rid the kingdom of him (for fear of later victimization by him?). Edward was clearly not able to be portrayed in the lifetime of people who had known him as a passive, godly youth in the usual manner of hagiographers, though his rashness would have been in keeping with other headstrong teenage males of his dynasty (e.g. Edgar's brother Edwy, reckoned after his death in 959 as a hot-tempered, lecherous and sulky tyrant who had exiled archbishop Dunstan). Overcoming failings of character by an internal struggle could however be a 'plus' for a king who was to be favourably regarded by clerical writers, for example, Edgar, so the story could have come from stock clichés – though Edward would have been seen as a suitable subject for this trope.

Edward was crowned on 18 July, probably in 975, but there appears to have been strong antagonism to his Church allies and outbreaks of violence against Church-granted lands on his accession. Famine followed, implying divine displeasure and probably bringing hungry and superstitious recruits to the ranks of those determined to overset Edgar's grants.[12] Assorted monasteries were pillaged and monks expelled in violence that escalated in 976 and was thus widely supported by aggrieved lay personnel; the *Chronicle* accuses Aelfhere of co-ordinating it. The new king and his ministers were unable to control it; possibly it centred in Aelfhere's Mercia and Edward dared not leave Wessex. The pillaging and the famine cast a blight over his reign, and early in 978 a disastrous accident at a royal council meeting at Calne (Wiltshire) saw the floor of an upper-storey chamber fall in and assorted people be killed or injured. Archbishop Dunstan narrowly escaped as the beam he was standing on was not affected, which was seen as showing divine favour.[13]

On 18 March 978 Edward was murdered in Dorset, at 'Corfe gate' – probably this means the gate of the royal manor at what is now Corfe Castle, or Corfe as the 'gate' in the Purbeck Hills, but just possibly Corfe Mullen.[14] At the time there was no castle there as this is Anglo-Norman work and the first building was probably late eleventh-century, but it was a strategic site and possibly the later royal hunting-preserve (known after

1066 as a 'forest', i.e. land where forest law applied, not in the modern sense of 'woods') of Purbeck already existed. Nearby Wareham had been a royal residence for over a century; king Beorhtric was poisoned there in 802. Edward's legend said that he was visiting his stepmother Elfrida at her manor when her attendants – or even Elfrida in person – stabbed him, probably as he reached down from his horse to take a goblet. The life of St Oswald, the earliest account c.995, blames the attendants without mentioning the queen and implies that he turned up on impulse for refreshment or a night's stay after hunting nearby. The attendants stabbed him as he drank, and it is not said if she knew in advance. His horse galloped away carrying him, and he fell to his death; he either bled to death or broke his neck.[15] In 1931 a body of a young male in his late teens with injuries consistent to a fall from his horse was found buried in the ruins of Shaftesbury Abbey, Edward's eventual shrine; was this the king? By the 1120s William of Malmesbury, also placing the murder in the evening when the king called in after hunting nearby, was alleging that Elfrida had received him at the manor and distracted him with a cupful of drink while an attendant stabbed him in the thigh,[16] and from then on her personal part in the murder was generally accepted. Henry of Huntingdon also placed her at the scene and taking part in the killing; the anonymous *Passio Sancti Edwardi*, written at his shrine (Shaftesbury abbey) around 1100, and John of Worcester put her 'behind the scenes' as inciting murder by her retainers,[17] presumably expanding Byrtferth's story in the life of St Oswald. The mid-twelfth-century romancer Gaimar went further in *Lestoire des Engles* (lines 3991 to 4043) on unclear evidence (if any?), having Edward chase a runaway 'dwarf' servant to Corfe manor and demand his return from the Queen, rudely refusing her invitation to come inside whereupon she and her attendants stabbed him while he was drinking.

On the one hand the queen had been a generous patron of the Church, was the mother of the current King Aethelred, and was possibly still alive when the hagiography of St Oswald was written so the author had reasons to avoid mentioning her part in the attack. Indeed, once she had reconciled with the Church early in her son's reign she was a crucial political ally to Dunstan and his associate Bishop (St) Aethelwold of Winchester, which some nobles clearly resented as once the latter was dead (984) and Aethelred was adult (985/6) he was induced to curtail Church influence and the queen ceased to appear at court. But later accounts also suffered from hindsight, in that the turbulent Viking-afflicted and ultimately disastrous reign of Aethelred led to the conquest of England by King Swein 'Forkbeard' of Denmark and his flight to Normandy so this could seem to have been the result of Divine displeasure, originating from the 'original sin' of regicide that had opened his reign. He could not be blamed in person for the latter, but losing his throne was in a sense atonement and punishment for the murder of his half-brother and later stories embellished the misfortunes and misrule of Aethelred – with his failings now said to have commenced by sullying the baptismal font, as also recounted of the monk-persecuting Byzantine emperor Constantine V. In this vein, Archbishop Wulfstan of York blamed the killing in his famous 'Sermon On The Wolf' as the shocking crime, due to treachery to one's lord which was the ultimate Anglo-Saxon 'warrior code' sin, for the punishment of the Danish invasions. In fact, it is unclear what Elfrida would have been doing at Corfe unless she was a guest there; it was not a royal manor, but belonged to the abbess of Shaftesbury. But an acquisitive, manipulative and ruthless queen like her was capable of pressurizing the abbess to loan her the manor for a stay if she wanted to go hunting or carry out local visits, and what little we know of Elfrida from contemporary documents has her using her patronage of Church institutions for her own benefit (e.g. in appointing her allies to offices). Whether she was maligned unfairly or was privately encouraging her servants and other would-be clients to serve her cause by killing the king without bringing her into it, she seems to have escaped any Church censure unless her scrupulously generous patronage of the monastic order in coming decades was partly a 'pay-off' for the Church's goodwill. In terms of hard political reality Edward's death left his partisans with no candidate to challenge her son as King and no incentive to start a civil war, and they had to accept Aethelred as king – as she may have reckoned correctly in a dangerous gamble for the crown. Edward was at most eighteen or nineteen He was hastily buried at nearby Wareham without royal honours (did Elfrida assume his poor reputation would make the elite quickly forget him so she had no need to bother with a state funeral?) and Aethelred succeeded to the throne. But embarrassingly the locals were soon claiming that Edward's body was performing miracles and regarding him as a saint, and the site where his body had been found after he fell off his horse (Norden, a mile or so north of Corfe Castle) was then or later said to have been graced with holy 'signs'. The Church encouraged, if not instigated, the campaign, and a year later he was reburied at Shaftesbury amidst more appropriate splendour with the royal family and nobles in attendance. Earl Aelfhere led the ceremony – did he force the issue to obtain a political truce? The shrine remained a centre of pilgrimage for centuries. As 'king and martyr', the first of two royal Edwards of England to be sanctified, Edward was the only post-Alfredian king to have a church which still survives – dedicated to him, at Corfe Castle.

(3) King Edmund 'Ironside', 1016: murdered, and if so by whom?

The second son of king Aethelred 'Unraed' (ruled 978 to 1013 and 1014 to 1016) by his first wife Aelgiva. From his activities Edmund was adult by 1013, so he was probably born by c.990. Aethelred had been struggling with a second wave of major raiding and later invasions by Scandinavians since his regency in the early 980s, with the main assaults following the defeat of his local levies in Essex under 'ealdorman' Byrtnoth by a large 'Viking' army under an unrecorded commander at the battle of Maldon in 991 (as commemorated by the heroic *Song of Maldon* poem) and then another invasion in 994. He later became notorious for his resorting to the payment of large sums of money, the so-called 'Danegeld' i.e. 'Dane-tax', to the raiders to leave rather than fighting them, though in fact this tactic of avoiding the danger of a catastrophic defeat by a larger and well-trained army under capable leaders had been resorted to by King Alfred himself in 871. When Aethelred instituted it in 994 to pay off the formidable future king Olaf Tryggvason of Norway, the warlord who may have won at Maldon and had a much more hardened and better-led army than him, this was by the advice of leading Churchmen led by archbishop Sigeric, among the civilian leaders of his regime[18] – and critics tend to forget that until 991 the English army had not fought a major campaign since 954. The inexperienced and possibly timid king faced two of the era's best Scandinavian commanders in Olaf Tryggvason of Norway (ruled c.994 to 1000) and Swein 'Forkbeard' of Denmark (ruled c.980 to 1014) at different times, and probably the unified and aggressive kingdom of Denmark had a highly organized, trained and successful military system in the later tenth century so Aethelred's caution about tackling them was not unreasonable. But the English military machine had been used to a chain of victories within the British Isles for many decades, and it had also had a large and well-maintained fleet under Edgar that had overawed its neighbours – which Aethelred seems to have let run down, possibly due to the cost. Worse, the English leadership never seemed able to win battles even when it had had experience, and quarrels among its leadership and avoiding battle seem to have become endemic and presumably pointed to poor morale, factional disputes, a lack of capable generals, and incompetence. Even if the king has been blamed unfairly for this, the *Anglo-Saxon Chronicle* (our sole continual source for events) was unremittingly hostile to him, albeit with a degree of hindsight as this section was probably written c. 1012–16, and the armed forces may have been run down in his regency, he was clearly a poor performer in the vital role of defending his people. The kingdom suffered firstly 'hit and run' raids from 980 and then a succession of invasions and defeats by larger roaming Scandinavian forces from 991, although Aethelred did manage to buy off Olaf Tryggvason with a peace-treaty and persuade him to accept baptism as an ally (like Alfred had done with Guthrum, but not from a similar position of strength). The record of the wars from 994 to 1002, i.e. before the main 'national' Danish army was brought in to ravage England by Swein and the English may have faced a tactically and numerically superior foe bent on plunder and conquest, is already full of English disasters and seeming incompetence.[19]

In 1002 Aethelred allied to Duke Richard II of Normandy across the Channel, a potentially predatory state of Viking settler origins, and married his (teenage?) sister Emma as his second wife – which meant that the Normans now ceased to allow the Vikings raiders to use their land as a base. This was followed by one of his all too frequent miscalculations, however. He now endeavoured to rid himself of another supposed threat, that of the Danes resident in England linking up with the unchecked Scandinavian army. He ordered the notorious 'St Brices' Day Massacre' (13 November 1002), presented in retrospect as a concerted effort to wipe out the Danes by simultaneous massacre which predictably failed to kill all its intended victims and only led to a heightening of hostility between English and Danes including those of the latter resident in the 'Danelaw'. It may not have been as wide-ranging as later believed, as the only recorded massacre was in Oxford. Was it just an attack on resident traders and mercenaries as suspected spies? The survivors escaped demanding vengeance,[20] and Swein 'Forkbeard' (whose sister had been among the victims) arrived from Denmark with a large army to destroy opposition province by province. Given the location of most of Swein's support in the coming years, it is probable that Aethelred's killings loosened the ties of some settlers of Danish origin in Eastern England to the West Saxon dynasty, but the 'Danelaw' and East Anglia resisted ravaging as determinedly as Wessex, as seen at the battle of Ringmere. In 1003 Swein sacked Exeter and then marched east into Wiltshire and Hampshire. In 1004 it was the turn of East Anglia, and after a brief respite while England suffered from famine in 1005 the raiding-army returned to the south in 1006–7. The tax which eventually bought them off amounted to 30,000 pounds this time, and during the resulting respite Aethelred put a massive effort into raising a new fleet which he based at Sandwich for the 1009 raiding-season. Disaster followed as usual, this time due to accusations of treason against one of the fleet-commanders (Wulfnoth, probably father of the later Earl Godwin) who fled and turned pirate; after his defeat the fleet was left inactive and dispersed early. The feuding among Aethelred's councillors, leading to sporadic executions by the King, now centred on Eadric (later nicknamed 'Streona') the new Earl of Mercia, widely regarded as a disastrous choice and with a murderous career of repeated treachery to all sides. The ousting and desertion of Wulfnoth seems to have been due to Eadric's brother.[21] Given the number of betrayals and killings that this unsavoury character was linked to and the presumed cause – his constant attempts to remove his rivals – Aethelred's reliance on him seems to be the worst of his long-term misjudgements and a sign of undue partiality or incompetence. The *Chronicle* reckoned him as 'defeatist', by hindering the royal army's attempts to attack the enemy even when they were for once united and determined to do it in 1009.[22] So was this cowardice, over-caution, or a desire to stop his rivals gaining military glory? But Eadric was able to preserve the loyalty of his own followers for years at the height of the wars of the 1000s and he must have had a degree of charm and charisma as well as ability to dispense patronage effectively to attract such support. This 'Flashman-esque' chancer was later to be linked to his royal patron's son Edmund's death at a crucial point in the wars, though this may just be later gossip.

At different times he betrayed the hard-headed and successful generals Edmund and Cnut of Denmark and was apparently 'forgiven' by both of them, going on to betray Edmund a second time – Cnut took no chances and struck first, executing him.

The Danes ravaged East Anglia and the East Midlands through 1010, with the *Chronicle* lamenting that the English army was rarely in the right place to catch them, the troops of most shires fought independently and were routed one by one, and when the army had a chance to act it failed to do so.[23] Does this indicate a poorer 'high command' than under Alfred and his immediate successors, and was this their king's fault? His responsibility for the disasters remains a mystery, and it may be that his 'out-of-date' army was incapable of dealing with the aggressive, methodical, and well-trained Danes – but even so he appointed the leadership and did not inspire people as his son Edmund was to do. When the army did fight strongly, as at Ringmere in East Anglia (where the number of presumed local Anglo-Danes from the 'Danelaw' who fought loyally for their king shows that the 1002 massacre had not caused them to desert en masse) they were overwhelmed.[24] Aethelred's latest attempt to buy the invaders off with another huge tax was accepted but they contemptuously failed to keep their word once they had the money. The attack on Canterbury in 1012 left Archbishop Aelfheah a prisoner in the Viking camp, and when his ransom failed to arrive he was murdered by drunken Vikings at a feast. That atrocity led to a competent commander, Thorkell 'the Tall', deserting to Aethelred with forty ships, but by then the enemy were too numerous and spread out over England. In 1013 Swein returned to eastern England with a new army, based himself on the Humber, and secured the submission of the 'Danelaw' and Northumbria before marching south to enter Wessex again. Outright conquest was now his aim, and Aethelred shut himself in London; Swein was driven off by a determined English military effort. Deserted by more and more of his abandoned subjects, Aethelred sent his wife Emma to Normandy. As his position deteriorated he retired to the Isle of Wight and in midwinter 1013 fled to Normandy: Swein had won his kingdom.[25] But Athelstan and Edmund, his two eldest sons by his first wife, stayed in England, presumably to organise resistance.

Edmund suceeded his elder brother Athelstan as his father's heir at some point early in 1014, probably while Swein was in control of England

and Aethelred was a refugee in Normandy, and was bequeathed his best swords.[26] Edmund showed the vigour, military ability, and talent at attracting loyalty which his father lacked. He probably had some military experience in the wars of 1010–13 which saw his father's position steadily eroded and his provincial elites deserting to the Danish forces of Swein 'Forkbeard'. There is no record of him leaving the kingdom for exile in winter 1013–14, unlike his father, stepmother, and half-brothers, and he (or the sickening Athelstan?) possibly remained in loyal regions away from Swein's army. Swein then died suddenly at Gainsborough in Lincolnshire in February 1014 before he could take over all the kingdom, and the 'Witan' or royal council agreed to recall Aethelred – as the *Chronicle* tellingly puts it, provided that he would promise to govern more justly than he had done before.[27] Aethelred returned and took command of the army, and Swein's (first or second?) son Cnut, commanding the Danish army in the 'Danelaw', was deserted by the local English nobles as the king advanced and had to retreat to his fleet and sail off to Denmark. Given the timing of his emergence as a commander and apparent age at death in 1035 (forty?), Cnut may have been born c.995 – or earlier if the story that he was old enough to command at Norwich in 1004 is reliable. What is unclear is if he was the first or second son of Swein – his brother Harold was apparently king of Denmark to 1018. The English war was not over however. Edmund first appears in history in 1015, challenging his father's latest blunder of following the advice of Earl Eadric of Mercia in executing Si(g)ferth and Morcar, two leading nobles of the 'Danelaw'. The men were probably suspected of links to Cnut, but killing them alienated their supporters; Edmund carried off Siferth's widow Edith (Eadgyth), imprisoned at Malmesbury, and married her in defiance of his father's wishes. She may have been a substantial heiress in her own right, and his action led to much of Mercia (English and Danish, the latter led by Siferth and Morcar's supporters) transferring its allegiance to Edmund in September 1015.

Edmund raised an army, still technically loyal to his father, and when Cnut landed the latter's progress across Wessex unchallenged was aided by Aethelred falling ill. Eadric raised his own army in Mercia and met Edmund, but they failed to reach an agreement and Eadric, believed to be intending treachery, deserted to Cnut; Edmund remained in the Midlands while Eadric led his men into Cnut's seized territory in western

Wessex. In 1016 Cnut and Eadric marched north into Warwickshire to attack Mercia. Aethelred moved out of London to take his army north and join Edmund. But there may have been problems over raising and motivating enough men for the king, the two armies failed to achieve anything, and Aethelred returned to London. Edmund, outnumbered, marched north into Northumbria and achieved the support of Earl Uhtred, and they moved south into Staffordshire and Shropshire but avoided an open battle. Cnut, doing likewise, moved across the North Midlands up towards York, and Uhtred had to return home. He then submitted to Cnut, leaving Edmund to return to London. Aethelred died in London on 23 April, probably in his late forties, and Edmund was elected king. Cnut had now secured Northumbria and was sailing south, and Edmund chose to avoid being penned up and retired into Wessex to raise an army. The Danes arrived at Greenwich, and the Londoners held their fleet back at the bridge but were outmanoevured as Cnut dug a ditch around the Southwark end of the bridge and hauled his ships across. London withstood a siege, and a Danish army pursued Edmund into Wessex but was defeated by him at Penselwood. The men of Wessex had rallied to Edmund as they had not to his father, and a second success followed in a two-day battle in midsummer at Sherston (Wiltshire or Hwicce?). Cnut's men returned to London, abandoning the Wessex campaign, and Edmund followed with the third army he had managed to raise in a year (a sign of his charisma to his exhausted subjects). The besiegers retreated to Greenwich, and a few days later Edmund won a third victory at Brentford which was marred by numbers of the English being drowned in the Thames through carelessness. When Edmund returned to Wessex to raise more men the Danes made a second assault on London, but this was beaten off and they retired to eastern Mercia.[28]

Edmund now returned to the Thames valley, and drove a Danish raiding-army that had attacked Kent back from the Medway onto Sheppey and thence onto their ships. Sensing which side was winning, Earl Eadric surrendered to Edmund at Aylesford and was received back – a decision which the *Chronicle* calls the worst ever made for the English nation.[29] It seemed so in retrospect, but at the time Edmund probably needed Eadric's men and dared not execute him like the wiser Cnut did later lest they desert. Given the degree of regional autonomy seen in mid-late tenth-century England, with a few crucial secular lords given control of a wide area (e.g. the earldom of Mercia from the time of Aelfhere under Edgar and the earlier rule of Athelstan 'Half-King' in the East Midlands and East Anglia), the senior thegns of a region were probably more loyal to their immediate superior than to the king. This was not Aethelred's fault but the system which he had inherited; the problem was the uncertain loyalties of the senior lords to the King by 1016, which court feuds may well have exacerbated. The Danes retired into Mercia, and Edmund followed; they eventually met in a crucial battle at Ashingdon, Essex, on 18 October 1016. Edmund had raised five armies in a year and revitalised his war-weary people, using his nation's administrative structure for warfare and uniting his nobles in a way that Aethelred had failed to do; he had also made up for any initial military inexperience compared to Cnut. But in the battle that followed Eadric and his Mercians fled, with later stories that some of Eadric's men had raised a false shout that Edmund had been killed at a crucial moment and caused panic. The *Chronicle* says that Eadric was the first to flee, and not for the first time, along with the men of Magonsaetan (i.e. Herefordshire and Shropshire) who logically were not as experienced in fighting the Danes as those whose lands were closer to the coast and so often attacked. The implication in the wording is of cowardice by Eadric causing his betrayal of the king and the national cause by losing the battle – weakness, not calculated treachery.[30] William of Malmesbury c.1125 says that Eadric shamefully led the flight and lost the battle but not that it was deliberate. But it was later blamed on a deliberate ploy by Eadric which he had arranged with Cnut; according to Henry of Huntingdon Eadric raised the shout that the king was dead himself.[31] Edmund lost the battle with serious English losses including much of the leadership such as Ulfcytel of East Anglia, and the casualty list may imply a last desperate attempt by the loyal elite troops to turn the tide of battle rather than save themselves and fight again later – a tribute to their 'esprit de corps' and devotion to their leader. The flight of the Mercians was interpreted as deliberate desertion to aid Cnut by prior arrangement, but it may have been a genuine panic by the soldiers. As with other sensational interpretations of major Anglo-Saxon events, the more lurid claims only appear in the twelfth-century on uncertain evidence.

The decisive reverse forced Edmund, posssibly wounded and certainly outnumbered, to retreat into western Mercia; Cnut, joined by Eadric, followed him to Gloucestershire and on Eadric's advice the two leaders met at a safe site in the middle of the Severn ('Ola's Island') to negotiate terms. Cnut was either too cautious or had lost too many men to force another battle yet, and the treaty gave Edmund rule of Wessex and Cnut Mercia and Northumbria. Cnut returned to London. The truce gave the majority of the Anglo-Saxon lands to the English contender and the Danish lands to his Scandinavian rival. A lasting settlement was unlikely. But within a month or so, on 30 November 1016, Edmund died at Oxford.[32] Later stories had it that Cnut had treacherously had him assassinated, possibly by a poisoned statue with a spring or by sending someone to stab him on the lavatory; Henry of Huntingdon cited the latter story and identified the assassin as a son of Eadric 'Streona', sent by his treacherous father.[33] Eadric was clearly thought capable of anything, and notably Henry's other stories of this war – e.g. Cnut fighting a duel with Edmund at Ola's Island and generously deciding to offer him Wessex as he was such a courageous fighter – are equally unverifiable. Personal inter-champion duels on an island, the alleged tradition of 'holmgang', are more myth than reality. The more reliable early twelfth-century historian William of Malmesbury did not feel confident enough of the facts to say how Edmund had died.[34] In fact, he may have died of a wound from Ashingdon or a sudden illness exacerbated by the strain of the long war; many of his family were short-lived and his father, grandfather, and great-uncle had died relatively young. At all events, no version of the story was known well enough to be universally accepted, unlike the basic details of how his uncle Edward 'the Martyr' had died.

Edmund was no more than twenty-eight or twenty-nine, and possibly only 25 or 26. The lack of an adult English leader gave his surviving full brother Eadwig/Edwy no chance against Cnut, and Edmund's councillors recognized Cnut as king of all England; Edmund's widow Edith and infant sons Edward and Edmund fled to Scandinavia, whence the boys later ended up in Russia. A capable and possibly outstanding war-leader and an inspiring leader, Edmund had all the qualities that Aethelred lacked and might have proved a king of the quality of Alfred, Edward, and Athelstan had he succeeded in driving out Cnut.

Chapter Ten

The Succession in 1066: Were The Claims of William of Normandy Invented or Irrelevant?

The background: 1035 to 1052

The Norman conquest of 1066 was not the first time that the English crown had fallen to a foreign ruler who imported his own countrymen to rule his new subjects. The long Viking campaigns against Aethelred 'Unraed' in 1002, marked by internal dissension and vicious intrigue within the English nobility, had been noted by the inadequate response of the government and its inability or unwillingness to meet the enemy in open combat. The increasing boldness of the Viking armies, which rampaged unchecked across England and defeated the local militias on the rare occasions that they were challenged, encouraged King Swein 'Forkbeard' of Denmark to turn from ravaging to conquest and in the autumn of 1013 much of the country transferred its allegiance to him. The existence of large numbers of Scandinavian settlers in the 'Danelaw' (the East Midlands and East Anglia) and Yorkshire, many if not most of them of Danish origin and only finally incorporated into the new Kingdom of England in the 940s and early 950s, undoubtabedly helped the Danish successes. Aethelred's drastic resort to a co-ordinated attempt to kill all the Danes in England (probably soldiers and traders who were born in Denmark rather than settlers of Danish origin) would have alienated many of their kinsmen and added to his unsavoury reputation. Deserted by most of his supporters, Aethelred fled to his wife Emma's kinsfolk in Normandy and only returned when Swein died suddenly in February 1014. The unexpected death of the conqueror led to most of the English magnates backing Aethelred rather than Swein's young son Cnut, who had to leave England temporrily but soon returned to resume the Danish campaign. He and Aethelred's son Edmund 'Ironside' seem to have been evenly-matched and fought a long war in which the probably ailing Aethelred was eclipsed well before his death in April 1016. Edmund then succeeded to the throne in those areas still loyal to the English royal house, secured extra support with a series of victories, and seemed to be on the verge of expelling Cnut until he was defeated in battle at Ashingdon in Essex in October. Edmund still had enough military power to force Cnut to accept a division of England, with Cnut governing the areas of Scandinavian settlement, but this was soon ended by Edmund's death a month later.

Cnut then succeeded to the rule of all England and held it to his death in November 1035; he also married Aethelred's widow, his second wife Emma of Normandy. The infant sons of Edmund and the two older sons of Aethelred and Emma, Edward (posthumously known as 'The Confessor') and Alfred, were set aside and exiled. Cnut relied on a mixture of Scandinavian and English nobles as his council and provincial governors, though like William he had a powerful army of his own countrymen to fund which massive taxes were raised in England. The North was divided between the warrior Siward (possibly of local birth and Danish descent) in York and one of a local Anglian dynasty, the hereditary lords of Bamburgh, in Bernicia; all of Mercia eventually came under the rule of a local magnate, Earl Leofric, and Wessex was given to a Saxon nobleman from Sussex called Godwin (probably the son of a fleet-commander disgraced by Aethelred) who had entered Cnut's service. Cnut also made efforts to conciliate the English Church and posed as the defender of the existing social and legal order; he increasingly ruled as much like a traditional English king. On Cnut's death in November 1035 it was his son by Emma, Harthacnut (b. 1018?), who succeeded to Denmark and was backed by Emma as one of the two rivals contending to rule England with the support of rival groups of nobles. His rival was his half-brother Harold 'Harefoot' (Cnut's son by Aelfgifu of Northampton, of uncertain legitimacy according to his enemies), who was apparently born in England with a well-born Anglo-Danish mother so he had stronger local, 'Danelaw' kin support and may have been older. Harold was either in England in late 1035, unlike Harthacnut who was regent of Denmark for Cnut, or soon arrived from Denmark (where his mother and full brother King Swein of Norway had fled on their recent expulsion from Norway). Harold seems to have become ruler of Mercia and

Northumbria, where there was a strong Danish-descended elite, while Emma and her ally Earl Godwin held Wessex for Harthacnut who failed to arrive in England to back up his rights. Harold was able to take over all England in 1037, while Harthacnut was held up in Denmark fighting the new King Magnus of Norway (who had expelled Swein); Emma had no option but to submit or flee and did the latter, to Flanders. Godwin chose to stay and recognise Harold – who he may already have helped to dispose of a rival claimant, the 'Atheling' Alfred (Emma's younger son by Aethelred). Lured to England by the apparent hope of the throne and/or a forged letter seemingly sent by Emma but in fact by Harold, Alfred and his Norman retinue were heading along the Pilgrim's Way from Canterbury to visit Emma at Winchester when Godwin intercepted them and pretended friendship. But en route at Guildford his men suddenly overpowered and killed or enslaved Alfred's men, handing the prince over to Harold who fatally blinded him – which Godwin later assured Emma and her other son by Aethelred, Edward, he had not known about in advance.[1]

On Harold's death in March 1040 Harthacnut, who had been about to invade, took the throne; he recalled Edward from Normandy, and on his sudden death in June 1042 the principal magnates chose Edward as King. Edward, half-Norman and having lived in France for over twenty years, thus assumed the throne of an England with which he was unfamiliar – and where he had been selected by a group of great Earls all chosen by Cnut, some of them of Scandinavian origin, and the standing army of 'housecarls' was a creation of the Danish dynasty. Until 1047 his throne was under threat from King Magnus of Norway, who claimed that Harthacnut had promised him the succession in their peace-treaty of 1039 (but did this refer to the succession to England or merely to Denmark?) and was rumoured to be backed by Edward's mother Emma at the time of the latter's surprise arrest and disgrace in 1043. Edward in turn brought in a number of French (not exclusively Norman) courtiers and churchmen, giving the see of London (and in 1051 the archbishopric of Canterbury) to the Norman Robert of Jumieges and the see of Wells to the Lotharingian Giso. His grand new church of St Peter at Westminster, the main 'prestige' architectural project of the latter years of his reign, was built to a Norman plan and seems to have been a copy of the abbey of Jumieges. He appointed his own half-French nephew Ralph of the Vexin as earl of Hereford after the disgrace of Godwin's eldest son Earl Swein for abducting the abbess of Leominster (with or without her consent), turning pirate, and murdering his would-be intermediary cousin Earl Beorn. Ralph may well have been intended at one point as the childless Edward's heir, though his failure to keep the raiding Welsh at bay must have undermined his chances of being accepted by the King's council and he predeceased Edward. The King also brought in Norman knights to assist Ralph in fighting the Welsh, and they constructed the first Norman castles in England in Ralph's Earldom around 1050.

England had thus come under strong Scandinavian and Continental influence well before 1066, and already had one Scandinavian dynasty. The Norman ducal dynasty was also ultimately of Viking descent, though tempered by over a century of residence in northern France where their progenitor Rollo/Hrolf 'the Walker', a Viking captain at the head of a raiding army, had been granted the County around Rouen by King Charles 'the Simple' in the treaty of St Clair-sur-Epte in 911. Hrolf was the son of the Norwegian ruler 'Jarl' Rognvald of More, who was also the ancestor of the Earls of Orkney, and the new Duchy of Normandy was peopled by a mixture of Scandinavians and French. Its rulers and its warriors came to develop a distinctive style of martial vigour which combined Viking ferocity and ambition with local French military technology, and in the eleventh century Normans were to carve out a new kingdom in Southern Italy and Sicily at the expense of Byzantines and Muslims as well as taking over England.

William 'the Conqueror' (a posthumous sobriquet, his contemporary nickname being 'the Bastard' on account of his illegitimacy) made much of his claim as the chosen heir to King Edward from the time in 1051 when the King managed to rid his kingdom temporarily of the Godwin family. When Cnut died in November 1035 the sons of Aethelred and Emma, Edward and Alfred, had left Normandy and made armed expeditions to southern England during the impasse between Harthacnut and Harold 'Harefoot', presumably to stake their claims; their mother Emma had been holding Winchester and Wessex in her son Harthacnut's name while Harold was based in Mercia. Edward was apparently refused permission to land at Southampton and had to sail back to France; Alfred, landing at Sandwich and proceeding west along the Pilgrims' Way towards

Winchester, was intercepted at Guildford by Earl Godwin of Wessex, handed over to Harold by Godwin, and fatally blinded.

It is not known if Godwin intercepted and arrested Alfred by a pre-arranged plan with Harold, as at the time he was officially an ally of Queen Emma (and thus her son Harthacnut) not of Harold, or out of a calculated but not long-term desire to ingratiate himself to Harold as the chances of Harthacnut arriving in England soon were diminishing. Had he even changed his mind since Alfred's arriving in Wessex had first been mooted and he had then agreed to it? The Queen might also have wanted Alfred neutralised – arrested, not killed? – in case he challenged her youngest and favourite son Harthacnut's rights. Godwin may thus have arrested Alfred on the Queen's behalf, and Harold only heard about the arrest afterwards and required the Earl to handover his prisoner – which Godwin did as a goodwill gesture because Harthcnut was showing no hurry to come to England. Godwin would have reckoned that as Harthacnut was showing no urgency in intervening, Harold would now be recognised as king before long so he needed to show goodwill to him. Godwin may not have known that Harold intended to kill Alfred, though this was a reasonable assumption; and he may have told Emma that he would help or at least preserve Alfred, hence Edward's long-running anger at his 'treachery'. The incident must have soured relations between Godwin and Edward when the latter finally regained his throne, though the new king lacked English partisans among a nobility and court purged by Cnut and including many new Scandinavian personnel. Quite apart from being one of Cnut's most trusted followers, a rare example of an Englishman given a large Earldom as early as c.1020, Godwin had married Cnut's Danish sister-in-law Gytha and was thus related uncle by marriage to Cnut's nephew Swein Estrithson, king of Denmark after Harthacnut from 1042 (and to Swein's brother, English Earl Beorn).[2] Edward was heavily dependent on Godwin's goodwill, and was unable to avoid promoting the Earl's sons (Swein and Harold) and nephew Beorn Estrithson to English earldoms as they became old enough to govern; in 1045 he married Godwin's daughter Edith which meant that the next generation of royalty would be Godwin's grandchildren.[3] The sources are unclear whether despite this alliance Edward sought to rid himself of the earl at the first opportunity. The accession gift that Godwin gave Edward – a magnificent warship – might be interpreted as a compensatory 'weregild' for the death of Alfred.[4] But it is difficult at this distance to judge how much Edward blamed Godwin for his brother's death, given that one version of the *Anglo-Saxon Chronicle* puts the blame for the betrayal and murder on Godwin and another version on Harold 'Harefoot' – who thus may have violated a promise to Godwin not to kill Alfred. One version has it that Alfred was intent on gaining the throne on his expedition, which would have outmanoeuvred his elder brother Edward[5] – in which case Godwin arresting him was to Edward's ultimate benefit. The possibility arises of Emma having been prepared to welcome and aid Alfred in 1036 but not do so to Edward, though we do not know whose orders led to Edward's party being refused entry to Southampton and having to return to Normandy. Or did Edward later suspect his mother over this incident?

As Edward lacked experience or a body of long-standing English advisers he was heavily dependent on the holders of the three main Earldoms into which Cnut had divided England. This was a crucial difference between his position and that of the tenth-century kings of Wessex and England, to the King's detriment – though its creator Cnut had been able to dominate his Earls, aided by a large army and fleet, would a weaker successor have this ability? Cnut's action thus indirectly paved the way for the Godwin family's ability to defy the King in 1051–2 – and thus to Harold's succession and to the Norman Conquest? The main English royal residences were to the south of the Thames in the old heartland of the kingdom, Wessex, and kings rarely ventured into the other regions. Thus the Earl of Wessex had a special closeness to the sovereign, and Edward continued this pattern. Godwin, whose main estates were around Bosham in Sussex and who was probably the son of the eminent 'thane' Wulfnoth Cild, a Sussex landowner and commander of the fleet who had been banished in 1009 after a dispute with Aethelred,[6] was as much Danish as Anglo-Saxon in his loyalties and had proven indispensable to Cnut as a senior officer in his Baltic campaigns (and possibly as steward of his household?). But to assess his loyalties (and marital links via Gytha) as 'Danish' is not to say that this was antagonistic to the English monarchy or state. It was still only 170–80 years since the Viking 'Great Army' had destroyed all the old Anglo-Saxon kingdoms except Wessex and there had been substantial Danish settlement in East Anglia, the 'Five Boroughs' of the 'Danelaw' in the East Midlands, and

Yorkshire. This area had been under its own rulers until welded into the new English kingdom by Edward 'the Elder' in the 910s, and had then revolted against his successors on the death of Athelstan in 939; Edmund I had only temporarily recognised their independence under a powerful Viking warlord, Olaf Guthfrithson of Dublin, in 939–41 and had soon reconquered the 'Danelaw' but York had only been regained in 954. Indeed, the word 'Danelaw' reflects the practical reality, legally formalised by Edgar c.960, that the bulk of the population were now used to Danish legal practices not Anglo-Saxon ones and were permitted to keep them when the united kingdom was created. The areas of Scandinavian settlement had been the first to recognise their Danish countryman Swein as ruler in 1013, and had mostly supported Cnut against Edmund 'Ironside' in 1015–16; in 1035 they had recognised Cnut's locally-connected son Harold as King rather than accepting Harthacnut who was backed in the 'capital', Winchester. Managing the kingdom of England from 1042 required balancing the 'Anglo-Saxon' and 'Danish' landholders in which Godwin and Cnut's other senior Earls had the experience which Edward lacked. The threat of invasion from Magnus of Norway, who also claimed to be Harthacnut's heir under a private agreement with him, was such that until Magnus died in 1047 Edward needed an experienced military commander to meet that threat and kept Cnut's large – and expensive – fleet in readiness.[7] Once Edward had married Godwin's daughter Edith the earl could look forward to his grandson on the English throne, though there were no children of the marriage and it was later said by hagiographers that Edward had pledged to remain celibate if he regained his throne. Inferring that this was deliberate policy on Edward's part due to dislike of Godwin is unproveable, and the nature of the evidence is doubtful – the king was being considered for sainthood in the mid-twelfth-century when most of his early biographies were written and a holy abstention from sexual relations would be a valuable indication of his suitability.

Claiming that Edward had remained chaste could be post-facto explanation of the surprising lack of royal children in terms that would promote Edward's claim to be a saint. But Edward might have felt obliged to marry his most powerful earl's daughter but been unwilling to let the Earl's grandsons succeed to the throne. Once Edward had rid himself of the rest of her family he was quick to send Edith to the royal convent at

Wilton (or to an even more rigorous exile at Wherwell convent).[8] This however had a practical reason, given that she could pass on information from Court useful to her exiled family. It seems to have been the new Norman Archbishop Robert of Jumieges who was keenest on Edward divorcing Edith – though this also implies that Robert wanted Edward to be succeeded by a son, not by the Norman Duke William, in 1051.[9] By that reckoning, Robert was not acting as an 'agent' of Duke William despite his apparently relaying Edward's offer of the crown to William, but as a loyal friend to Edward – and so William's apparent 'support' in England as a potential heir in 1051–2 becomes even less likely.

A power-struggle erupted between Edward and Godwin in mid- or late 1051, as the earl refused to sack Dover (in his earldom) as the king demanded that he do in retaliation for the citizens killing some visiting members of the entourage of his brother-in-law Count Eustace of Boulogne. Eustace, second husband of Earl Ralph's mother Goda, had been returning from court when his followers tried to demand lodgings in Dover and a clash with the townsmen erupted; as Edward was still childless he may have had designs on the succession. (He later joined Duke William's expedition in 1066 against his Godwinson enemies, but in 1067 attacked Dover in obscure circumstances that may have indicated designs on the kingdom.)[10] The king's demand was in line with the practice of punishing attacks on people under the king's protection, as Harthacnut had had Worcestershire ravaged in 1041 for the deaths of some tax-collectors, but Godwin refused to obey and collected his and his sons' levies. Their force marched on the royal court at Glouceser and camped at Beverstone on the Cotswold ridge nearby, but Earls Leofric of Mercia and Siward of Northumbria brought their men to reinforce the king and Godwin was forced to accept mediation and attend a judicial investigation of his case in London. With the king evidently determined to produce judgement against him, he was stripped of his earldom and banished with his family; his elder sons Swein (recently restored to Hereford after dismissal for running off with the abbess of Leominster) and Harold were also stripped of their earldoms. Earldoms were duly given to Leofric's son Aelfgar (East Anglia) and other loyalists, and whether or not Edward had given the earldom of Hereford temporarily to his nephew Ralph of the Vexin when Godwin's eldest son Swein was banished in 1048–9 he now did so permanently. The current dispute between the king and Godwin over the Archbishopric of Canterbury was resolved in favour of the king's Norman Bishop of London, Robert of Jumieges. But in 1052 Godwin returned with a fleet from his allies in Flanders to ravage the South Coast, and Harold returned with more ships from Ireland to ravage Somerset en route to meeting up with his father at Portland. The two forces, unopposed by the royal fleet, sailed into the Thames to land at Godwin's manor of Southwark and this time the other major Earls would not back the King in a confrontation but insisted on Godwin's rehabilitation – possibly being opposed to the King's recent grants of office to Normans. Edward, in a humiliating position of being able to call on fewer troops under his direct command than his Earls, was forced to accept Godwin and his sons back, restore the Queen to Court, and banish (most of?) his Normans. Archbishop Robert fled to Normandy without resigning his see, and as a result the new Archbishop, a Godwin client called Stigand who currently held the see of Winchester, was never recognised as legitimate on the Continent.[11]

It is notable that the Norman chronicler William of Poitiers claims that the Archbishop took Duke William the news that King Edward had made his Earls swear to accept the duke as his heir, which is unlikely for the period after Godwin's return (given that Edward was currently at Godwin's mercy). The logical time for Edward to do this was either before Godwin's disgrace, in which case it would have formed part of Godwin's grievances against Edward, or after Godwin's exile. Other sources imply that the message was taken by Archbishop Robert as he journeyed to Rome to collect his 'pallium' (ceremonial sash/scarf of office) from the Pope in spring 1051, before Godwin's exile – Robert's date of return from Rome was June 1051. This is the reckoning of David Douglas and Stephen Baxter. (Did the transfer of hostages from the Godwin family to Normandy by Archbishop Robert occur then too?) The whole point of Godwin's stand against Edward was about removing foreign influence, and after Edward exiled the Godwin family Earls Leofric and Siward helped Godwin to return by not backing Edward so they were not pro-French either and may have opposed William being promised the crown. The *Anglo-Saxon Chronicle* says that the Archbishop fled London before Godwin returned to Court in 1052, so he was not there to witness any such ceremony of oath-taking.[12] This would make the Archbishop's delivery of the promise – and the hostages? – to William more likely to occur in 1051. Or did Robert tell William about an oath-taking ceremony (inaccurately?) to encourage his Duke to turn on Godwin's family for treachery to their solemn promise if William was not made Edward's successor? Was the story of an oath-taking ceremony just later, post-1066 'spin' by Duke William and his loyal chroniclers? Whenever it occurred, Robert handed over Godwin's captive/hostage youngest son Wulfnoth and his grandson (Erik?, son of Earl Swein), as hostages to the Duke – which may have led indirectly to Earl Harold's crucial visit to Normandy in 1064/5 in an effort to retrieve them. But if Edward had either forced Godwin to deliver the hostages to William – to tie him into his own plans for the succession – or taken them prisoner when Godwin was expelled from England in 1051 and then sent them to William, it failed to secure the Godwin dynasty's backing for the duke as heir long-term. For that matter, Edward's summoning his nephew Edward 'the Exile' home in 1054–6 (see below) may well imply that Edward changed his mind later himself.

Godwin did not have long to enjoy his triumph, as he died at Easter 1053 (possibly while arguing with Edward at a feast over his responsibility for Alfred's death) and Harold succeeded to Wessex.[13] Harold's relations with Edward seem to have been less fraught; he was able to secure Northumbria for his brother Tostig when Siward died in 1055 despite the availability of male kinsfolk from the local Bernician dynasty of Earl Uhtred. Cnut and Harthacnut had divided Northumbria between the 'Danish' (or Anglo-Dane) loyalist Siward and this family's nominee Eardwulf; Edward, either from inexperienced partisanship or 'centralising' motives, gave it all to Tostig. The opposition of this family to Tostig is apparent from his suspected involvement in the murder of one of them, Cospatrick, at court to complain about Tostig's harsh rule, in December 1064. East Anglia, Harold's own Earldom in 1045–51 went to Harold's next brother Gyrth when Aelfgar succeeded Leofric in Mercia in 1057. Aelfgar, briefly given East Anglia during Harold's exile in 1051–2, was restored to it when Harold succeeded to Wessex and then succeeded Leofric in Mercia; he faced two attempts from the Godwin family to deprive him of his rank and exile him, one before and one after Leofric died (1055 and 1058).[14] The fact that Aelfgar fought his way back to England successfully, on the second occasion with an army of men from Gwynedd and Norway, is as significant as the Godwin family's similar success in 1052. On neither occasion could the royal army outface a determined exile with local partisans and foreign mercenaries – even in 1058 with Aelfgar's sympathetic father Leofric dead and Harold to assist the king. Again, in 1065 the Northumbrian rebels who had driven out Tostig and brought in Aelfgar's son Morcar to rule them, marching south to coerce Edward, succeeded in inducing him and Harold to accept the 'fait accompli'.[15] Harold was a successful general, in command of the famous regiment of 'housecarls', who destroyed the military power of the newly-unified Welsh state under Gruffydd ap Llewelyn in a massive assault in 1063. He won against the most experienced and ferocious Viking warlord of the age, Harald 'Hardrada' of Norway, at Stamford Bridge in 1066. Yet even he could not keep the House of Leofric out of reasserting their control of Mercia in 1058, or risk taking on them and the Northumbrian rebels in 1065 though it is possible that on the latter occasion he may have preferred to see his potential rival, Tostig, lose power.[16] This would indicate that the military power of and national backing for the Godwin dynasty in England was rather less than the extent of their lands and Earldoms might suggest.

William's visit to England in 1051/2: real or invented?

Some time during Godwin's exile Duke William had visited Edward's court, and Norman writers subsequently claimed that he had been promised the throne then. (The visit is recorded in the 'C' version of the *Chronicle* but not the 'D' one, so it was not that well-known.)[17] The throne was not Edward's to give away as the Council ('Witan') made the final choice on a king's death, but he could make a recommendation and if he had required his earls to take an oath to William's succession in 1051 he was already trying to bind them to follow his wishes not repudiate them once he was gone. It had passed out of the direct royal line to foreigners without a blood claim before, as with Cnut in 1016 and his father Swein in 1013 (both by conquest) and possibly been promised to Magnus of Norway around 1039 by Harthacnut in the peace-treaty to end their war over Norway. Neither had had children (both were to be succeeded by older male kin); Harthacnut had not been in possession of England, so he may only have meant the promise to refer to Denmark. At the time he had little experience of England, having left it as a child, and may not have known (or cared?) that its throne was passed by election by the 'Witan', not solely by royal wishes. A semblance of legality was usually followed in England, as when the flight of Aethelred to Normandy from Swein's advancing armies in 1014 led to his abandoned Councillors formally inviting Swein to assume the throne – and by their invitation to him to return on Swein's death, provided that he ruled more justly than before.

There was no strict rule of primogeniture or of succession of the closest male relative, so the exclusion of Edward's closest relative – his sister's son Ralph of Mantes, who was proving an incompetent Earl of Hereford unable to stop Welsh raiding – was not surprising. (Ralph was half-French but not a potential ally of William, as his father's and older brother's county of the Vexin was sandwiched between Normandy and the French king's lands and was resisting William's influence.) As the kingdom had passed to Danes in 1014 and 1016 the choice of another successful warlord capable of holding the country together, Edward's closest relative in his mother's Norman ducal family, was logical. Crucially, at the time Edward did not know the whereabouts of his only surviving royal Anglo-Saxon male kin, his half-brother Edmund Ironside's sons – though he had not tried to find them either and had had a decade to do so. If he considered the succession at all in 1042–51, he was thus presumably intending to have sons – even when he married the possibly unwelcome Edith, Godwin's daughter? Once he had rid himself of Godwin he sent Edith to a nunnery, usually the forerunner of divorce – and according to some sources his principal (Norman) cleric Archbishop Robert was hoping he would re-marry and thus have sons by a second wife until Godwin forced his and Edith's restoration by invading in 1052. So did Robert (or even Edward?) not intend William to be the heir as of 1051–2? By this argument, Edward was looking for a second wife not an adult heir at this stage. There were however two advantages for Edward choosing William as his heir in 1051–2 rather than waiting to get Papal approval for a divorce, remarry, and have a son old enough to succeed him. In the first place, William was the lord of Normandy, the area of France closest to southern England (where Godwin's power-base lay, in Sussex) and had harbours available for Godwin and his sons to use in a cross-Channel invasion. Even if the ruler did not aid such an attack, semi-autonomous and adventurous barons might lend Godwin troops or ships – and the Vikings had used Norman harbours as bases while raiding England in the

990s. Godwin was currently in Flanders (ruled by Count Baldwin), also with harbours and a naval tradition but further away – but he could still call on Normandy for aid, as his third son Tostig was married to Baldwin's daughter Judith, sister of William's wife Matilda. Edward had crossed to England from Normandy with troops in 1036 to challenge Cnut's son Harold 'Harefoot' after their stepfather King Cnut died, so Edward was aware of its possibilities for aiding an invasion. Keeping William sweet by promising him the throne would diminish this danger – and Edward could change his mind later when he had no need of William's aid, and/or he had a son by a second marriage. Indeed, the early twelfth-century 'English' (as opposed to Norman in cultural orientation) historian Eadmer recorded that Edward had promised William the succession before he left Normandy for England on his recall by his half-brother Harthacnut in 1041, though William's alleged services and hospitality to Edward as an exile were not that significant as a cause of this as the young Duke was only a politically powerless boy (aged thirteen at the most) and his duchy was riven by civil war at the time.

By 1051, William was also a proven strong and capable ruler. His minority since his accession at the age of seven or eight in 1035 troubled by endemic feuding among the turbulent Norman aristocracy and at times virtual anarchy, he had ruthlessly reasserted ducal power since his teens, restored order, and won a major battle over his remaining challengers with the help of the French King Henry at Val-es-Dunes in 1047. Edward would have known his distant cousin from his youth, seen the early stages of his emergence as a capable ruler until 1041, and been in close touch with events since then via the Norman clerics and knights at his court. Once he had rid himself of his Godwin wife and the chance of a half-Godwin heir in 1052 William was a potential ally, known to him unlike other experienced foreign rulers (e.g. the ferocious Harald 'Hardrada' of Norway or Godwin's nephew Swein Estrithson of Denmark) and was likely to prove a stronger ruler than Earl Ralph who had not made a good start as Earl of Hereford in fighting the Welsh. Granted that other foreign – Scandinavian – rulers had been interested in or allegedly been promised the throne, it would not be unusual for Edward to promise it to his cousin who was proving a capable ruler in Normandy. At this point, around 1051, William married Matilda of Flanders, who was descended in the female line from King Alfred so their children had a legitimate (if remote) claim to England. Given William's ruthlessness in striking hard bargains, he was capable of insisting on recognition as Edward's heir in return for support against the Godwins in 1051–2; it is not dissimilar from the 'deal' apparently made by Harthacnut with his powerful and potentially hostile neighbour Magnus of Norway in 1039 at the end of their long war over the rule of Norway (taken by Magnus from Harthacnut's half-brother Swein in 1035).[18] On both occasions, the party making the concession of the succession to his neighbouring ruler did not publicise it; the latter did so years later. The logical new heir to England from a strictly genealogical perspective was the exiled elder son of Edward's half-brother Edmund 'Ironisde' (d. 1016), who Edward was to seek out and bring home in the mid-1050s. But this man, Edward 'the Exile', had ended up in remote Russia, as a guest of 'Grand Prince' Yaroslav of Kiev, after being exiled as a baby by Cnut. (The latter may even have asked Yaroslav to kill him as a favour and been ignored.) He had since then moved on to Hungary in 1046/7 to aid the seizure of the throne by the exiled prince Andrew.[19] Edward may not have known where his namesake was, as he subsequently had to send Bishop Ealdred of Worcester on a mission across Europe to seek him out rather than being able to locate him quickly.[20] In 1051 he did not seek out his nephew as soon as he had rid himself of the Godwins, but the endeavours of Archbishop Robert to arrange a divorce from Edith would suggest that Edward re-marrying to provide an heir was the more active option. Only when Edith was restored to Court in 1052 to satisfy the returned and triumphant Godwin and Godwin – who may still have expected to have royal grandchildren via her marriage – died did the search for the missing 'Atheling' resume.

At the time of the Godwins' exile in Flanders in 1051–2 the diplomatic and military usefulness of Duke William, their Channel coast neighbour so able to provide ships to match their fleet, may have seemed more important. Did Edward need William's ships as his own captains were unreliable? This would have been logical, as the exiled Godwin had been Earl of – and thus chief patron for – the south coast ports, including the emerging 'Cinque Ports' of which Sandwich was the main fleet-base as England faced Viking threats in the mid-late 1040s. Godwin (probably son of Edward's father Aethelred II's admiral Wulfnoth) had taken command of the fleet then, and when he sailed his rebel fleet across the Channel in 1052 to link up with his son Harold's own ships from Dublin the royal fleet proved useless and/or unreliable. The two Godwin fleets linked up, and advanced unopposed to the Thames estuary to sail upriver to London and land the Earl at Southwark. Evidently Edward's own captains could not stop Godwin, probably due to disaffection from the local naval levies of Wessex; and if Edward had been expecting naval help from Duke William the latter let him down.

Some historians have claimed that William was still too busy fighting Norman rebels to visit England in 1051/2, and no Norman source mentions this visit which would surely have been made much of after Edward's death had William been able to prove that it – and the promise of the throne – had taken place. There may have been time for William to leave his turbulent duchy for a quick visit to Edward in Winchester or London, possibly without announcing it in advance so that he could be back before many restive Norman nobles in outlying districts were aware that he had left the land and could thus risk a revolt. But if he visited England and was promised the throne in 1051, this may account for his soon having Godwin's captive son Wulfnoth and grandson Erik as hostages. They seem to have been in Edward's hands in 1052 rather than being in exile with their relatives, and Harold was seeking their return from Norman custody by 1064/5 – though it is equally possible that an alternative version of events is correct, that Archbishop Robert kidnapped the two as he fled on Godwin's return in 1052 and handed them over to William. The return of Edith to the king's side as part of the terms of their rehabilitation would have revived hopes by Godwin that she would provide an heir. She was probably still in her twenties in 1052, though Edward was around forty-nine.

The family's military power and readiness to use it in their dynastic interests meant that any suggestion of William being allowed to succeed to the throne after their return in 1052 was unlikely. It is only one Norman source, William of Poitiers, who claims that Edward made his lords (Godwin included) swear to accept the duke as his heir in 1052–3 – and this is unreliable as he says that Archbishop Robert, who was in reality already in exile, took this news to the duke. If Duke William did hear from the Archbishop that oaths had been taken to him as heir, this would have occurred before Godwin's return – unless the Archbishop exaggerated the story of an oath being taken to encourage the duke to attack England (and thus ruin Robert's enemies the Godwins) if the Norman succession did not occur. Godwin, and after his death his eldest surviving son Harold as the new Earl of Wessex, were unlikely to accept the vigorous and ruthless William as their new sovereign. In addition the Godwins' return had led to the flight from England of Archbishop Robert, who was illegally replaced with the Godwins' protege Bishop Stigand of Winchester, which could be used as a grievance in protesting to the Papacy. Some of the Norman knights imported to Earl Ralph's territory and other Frenchmen with official positions of royal favour also seem to have fled, though there was no general expulsion of French (or just Norman) personnel as some alien courtiers and Bishops remained in England. It is thus too simplistic to imply that the Godwins' return meant a purge of 'Norman influence' and resulting hostility between the refugees' lord Duke William and the Godwin family, though the exiled Archbishop Robert no doubt denounced his evictors to his countrymen and it was a bonus to William's later anti-English diplomacy in 1066 that Stigand failed to obtain Papal recognition for his illegal usurpation of the arch-see. He did travel to Rome in 1058 to obtain the necessary Papal sanction and 'pallium' of office, but unfortunately the Pope who had accepted his claim (Benedict IX) was overthrown soon afterwards and all his acts were declared invalid.

Search for an heir, 1052–66: and the precedents for Harold's non-dynastic succession.

It is unclear if Harold was actively seeking the throne in the mid- and late-1050s, by which time it must have been apparent that Edward and Edith would have no children. But Edward was not considering him as a successor, given the action which he took. Edward turned to the last male of the old West Saxon dynasty apart from Ralph and his brothers Count Walter of Mantes and Bishop Fulk of Amiens. Edward 'the Exile', the survivor of the infant sons of Edmund 'Ironside', (King Edward's half-brother) exiled in 1016, was currently living in Hungary where he had arrived with the expedition sent from Russia to install King Andrew in 1046/7. He appears to have had estates there, and to have married a kinswoman of Andrew's ally the German Emperor Henry III. (The identity of this lady, Agatha, has been hotly disputed – but it is clear that English sources were incorrect in making her a daughter of the late Hungarian king, St Stephen.) Having sent senior diplomatic emissaries (including Bishop Ealdred of Worcester) across Europe to locate Edward 'the Exile' in 1054, the king invited him back to England – clearly with a promise of the throne. This would indicate that, whether or not Godwin and Harold had imposed an effective veto on William being made heir, Edward was looking for an alternative candidate. But the 'Exile' – aged only around forty-one – died soon after his arrival in London early in 1057, without seeing the king, and his claim passed to his son Edgar 'Atheling' whose age is unclear but who was still too young to fight in 1066 so he was probably only an infant. Much has been made of the lament in the *Chronicle* that he was 'not allowed' to see King Edward[21] – who prevented it? Earl Harold or Duke William, by poisoning him? – but this probably refers to the intervention of God, not sinister Godwinson or Norman plotters.

Under-age kings were rarely chosen by the 'Witan' council unless there was no other candidate available, as in 975, and with Ralph's death in 1057 there was no other blood-relative in England to consider (nobody seems to have bothered with his sons, who were probably too young). Though nothing was made public about Edward's choices, his marriage remained childless – he could not very well have put Edith aside as barren after 1052 without angering her brothers, though he had not hurried to divorce her and remarry while he had the chance in 1051–2. It is possible that Edward hoped to be able to live until Edgar was an adult, and if the latter was born around 1052/3 that was plausible. In 946 the infant sons of the late King Edmund I had been superseded by his younger brother, at a time of military threat from the Dublin and Norse Viking rulers; in 975 a boy of at most thirteen or fifteen (Edward 'the Martyr') succeeded. Peaceful succession from outside the immediate royal dynasty had not occurred in Wessex since 786 (Beorhtric). Evidence for the other pre-Viking Saxon kingdoms is unclear but it appears that such non-dynastic rule by a well-placed 'strongman' was possible, and the precedents in the Viking-settled areas of England were for seizure of a vacant throne by external invaders (usually from Dublin or York). The area of most cultural impact on eleventh-century England was Scandinavia, where hereditary succession was the norm in Denmark and Sweden; in turbulent Norway the monarchy was less firmly rooted but most tenth-century and eleventh-century seizures of power were by a nobleman with Royal blood (e.g. Olaf Tryggvason in c.990 and St Olaf c. 1015) or by a neighbouring invader (Cnut on behalf of his son Sweyn in 1028). In King Edward's French cultural world, to which he would have looked for legal norms, his mother's Duchy of Normandy and most senior French provincial 'mini-states' were strictly hereditary. The French kingship itself had been 'usurped' from the Carolingian dynasty in the infancy of King Charles 'the Simple', during a military emergency (Viking invasion), by a capable adult provinical magnate – Count Odo of Paris – with his peers' support in 888. This was the most similar precedent for Harold's usurpation. It had been returned to Charles, now a teenager, on Odo's death in 898, usurped again by Odo's brother Robert by revolt in 922, and seized back by Charles' son Louis IV (backed by Athelstan of England) in 936; in 987 the last of the Carolingian kings, Louis V, had died and a male relative been ignored as Robert's grandson Hugh Capet took the throne for his family (as it turned out, permanently). The 'Capetians' did have Carolingian blood, but only in the female line – an argument which in England supported Duke William (or technically his children), not Harold. The succession of Earl Harold, without any royal blood, to the English throne would thus have been unusual in terms of contemporary precedent and it is unlikely that Edward, a man 'conditioned' by his admiration for French culture and ecclesiastical/legal procedures, would have looked on it with favour. There is no hint at the time that Harold was considered as having any West Saxon royal blood, though this unproveable genealogical claim – connecting his paternal grandfather Wulfnoth 'Cild' to the house of King Alfred's older brother Aethelred I – was to surface in a later period. It would have been a major boost to his legality as king in 1066 and so have been likely to appear in the *Anglo-Saxon Chronicle*, unless it was deliberately suppressed. Harold's succession would represent a triumph for naked power over legalism, and was only conceivable as an emergency measure.

It was Harold to whom Edward finally bequeathed the care of his kingdom in January 1066, according to all the sources[22] – though some of the versions of the *Anglo-Saxon Chronicle* state this more explicitly than others. The 'E' version says that he was both 'granted' it by Edward (as opposed to it being 'committed' to him) and then elected to it by the 'Witan'/Council, which points out that an election was needed in

Anglo-Saxon England to formalise a grant – as the 'Witan' had deposed Aethelred II for misrule in 1014 and elected Harthacnut's presumed heir Edward in 1042. (Thus, technically speaking any grant of the kingdom to William by Edward in 1051/2 would have had to be ratified by the Witan on 5/6 January 1066 to be legal.) Edgar could have been titular ruler aged twelve to fourteen had Edward or the Witan chosen him.. But he was only chosen by the Council in ?November 1066 as a last resort when Harold was dead and Duke William approaching London.[23] It is uncertain if the earl had been angling for the crown ever since 1053 or if his acquiescence in the rebellious Northumbrians' deposition of Earl Tostig in 1065 was reluctant or was a chance to rid himself of a potential rival. (Tostig is supposed to have been the Queen's favourite brother and the two of them to have arranged the murder of Tostig's local rival Cospatrick at court in 1064.) Harold had reasons for not fighting the advancing rebel army of Northumbrians as it marched across Mercia towards the court in autumn 1065 but negotiating a peaceful deal – not least the fact that bloodshed would weaken his army ahead of a Norman or Norwegian invasion. The rebels had cunningly chosen Morcar, brother of Earl Edwin of Mercia and son of Harold's late foe Earl Aelfgar, as their new earl so Harold could not rely on Edwin supporting him; if it came to a battle would the Mercians side with Northumbria? War could pit the 'House of Godwin' against the family of Leofric, as in 1051–2, 1055, and 1058 – and in each of those three crises the senior earls of England had chosen to negotiate, not fight. The exiled invader Godwin had thus forced his reinstatement by an armed incursion in 1052, and the exiled invader Aelfgar had forced his reinstatement the same way in 1055 and 1058. Harold's acceptance of the demands of the rebels to keep Morcar in power was thus the 'usual' resolution for such an armed confrontation with rebels in the period, and it preserved lives and English unity. But Edward was clearly far from pleased, as shown by his angry reaction,[24] and Tostig had to stay in exile and seek foreign support for another attempt to regain Northumbria in 1066. In retrospect, it could seem that Harold had got rid of a rival for the English throne by refusing to force his brother's return to power.

William's reaction. But did Edward blame Harold for not fighting to restore Tostig to power, or just blame the Northumbrians for defying his chosen earl and Earl Edwin of Mercia for helping them not helping Harold?

William gave the impression of a wrathful reaction to being cheated of his rights when he heard of Harold's succession, according to his own writers. This may be propaganda to earn sympathy, although the post-1066 Norman writers were probably unware of the legal situation in England concerning the Witan having to ratify any grant of the kingdom to a successor chosen by the king. They were thus probably not told to keep quiet about that by their sovereign William as a piece of 'Norman spin' to cover up a plot to blacken Harold's actions. William claimed to have been denied the throne, as Edward had wished and had informed him as late as Harold's visit, by the faithless oath-breaker Harold and rallied support across Europe for an invasion. He included the Papacy in his campaign, with the aid of the fact that Archbishop Stigand could be denounced as illegal for replacing the illegally expelled Archbishop Robert in 1052 and William could promise to install a proper Archbishop in line with recent (post-1040s) Papal promotion of 'suitable' candidates for senior Church offices (i.e. unimpeachably moral clerics of good reputation and pro-Papal views) instead of the dubiously holy 'place-men' of local secular dynasts. Reformist Emperor Henry III (d. 1056) and his widow Agnes of Poitou had been installing such men in their domains since the mid-1040s backed by the Papacy; now William would 'clear out' the worst offenders in unreformed England, as he and his new (north Italian) Archbishop Lanfranc were to do in 1070. William duly acquired a blessed Papal banner for his cause from Alexander II.[25] The precedent for a Papal banner – that granted to the new Norman Dukes of Apulia – suggests that William's representatives in Rome suggested the idea from seeing what had happened in the 'other' Norman state, as bolstering his legitimacy in the manner which had been so useful to Duke Robert 'Guiscard', the new and usurping Norman lord of Apulia. The grant of a banner to the Duke of Apulia had followed years of local Norman defiance of the Papacy's temporal and religious claims in this anarchic area, as the bands of Norman adventurers who had moved into the region (formerly a mixture of a Byzantine province and independent Lombard coastal city-states) coalesced into a duchy under the leadership of the sons of Tancred de Hauteville, a minor Norman knight. The first Duke, Robert 'Guiscard' ('the Fox'), and before his succession in 1057 his older brothers, had defied the Papacy and encroached on its local vassal, the town of Benevento; and when Pope Leo IX had led an army on Apulia in 1053 he had been defeated and captured and humiliatingly forced to agree to Norman demands. The Papacy had failed to use either the declining local Byzantine military authorities or the Lombards to rid the region of the Normans. Giving a consecrated banner to Duke Robert recognised the inevitable and transformed him from a robber-baron into a Papal vassal, who in return for Papal support would recognise the Pope as his overlord – a legal master-stroke possibly suggested by the new architect of aggressive Papal legal 'soft power', Cardinal Hildebrand.

The similar grant to Duke William thus saw this use of the Normans as 'Papal vassals' extended to northern Europe. In the eyes of the Papal bureaucracy, led by Hildebrand, it would make him the Pope's vassal and add to local Papal legal rights in a kingdom whose rulers and Church had had little to do with the Papacy for decades. Stigand's continuance in office was clearly an affront to them, and indeed ever since the reform of the formerly corrupt and favouritism-prone Papacy in the late 1040s (led by the German 'Holy Roman' Emperor Henry III) the Papal bureaucracy had been trying to remove allegedly worldly or corrupt bishops who were seen as the secular-minded allies of their local lords, not loyal and holy Papal servants. Stigand, a Godwin dynasty client intruded into a stolen archbishopric whose incumbent had had to flee for his life, was a clear candidate for this targeting. Possibly William's envoys even claimed that Harold had broken his oath on holy relics to support William's accession (see later) and was thus affronting the Church. William's half-brother Odo of Bayeux, as the local bishop if the oath was sworn at Bayeux, would logically have sent (or invented?) details of the oath-taking. But what little non-Norman evidence is available is silent on the question of Edward's intentions from 1052–66 – and crucially on the matter of whether Harold had been ordered by Edward to swear allegiance to Duke William as the heir to the throne.

The Bayeux Tapestry and the question of Harold's visit to Normandy. Invented or distorted?

Literary Norman propaganda presented Harold as a usurper who had broken his oath to support William's claim and been punished by God.[26] It is debateable whether the famous journey to Normandy that Harold made in 1064/5, the opening part of the story of the Conquest in the Bayeux Tapestry, was a mission from Edward to confirm Willlliam's heirship as the Norman writers William of Poitiers and the author of the *Carmen de Hastingae Proelio* later claimed.[27] William of Poitiers has it that William was promised the throne by Edward in 1051 and, after the Duke had gone home, made his earls and archbishop Robert take an oath to this effect – though as this was before Robert's expulsion on Godwin's return Godwin and his son Harold were clearly not involved. (Did he cover this crucial fact up so as to make Harold seem more of a traitor, or not realise it?) Harold's embassy in 1064 or 1065 (at a time of dearth in Normandy so logically before the late summer's harvest) was thus to confirm the earlier grant, and the author of the '*Carmen*', Guy of Amiens, has it that Edward sent a ring and sword to William with Harold's embassy as a token of heirship. Poitiers then adds on a second reference to events of 1051 and 1066 in William's speech to his men before the battle of Hastings, when he tells them that Edward invited him to England, promised him the heirship, and later sent Harold to Normandy to confirm this. By his account, Harold took a voluntary oath to William – i.e, this was not part of the planned embassy as then Edward would have told him about the oath being a necessary part of it beforehand. He promised to act as the Duke's proxy in England until Edward died and then to deliver the kingdom to him, together with the 'castrum' of Dover – presumably the old Roman fortress on the cliffs above the harbour as there was no castle (a Norman not English form of building) in Dover until 1066. Harold went back on his promise in 1066, out of ambition and greed, but is not definitely stated as planning to deceive William all along – though implicitly William was naïve and nobly honourable to trust him in the first place.

The *Anglo-Saxon Chronicle*, which retails the events surrounding Edward's attempt to bring Edward 'the Exile' back in 1054–6, is silent on the embassy – which could indicate that the post-1066 compilers, writing under Norman control, knew that William's story was invented or exaggerated and so left it out. Alternatively they may just not have known the full details and have heard differing versions so it was omitted sooner than risk recording a falsehood. It is unclear if Harold even intended to go to William's court; he apparently sailed from his family estate at Bosham on Chichester Harbour (whose hall and church are shown on the Tapestry) but was caught in a storm and so may have been heading elsewhere before being shipwrecked in Ponthieu. One source (William of Malmesbury, c. 1125) claimed that he was out on a fishing-trip when his vessel was blown across the Channel to Normandy[28] – though this begs the question of why the Tapestry then refers to a preceding meeting with the king where Harold is clearly being given instructions. The argument that the Tapestry was commissioned by William's half-brother Bishop Odo, Earl of Kent, from needlewomen in Canterbury as a piece of 'official' propaganda commemorating the Conquest is not now as certain as it once was. Andrew Bridgeman (*1066: the Hidden History of the Bayeux Tapestry*, Harper Collins, 2004) thinks that Eustace of Boulogne may have been its patron.[29] The number of references to Odo and his retainers make him a more likely patron, and the dedication of Bayeux Cathedral a plausible occasion for the Bishop to commission the Tapestry. The style of the needlework is probably English and has links with that of contemporary Canterbury; the theory that the mysterious details added in the margins are a scurrilous English commentary on the 'official' story put out in the main 'text' is less clear. The Tapestry first appears 'in situ' at Bayeux Cathedral in 1476, and is likely to have been brought there at latest before Odo left for the First Crusade in 1097. He had been deposed as Earl of Kent and imprisoned by the Conqueror in 1082 and only briefly returned to local power on the king's death in September 1087, before leaving England for good after a failed revolt against Wiliam II; thus it is probable that if he commissioned (instead of just acquiring) the Tapestry it was done before 1082. A connection has been made between the careful inclusion of the Norman abbey of Mont-St-Michel (near where Harold aided William on campaign in ?1064) in the Tapestry and the presence of its ex-abbot as Abbot of St Augustine's, Canterbury in 1072–7. Did he suggest the inclusion of his old abbey? The date of the commissioning would therefore be pre-1077. The Tapestry is unlikely to have blatantly invented the story of a visit which never took place.

Post-1066 England was not a twentieth-century-style Soviet police state, and not all the 'Norman' writers who mention the visit were so strictly under Royal patronage that they had to write whatever was commanded by either William or Bishop Odo. The enthusiastic glorification of William's 'heroic' and justified attack on the 'oath-breaking usurper' in William of Poitiers' work and the '*Carmen*' indicate a natural desire to please the works' patrons and denigrate their enemies. The notion of the hero's enemy as an oath-breaker, an ultimate sin to an era where rulers had to rely on their vassals to carry out promises of loyalty given on oath to avoid chaos, is similar to that in the *Song of Roland* – though Harold is presented as a (flawed) hero who rescues William's men from a quicksand at Mont-St-Michel.

But if these works had been part of a systematic campaign of lying 'Norman propaganda' there would only be one version of events, on which all the Norman sources would agree. Instead, there is confusion about what exactly happened on Harold's visit to Normandy. This indicates that there was only a generalised 'official version' of events, namely that Harold had sworn and then broken an oath, rather than a ruthless attempt to put over one invented story. Logically, the different versions of where the oath was sworn and in what circumstances suggest that the writers who mention it heard from different sources, often at 'second-hand'. (The Tapestry naturally has it at Bayeux, suggesting an effort to glorify the cathedral as the site of the incident and so please Bishop Odo.) Similarly, Duke William evidently did not have a careful plan at the time to stage the event in public in front of an array of witnesses – nobles and churchmen – who could then testify to Harold's treachery if the earl broke his oath. But the sending of a Papal banner to assist and bless his cause in 1066 would also indicate the probability that some – believable – witnesses sent to Rome persuaded Pope Alexander that Harold had broken a solemn oath. Why else would the Papacy have become involved in a succession-dispute so far away? Intervening in a succession-dispute in northern Europe was unprecedented, even if Harold had insulted the Papacy by refusing to remove Stigand as archbishop (and Stigand had committed the indiscretion of turning up in Rome to seek Papal approval in the late 1050s when an 'illegal' Pope was in office so their agreement was cancelled when the latter was removed).

The claim that Harold was not sailing to anywhere in France when he was blown ashore in Ponthieu is unlikely. It would have to be a very strong northerly wind to catch Harold's supposed fishing-vessel off the Sussex coast and blow him all the way to Ponthieu near the mouth of the Seine. Harold was an experienced sailor, having commanded an Irish-Viking naval attack on the west county in 1052 as he joined his father's successful attempt to force his way back to power. He was not likely to have ventured so far from land in uncertain weather – or not with a large collection of vassals and the mysterious female shown in his entourage on the Tapestry, 'Aelgifu'. Taken in combination with the scene of King Edward with Harold in the tapestry, it is probable that the Earl's voyage – too 'unofficial' to merit a mention in the *Chronicle*? – was intended for a destination across the Channel. Was he heading for his family allies in Flanders – whose count's daughters were married to Tostig and Duke William – and ended up on the French coast further west by accident? This was implied by early twelfth-century English historian Henry of Huntingdon (though he was inaccurate on some 1060s details and made Tostig Harold's elder brother). Harold was shipwrecked and seized by William's eastern neighbour and vassal Count Guy of Ponthieu, who held him hostage (presumably for ransom) until William forced him to hand the earl's party over to him. An alternative suggestion is that Harold *was* heading for Normandy, but he was trying to persuade the duke to release his hostage brother Wulfnoth and his elder brother Swein's son Haakon, left in England when the Godwins had fled in 1051 and then handed over to William by Edward in 1051/2. This claim was made by the English chronicler Eadmer in the early twelfth century,[30] later in date than the other evidence but at a time when telling the truth as opposed to the 'official Norman version' would be less dangerous. William duly returned Haakon when Harold left for home, but kept Wulfnoth as an 'insurance policy' for Harold's co-operation – and indeed Harold's unfortunate youngest brother remained in Norman custody until William died in 1087.

Why does the Tapestry show a hunched-up Harold looking rather sheepish or apologetic in front of a finger-wagging, admonitory King Edward at their interview after he sailed? Eadmer indicates that Edward had warned him against going, telling him that he would not get Wulfnoth released but be pressurised into aiding the Duke's plans.[31]

This would fit in with the picture in the Tapestry – and if the latter is allegedly peddling a falsified 'Norman' version of events it surely has no reason to show Edward as being displeased at Harold's intentions, the mission to Normandy being at Edward's own request. Indeed, shortly before the visit William had overrun Edward's nephew Count Walter of Mantes' lands and arrested him, and he then died in prison (naturally or not), so arguably Edward had reason to suspect William's plans at the time. Harold is shown in the picture as cringing before the king, which – apart from a propagandist desire to show him as an unworthy character – should indicate that he and the king were not just having an amicable discussion about the nature of the mission. Is Edward supposed to be warning Harold not to play him or William false, or warning him that William would use him for Norman political purposes? Did the Tapestry's Norman patron intend one meaning, favourable to William, but the actual creators left it ambiguous?

In one theory, Edward had given up his plan to make William his heir and was thus in favour of either Edgar 'Atheling' or Harold himself. The accession of an under-age claimant (too young to govern or to command armies) was problematic at a time of international tension with a thwarted William threatening invasion. Edgar had less hope of being accepted by the Witan until he was an adult, which would not be for a few years after 1066. So was Edward alarmed at Harold's intentions to sail to Normandy and negotiate with the duke, fearing that Harold would be trapped into supporting William's claim? The reason for the mission in this case would be that Harold was seeking to persuade William to return his hostage brother and nephew. Edward – wanting either Harold or Edgar to succeed him – would be aware that the Duke had not given up his hopes of securing the succession which Edward had rashly promised him in 1051/2. One late source, the early twelfth-century chronicle of the abbey of St Riquier in Ponntheiu, indeed has it that Harold broke an oath to Edgar 'Atheling' by taking the throne (i.e. presumably Edward wanted the latter to succeed him in 1064–5), but it is unclear what if anything this has to do with the oath taken in Normandy.

Nor is it clear what the attitudes of the other earls were to the succession at this point, as they had the greatest 'say' in the 'Witan' and could have vetoed any grant by Edward to Harold. Ralph of Hereford, an alternative heir, had died in 1057 and his earldom been taken over by Harold, whose brothers Tostig and Gyrth had taken on Northumbria (after Siward) and East Anglia (on Harold's succession to Wessex). Leofric's son and successor Aelfgar, who had been twice exiled from England since Harold became Earl of Wessex but had fought his way back to his earldom of Mercia with armed assistance from Vikings, Dubliners and Gwynedd, can be accounted a foe of the Godwins but had died around 1062. His elder son Edwin, young and inexperienced, succeeded him and in 1065 was to stand aside from backing the king as the rebellious Northumbrians evicted Earl Tostig and chose Edwin's brother Morcar as their new earl. Indeed, his calculated failure to join Harold as the rebels invaded Mercia forced the latter to negotiate and to accept Tostig's exile as easier than a civil war – which option would only kill off many warriors and facilitate a Norman or Norwegian invasion. It is unclear if Harold tried to save Tostig's earldom in the negotiations and had to give way in the face of obstinacy by the Northumbrians backed by Edwin and Morcar, which is what the king's semi-official biography of c. 1070 implies, or if he deliberately abandoned Tostig (as a potential rival of his for the throne?). In any event, Tostig was exiled (to his father-in-law's county of Flanders where he and his father had taken refuge from the king in 1051–2) and was angry enough at Harold not intervening on his behalf to invade England when Harold was king.

For that matter Edward may have changed his mind about William since 1051, when he needed his help against Godwin, and had doubts over William by the time of Harold's visit to Normandy. His sister's son Count Walter of Mantes – brother of Ralph and thus another claimant to the throne – had been captured by the Normans in a border-war in 1063 as William took over Maine and died mysteriously in custody, with early twelfth-century Anglo-Norman historian Orderic Vitalis having heard that William was believed to have poisoned him in prison. This may give a reason for believing that Edward in 1064/5 was not likely to blandly send Harold to Normandy to confirm the 1051 grant of the succession to William, and that the Norman insistence on this is incorrect – though that may be due to the late eleventh-century Norman writers such as William of Poitiers and William of Jumieges not being aware of English politics pre-1066 rather than just 'lying Norman propaganda' as some twentieth-century commentators assumed. The visit does seem to have taken place and is hardly likely to have been invented given the disparate accounts of its incidents (which thus were not just 'created' as a useful story by William of how the lying oath-breaker Harold had cheated him of the succession). That has been doubted too, though the actual date is still unclear and has been confused by doubt over whether Harold's 'midwinter attack' on the court of his enemy king Gruffydd ap Llywelyn of Gwynedd/Powys (Edwin and Morcar's brother-in-law) at Rhuddlan was in midwinter 1062–3 or 1063–4. The resultant campaign saw Harold and Tostig ravaging Gwynedd for months until Gruffydd's men gave up and some of them killed their leader and sent his body to Harold to end the war, which was apparently in July/August (1063 or, as the latest reckoning by David Bates proposes, 1064). In the latter case, the visit to Normandy would be in late summer or autumn 1064 to give time in 1065 for the prolonged Northumbrian crisis; the visit coincided with a shortage of corn in Brittany which would imply that it was before the harvest made the year's grain available.

By the time that the events of the visit came to be recorded in chronicles and the Tapestry all were agreed that Harold had sworn an oath to William, promising to 'be his man' as a feudal vassal and to support his claim to the English throne. Even the *Vita Aedwardi Regis*, the semi-'official' account of Edward's reign commissioned c. 1070 by his widow, made an oblique reference to Harold being 'too free with oaths' and his having escaped all attempts to ambush and trick him on his Continental visit, which imply that he was tricked into giving an oath and later broke it. One – Norman – account has it that he was to put the crucial town and fortress of Dover into William's hands to aid his occupation of the country on Edward's death, though if so this was not carried out. In return he was promised the hand of one of William's daughters, which one is unclear – 'Agatha', who is named, did not exist.[32] Possibly Adeliza was meant, and/or Harold was planning to marry the mysterious woman 'Aelgifu' (who was in his party and is named but not identified genealogically in the Tapestry) off to one of the duke's nobles or sons. Harold may already have been married by local Anglo-Danish 'common law' custom to the mother of his children, Edith 'Swan Neck' – his sons were old enough to fight in 1068 – but the Church does not seem to have accepted this and early in 1066 Harold was able to conduct an unhindered dynastic marriage to the sister of Earls Edwin and Morcar. The woman in question, Edith of Mercia, was indeed the widow of King Gruffydd ap Llywelyn of Gwynedd and Powys (and by conquest of Dyfed) in Wales who Harold had overthrown and hunted down until he was killed by his own men in summer 1063/4. No doubt Norman viewers could interpret the crucial scene of the oath-swearing in the Tapestry in the orthodox manner, as showing that Harold was ordered by Edward to swear allegiance to the duke and the scheming oath-breaker went back on his promise. But is there an alternative explanation that the Tapestry's makers did not dare to reveal too openly?

William clearly took the opportunity of having Harold at his court as a 'guest' to trick or blackmail him into swearing to uphold his claim to the throne. The later English writer Eadmer has him saying he would only allow Harold to leave his custody when he swore to back the Norman's claim to the throne and hand over Dover to him. It is recorded that he went as far as to hide the holy relics on which Harold was tricked into swearing under a cloth on the table on which Harold put his hand during the oath, making breaking it more serious than Harold assumed when he was persuaded to swear.[33] Or did Harold merely swear allegiance to William as his 'lord' as part of the customary ceremony of doing homage to the man who had just knighted him on their joint campaign to Brittany? In Norman 'feudal' terms, that would make him obliged to uphold his lord's interests. The Tapestry shows William as 'officially' giving Harold weapons and a helmet and standard in what is clearly the Northern French ceremony of knighthood, following the recent Breton campaign. Harold may have assumed that taking an oath was a necessary politeness to accompany homage and only applied to him serving William as his 'man' while in Normandy – only to be informed that it applied to William's claim to the throne of England too. The Saxon sources are silent on this, but the *Chronicle* post-1066 could not have accused the compilers' new masters of dishonesty. The Norman sources are at variance, as if the actual ceremony of swearing allegiance – presumably in the ducal hall or chapel at Rouen, but placed at Bonneville by one story[34] – did not have many witnesses. Hence William and his partisans could make up differing accounts of it as their political cause required and present Harold's treachery as being as serious and blasphemous as possible.

The affair was so open to reinterpretation or embellishment that the terms of Harold's forced alliance were unclear. Was he promised one of William's daughters as his wife, and if so which one? And if he agreed to betroth his sister – presumably the unmarried Aelgifu – to one of

William's leading lords, is this the same woman who appears under that name in an enigmatic scene in the Tapestry hinting at scandal involving 'a certain cleric'[35?] The scene comes as part of the events in Normandy during Harold's visit, and thus implies that this Aelgifu was in Normandy with Harold and the scandal occurred at the duke's court; his sister seems an unlikely member of a 'political' embassy (let alone a fishing-trip). It would seem illogical for the reference to be to the old scandal of Aelgifu, Cnut's 'common-law' wife from Northampton, who was supposed to have passed off another man's son as Cnut's in order to get the 'bastard' (i.e. Harold 'Harefoot', king in 1036–40) the English crown. This has been suggested as a solution, but what relevance could it possibly have to events at William's court in 1064/5? Possibly Eadmer, an Englishman writing in the following century when the circumstances of Harold's visit to Normandy was of less immediate political import, could tell the truth easier than the earlier writers.

Edward's apparent commendation of the kingdom to him on his deathbed is found both in the 'official' *Vita Aedwardi*, written c. 1070 for his widow Edith, and in the various versions of the *Anglo-Saxon Chronicle* (Canterbury, Abingdon, and Northern) and is even admitted by William's Norman panegyricist William of Poitiers. It can be trusted as a genuine record of the king's words, and probably interpreted as a definite recommendation for the succession – though the visions of immanent Divine wrath on England that the *Vita* says the dying King had[36] would have encouraged him to think that England would now need a strong, adult ruler. In January 1066 Harold could secure the crown as the 'man on the spot' with military backing, brushing aside any possibility that he should be regent for Edgar Atheling as the 'legitimate' claimant. This, as explored above, would have had overwhelming legitimacy on legal grounds, and on those of precedents and of current European practice. But legitimacy was useless without an army, and Edward himself had once been the victim of a king of England ignoring his superior legal claim as Cnut left his throne to one or other of his own sons in 1035. The heirship had apparently been promised to an allied foreign prince with no blood-connection to the royal line in 1040 – his half-brother Harthacnut had supposedly made a promise to Magnus of Norway. Kingdoms could be annexed by a foreign ruler with the troops available in the Scandinavian world, as Cnut had done to England in autumn 1016 and Norway in

1028, Magnus tried to do to Denmark in 1041–7, and Harald Hardrada and Swein Estrithson tried to do to England (1068 and 1069). The latter two had some distant genealogical claims, as Harald was related to Erik 'Bloodaxe' of Norway, Viking ruler of York in the early 950s, and Swein was Cnut's nephew. Duke William was acting within the constraints of Scandinavian politics in claiming England by the sword, with or without a promise of the heirship made earlier. But that sort of action was not the norm in the more legally-constrained, 'civilised' states of 'feudal' central and western Europe, especially his own region of northern France. Nor did his succession and his coronation in December 1066 pass unchallenged, given the level of unrest which followed. Was the whole question of his right to the throne based on a fraud? Notably, on his death-bed in Rouen in September 1087 William claimed that he had received the crown from God and was therefore returning it to Him.[37] This was an admission that he had won the realm of England by the sword as his Scandinavian predecessor Cnut had done, with no reference to it having been legally his due to a bequest by his kinsman Edward – though in any case he had had to fight for it, rightful heir or not. But it is noticeable that after 1066 the question of William's claim being based on the bequest by King Edward was framed in – Norman, Continental – legal terminology that assumed that the late king had had the right to bequeath the throne to anyone in the first place. The king in Anglo-Saxon England had a right to recommend an heir, and it is apparent that Edward had several rival heirs in mind at different times – William, Edward 'the Exile' and his son Edgar, and possibly Harold if his commending the kingdom to him in January 1066 meant the throne not a regency for Edgar. But the final choice lay with the Witan, who had deposed Edward's father Aethelred in 1013 in favour of the conquering Swein 'Forkbeard', invited him back in 1014, and chosen Edward himself in 1042. The leadership of England did submit to William at Berkhamsted as he approached London in late 1066, but this was as much accepting the inevitable as choosing Swein had been in 1013. The Norman 'historians' post-1066 did not understand the legal norms of succession in England and the Anglo-Norman ones like Orderic and Eadmer probably knew little of that too, though this is probably a matter of genuine ignorance (and looking on the 'losing side' in 1066 as being culturally backward) rather than deliberate suppression of the truth.

Notes

Chapter One: Ambrosius and Over-Kings

1. Zosimus, Historia Nova, ed. L. Mendelssohn (Leipzig 1887), book 6, chapter 5.
2. Nennius, chapters 31, 43–7. And see David Dumville, 'Nennius and the Historia Brittonum' in *Studia Celtica*, vol 10–11 (1975–6), pp. 78–95.
3. Oliver Rackham, *History of the Countryside* (Phoenix 1986); Petra Dark, *Britain and the end of the Roman Empire* (Tempus 2000); Richard Reece, 'Town and Country: the End of Roman Britain' in *World Archaeology*, vol 12, 1980, pp. 77–92; D.N. Brook, 'A Review of the Evidence for Continuity in British Towns in the Fifth and Sixth Centuries' in *Oxford Journal of Archaeology*, no. 5, part 1, 1986, pp. 77–102; Francis Pryor, *Britain AD*.
4. Rackham, p. 75; Dark, pp. cit.
5. Gildas, chapters 18–19 and 21.
6. Gildas, chapter 23.
7. Geoffrey of Monmouth, *A History of the Kings of Britain*, ed and trans. Lewis Thorpe (1966) pp. 149–51.
8. V. E. Nash-Williams, *Early Christian Monuments in Wales* (1950) pp. 123–5.
9. Geoffrey of Monmouth, pp. 153–5.
10. M. Jones, 'The Gallic Chronicle Exploded?' in *Britannia*, vol 22, 1991, pp. 211–16.
11. Nennius, chapter 31.
12. For the conventional view of the Saxon Shore fortresses as military bases, see: Stephen Johnson, *The Roman Forts of the Saxon Shore* (London 1976). For alternative modern theories: Andrew Pearson, *The Roman Saxon Shore Fortresses: Coastal Defence of Southern Britain* (Tempus 2002).
13. See R. Collingwood and J. N. Myres, *Roman Britain* (Oxford UP 1932).
14. Geoffrey of Monmouth, pp. 149–51.
15. See discussion in Mike Ashley, *The Mammoth Book of King Arthur* (Robinson 2005) pp. 42–4. Owain is also named as one of the chief councillors of Britain in the Welsh *Triads*, no. 13.
16. Gildas, chapter 25.
17. Nicholas Higham, *King Arthur: Myth-Making and History* (Routledge 2002); Thomas/Caitlyn Green, Concepts of Arthur, pp. 145–6.
18. Ibid.
19. Nennius, chapter 30.

20. Ibid, chapter 31.
21. Oliver Padel, 'The name of Arthur' in *Cambrian Medieval Celtic Studies*, vol 27, pp. 1–31.
22. Gildas, chapter 25.
23. Geoffrey of Monmouth, pp. 151, 155, 186–9.
24. Jack Lindsay, *Arthur And His Times* (Frederick Muller, 1958) p. 65.
25. John Morris, *The Age of Arthur* (Weidenfeld and Nicolson 1973) p. 363.
26. Gildas, chapters 30–1.
27. Ibid.
28. Roger Bland and Catherine Nixon, 'The Hoxne Late Roman Treasure' in *Britannia*, vol 25, 1994, and also their *The Hoxne Treasure – The Illustrated Handbook* (British Museum 2005).
29. Nennius, chapter 66.
30. Morris, p. 73.
31. Gildas, chapter 20.
32. Morris, p. 73.
33. Geoffrey of Monmouth, pp. 167–9.
34. *Annals of Ulster*, sub anno 549: at: 'celt.ucc/ie/published/T100001A'.
35. *Annales Cambriae*, sub anno 516/18.
36. Geoffrey of Monmouth, pp. 197–9.
37. Morris, p. 100.
38. Ibid.
39. *The Anglo-Saxon Chronicle*, ed. Michael Swanton (Phoenix 2000) pp. 14–15.
40. Morris, p. 100.
41. Brut Tyssilio.
42. Baram Blackett and Alan Wilson, *Artorius Rex Discovered* (1985) pp. 217–24.
43. S. Blake and S. Lloyd, *The Keys to Avalon* (Rider 2000), pp. 85–8.
44. Geoffrey, p. 195.
45. Geoffrey, pp. 262–81.
46. See P. Bartrum, *Early Welsh Genealogical Tracts* (Cardiff 1966).
47. Morris, p. 192.
48. *Annales Cambriae*, sub. anno. 573.
49. Nennius, chapter 62.
50. Morris, pp. 17, 19, 66.
51. Ibid, p. 54.

Chapter Two: Hengest

1. Bede, *The Ecclesiastical History of the English People*, ed Judith McClure and Roger Collins (Oxford UP 1969), book 1 chapter 15, pp. 26–7.
2. Procopius, *De Bello Gothico*, book 4 chapter 20.
3. J.N. Myres, *Oxford History of England*, vol 1 pp. 324–6.
4. See 'canterbury-archaeology.org.uk/stmartin/4590809556'.
5. Bede, book 1, chapter 25, p. 39.
6. As note 1.

7. Bede, book 2 chapter 5, p. 78.

8. H.M. Chadwick, *The Origins of the English Nation* (1907) pp. 44–5; H. Moisl, 'Anglo-Saxon genealogies and Germanic oral tradition' in *Journal of Medieval History*, vol 7 (1981) pp. 219–23 and 235–6; Patrick Sims-Williams, 'The settlement of England in Bede and the Chronicle' in *Anglo-Saxon England*, vol 12 (1983) pp. 1–41.

9. Bede, book 1, chapters 15–17; pp. 27–31.

10. Ibid, book 1, chapter 22, p. 36.

11. Ibid, book 1, chapter 17, p. 29.

12. A. Everitt, *Continuity and Colonization: the Evolution of Kentish Settlements* (1986) pp. 93–117.

13. Strabo, *Geography*, ed G. Augac (Paris 1990), book 4 chapter 3 and book 4, chapter 5; Diodorus Siculus, *History*, ed C.H. Oldfather (1939) book 5, chapte 21; Caesar, *De Bello Gallico*, book 5, chapter 22.

14. Ptolemy, *Geography*, ed C. Muller (2 vols, Paris 1883–1901), book 2, chapter 3.

15. Nennius, chapter 37.

16. V.E. Nash-Williams, *Early Christian Monuments in Wales* (University of Wales Press, Cardiff 1950) pp.123–5.

17. J.E. Turville-Petre, 'Hengest and Horsa' in *Saga-Book of the Viking Society*, vol 14. (1957) pp. 273–90; David Dumville, 'Sub-Roman Britain: History and Legend' in *History*, new series, vol 42 (1977) pp. 173–92; ibid, 'Kingship, genealogies and regnal lists' in P. Sawyer and L. Wood, eds, *Early Medieval Kingship* (1977) pp. 72–104; Patrick Sims-Williams, 'The settlement of England in Bede and the Chronicle' in *Anglo-Saxon England*, vol 12 (1983) pp. 1–41.

18. Bede, book 2, chapter 5, p. 78; P. Wormald, 'Bede, Bretwaldas and the origin of the Gens Anglorum' in S. Bassett, ed, *The Origins of Anglo-Saxon Kingdoms* (Leicester U.P. 1989) pp. 53–74, at p. 59.

19. Nicholas Brooks, 'The creation and early structure of the kingdom of Kent' in S. Bassett, ed., as above, p. 59.

20. Scott Gwara, *Heroic Identity in the World of Beowulf* (Brill 2008) p. 163; J. R. R. Tolkien, *Finn and Hengest* (Harper Collins 2006).

21. Bede, book 1, chapter 25, pp. 26–7.

22. *Anglo-Saxon Chronicle*, ed. Michael Swanton, pp. 12–14.

23. Nennius, chapters 31, 36–9, and 43–6; analysis in Dumville, op. cit.

24. Mike Ashley, *The Mammoth Book of King Arthur* (Robinson 2005) pp. 119–22.

25. Sims-Williams, op. cit., at pp. 24–5.

26. *Anglo-Saxon Chronicle*, ed Swanton, pp. 14–15.

27. Geoffrey of Monmouth, pp. 191–3.

Chapter Three: Cerdic

1. For the problems concerning the historicity of the *Chronicle* version of early Wessex history as opposed to the archaeology, see particularly Barbara Yorke, 'The Jutes of Hampshire and Wight and the origins of early Wessex'

in Steven Bassett, ed., *The Origins of Anglo-Saxon Kingdoms* (Leicester U.P. 1989) pp. 84–96.

2. See reference in Bede, *Ecclesiastical History of the English People*, ed. Judith McClure and Roger Collins (Oxford UP 1969) book 4, chapter 15 (p. 197).

3. On the question of the construction and reliability of the genealogies, see note 1 sources and Kenneth Sisam, 'Anglo-Saxon Royal Genealogies' in *Proceedings of the British Academy*, vol 39 (1953) pp. 287–348, especially pp. 300–07 on Wessex. Also see J. Lindsay, Arthur and His Times (Muller 1958) pp. 66–7.

4. *The Anglo-Saxon Chronicle*, ed. Swanton, p. 66.

5. 'Caer Faddon' is the name for the battle of Badon in the twelfth-century 'Dream of Rhonabwy'.

6. Nennius, chapter 49 for Vortigern's Gloucester-connected genealogy.

7. C. Barber and D. Pykitt, *Journey to Avalon: the Final Discovery of King Arthur* (Blorenge Books 1993), p. 105

8. *Anglo-Saxon Chronicle*, pp. 14 and 15.

9. As n. 7.

10. *Anglo-Saxon Chronicle*, pp. 14 and 15 ('495' to '514' entries) and 16–17 ('519' to '534' entries).

11. Ibid, p. 16.

12. See David Dumville, 'The West Saxon Genelaogical Regnal List and the Chronology of Early Wessex' in *Peritia*, vol 4 (1985) pp. 21–66; also Dumville, 'Kingship, genealogy and regnal lists' in P. H. Sawyer and Ian Wood, eds, *Early Medieval Kingship* (1977) pp. 72–104 and D. P. Kirby, 'Problems of early West Saxon history' in *English Historical Review*, vol 80 (1961) pp. 10–29.

13. Dumville article, in *Anglia* (1986), also as in n. 12.

14. H. M. Chadwick, *Origins of the English Nation* (1924) p. 21.

15. *Anglo-Saxon Chronicle*, pp. 18 and 19 (Ceawlin) and pp. 20, 21 (Ceol).

16. Wessex Genealogical Regnal List, sub anno '494' and '500' (Cerdic).

17. *The Chronicle of Aethelweard*, ed. A. Campbell (1962) p. 12.

18. O. G. S. Crawford 'Arthur and his battles' in *Antiquity* (1935).

19. Gildas, chapter 26.

20. Barbara Yorke in Bassett, op. cit, p. 94.

21. Bede, ed. J. McClure and R. Collins, book 4, chapter 16 (pp. 197–8).

22. *Anglo-Saxon Chronicle*, sub anno '477' (pp. 14, 15), '485' (ibid), and '491' (ibid).

23. See D. P. Kirby, 'Problems of early West Saxon history' in *E H R* vol 80 (1973) pp. 10–29 and S.C. Hawkes, 'The Early Saxon period' in T. Rowley et al, ed, *The Archaeology of the Oxford Region* (1986) pp. 64–108.

24. *Anglo-Saxon Chronicle*, pp. 18, 19.

25. Ibid, pp. 16, 17.

26. Bede, ed McClure and Collins, book 2, chapter 5 (p. 78).

Chapter Four: Mercia

1. Bede, book 2, chapter 5; P. Wormald, 'Bede, the Bretwladas and the Orgins of the Gens Anglorum' in Wormald et. al., *Ideal and Reality*, pp. 99–129; S. Keynes, 'Raedwlad the Bretwalda' in C. B. Kendall and P. S. Wells, *Voyage to the Other World: the Legacy of Sutton Hoo* (Minneapolis 1992).

2. David Dumville, 'The Tribal Hidage: an introduction to its texts and their history' in Stephen Bassett, ed, *The Origins of Anglo-Saxon Kingdoms*, pp. 225–30; J. Brownbill, 'The Tribal Hidage' in English Historical Review, vol 40 (1925) pp. 49–103; R. H. Hodgkin, *A History of the Anglo-Saxons*, 3rd edition (2 vols, 1952) vol 2 p. 389; C. Hurt, 'The Tribal Hidage' in *Transactions of the Royal Historical Society*, 5th series, vol. 21 (1977), pp. 133–57.

3. Bede, book 2, chapter 24.

4. D. Dumville, 'Essex, the Middle Angles and the expansion of Mercia in the SE Midlands' in Bassett, op. cit., pp. 123–40 especially pp. 125–20; Nicholas Brooks, 'The formation of the Mercian kingdom' in ibid, pp. 159–70, especially pp. 159–60.

5. J. Campbell, Bede's 'Reges and Principes' (Jarrow Lecture for 1979), reprinted in Campbell, *Essays in Anglo-Saxon History* (1986) p. 85–98.

6. Brooks in Bassett, op. cit., pp. 162–4.

7. W. Davies, 'Annals and the Origin of Mercia' in *Mercian Studies*, ed. A. Dornier (1977) pp. 17–29. For the regions, see: M Fowler, 'Anglian settlement of the Derbyshire – Staffordshire Peak District' in *Derbyshire Archaeological Journal*, vol 74 (1954) pp. 134–51; A. Ozanne, 'The Peak dwellers' in *Medieval Archaoelogy*, vol 6–7 (1962–3) pp. 15–52; T. H. McClough, A. Dornier and R. A. Rutland, *Anglo-Saxon and Viking Leicestershire* (1975); S. Losco-Bradley and H. M. Wheeler, 'Anglo-Saxon settlement in the Trent valley: some aspects' in *Anglo-Saxon Settlement*, ed. M. L. Faull (1984) pp.101–14; J. N. Myres, *The English Settlements*, 2nd ed (1986) pp. 182–6.

8. *Felix's Life of St Guthlac*, ed. B. Colgrave (1956), chapter 2.

9. D. Dumville, 'The Anglian Collection of royal genealogies and regnal lists' in *Anglo-Saxon England*, vol. 5 (1976) pp. 23–50.

10. Sir Frank Stenton, *Anglo-Saxon England* (1989 edition) pp. 39–46.

11. Kate Pretty, 'Defining the Magonsaete' in S. Basett, op. cit., pp. 171–83; H.P.R. Finberg, 'The princes of the Hwicce' in *Early Charters of the West Midlands* (1961) pp. 167–80; Finberg, 'St Mildburg's Testament' in ibid, pp. 197–217; Finberg, 'The princes of the Magonsaete' in ibid, pp. 217–25; D. Hooke, *Anglo-Saxon Landscape: The Kingdom of the Hwicce* (Manchester 1985). For a more doubtful view of the 'British' Magonsaete, see Margaret Gelling, *The West Midlands in the Early Middle Ages* (1992) and Sheila Waddington thesis 'The origins of Anglo-Saxon Herefordshire', University of Birmingham Ph D thesis 2013.

12. Bede, book 3, chapter 24; ed McClure and Collins, p. 150.

13. Ibid.
14. R. W. Chambers, *Beowulf*, 3rd edition (Cambridge 1959) pp. 31–40.
15. Bassett, op. cit., p. 164; F. Stenton and A. Mawer, eds, *The Place-Names of Worcestershire* (English Place-Name Society, vol 4, 1927) p. xxii.
16. Bede, book 2, chapter 14; p. 97; also N. Brooks, 'The formation of the Mercian kingdom' in S. Bassett, op. cit., at p. 166.
17. *The Anglo-Saxon Chronicle*, ed. M. Swanton, p. 24.
18. Ibid.
19. N. Brooks in S Bassett, op. cit., p. 160; also P. Hunter Blair, 'The Northumbrians and their southern frontier' in *Archaeologia Aeliana*, 4th series, vol 26 (1948) pp. 98–126.
20. Bede, book 3, chapter 9, p. 124; *Anglo-Saxon Chronicle*, pp. 126, 127.
21. W. Davies, 'Annals and the origin of Mercia', op. cit., at p. 21.
22. Anglo-Saxon Chronicle, p. 24.
23. Ibid, p. 25.
24. Bede, book 2, chapter 20; p. 105.
25. Ibid, book 2 chapter 9; p. 85; *Anglo-Saxon Chronicle* p. 25.
26. Bede, book 2 chapter 12, pp. 91–4.
27. Ibid book 2 chapter 9, p. 84.
28. Ibid, book 2 chapter 20, p. 105; *Anglo-Saxon Chronicle*, pp. 24, 25.
29. Bede, p. 105.
30. Ibid, book 3, chapters 1–2; pp. 110–112.
31. Ibid, book 3, chapter 7; p. 120.
32. N. Brooks, in S. Bassett, op. cit., p. 165.
33. Brooks in Bassett, pp. 166–7.
34. Marwynad Cyndylan, in *Canu Llywarch Hen*, ed. Ifor Williams (1935) pp. 50–2; also D Dumville, 'Sub-Roman Britain', op. cit., at p. 186.
35. Bede, book 3, chapter 16; p. 135.
36. Ibid, book 3, chapter 7; p. 120.
37. Ibid, book 3, chapter 21; p. 144.
38. Ibid.
39. Bede, book 3, chapter 24; pp. 150–2.
40. Ibid; also *Anglo-Saxon Chronicle*, pp. 29, 32.
41. Ibid, pp. 32, 33.
42. John Blair, 'Frithuwold's kingdom and the origins of Surrey' in S. Bassett, op. cit., pp.97–107.
43. Bede, book 4, chapter 5; also D. P. Kirby, *The Earliest English Kings* (Routledge 1991) pp. 115–16.
44. *Anglo-Saxon Chronicle*, pp. 34, 35.
45. Kirby, op. cit., pp. 115–16.
46. Roger Bland and Kevin Leahy, *The Staffordshire Hoard* (British Museum Publications, 2005).

Chapter Five: Northumbria

1. Bede, book 2, chapter 2, pp. 73–4; book 1, chapter 34, pp. 61–2.
2. See D. Dumville, 'The origins of Northumbria: some aspects of the British background' in S. Bassett, op. cit., pp. 213–22; also K. Hughes, *Celtic Britain in the Early Middle Ages: Studies in Scottish and Welsh Sources* (1980) and D. Dumville, 'On the North British section of the Historia Brittonum' in *Welsh History Review*, vol 8 (1976–7) pp. 345–54; Ifor Williams, *The beginnings of Welsh Poetry* (1972) pp. 70–88; T. Charles-Edwards, 'The origins of Northumbria' in *Archaeologia Aeliana*, 4th series, vol xxv (1947) pp. 1–51; Charles-Edwards, ' The authenticity of the Gododdin: a historical view' in *Artudiaethau ar yr Hengerdd*, ed. R. Bromwich and R. B. Jones (1974) pp. 44–7; Kenneth Jackson, *The Gododdin: the oldest Scottish poem* (1969) pp. 69–75; D Dumville, 'Early Welsh poetry: problmes of historicity' in *Early Welsh Poetry: studies in the Book of Aneirin*, ed. B. F. Roberts (1988).
3. Bede, book 3, chapter 3; pp. 113–14.
4. *Early Welsh Genealogical Tracts*, ed. P. C. Bartrum (1966); M. Miller, 'Forms and uses of pedigrees' in *Transactions of the Honourable Society of Cymmrodorion* (1978) pp. 195–206; Miller, 'Royal pedigrees of the insular Dark Ages: a progress report' in *History in Africa*, vol 7 (1980) pp. 201–24; also Dumville, op. cit., especially his 'Sub-Roman Britain: History and Legend' in *History*, new series, vol 62 (1977) pp. 173–92 and 'Kingship, genealogies and regnal lists' in Swayer and Wood, op. cit., pp. 72–102.
5. *Anglo-Saxon Chronicle*, pp. 16, 17.
6. Bassett, p. 218.
7. *Anglo-Saxon Chronicle*, p. 16.
8. D. P. Kirby, op. cit., p. 68. D. Dumville, 'The Anglian collection of royal pedigrees' in *Anglo-Saxon England*, vol 5 (1976) pp. 32, 36.
9. M Miller, 'The dates of Deira' in *Anglo-Saxon England*, vol 8 (1979) pp. 35–61.
10. Kirby, p. 68.
11. *Florentii Wigornensis monachi Chronicon ex Chronicis*, ed. B. Thorpe (2 vols, London 1848), vol 1, pp. 6,8.
12. Nennius, chapter 28.
13. Kirby, p. 61.
14. William of Malmesbury, *The Kings Before the Norman Conquest*, ed Joseph Stevenson (Llanerch Press reprint, 1989) p. 37.
15. Taliesin, poem VI, 1.3 and poem III, 1.11; see J E Carwyn Williams, ed, *The Poems of Taliesin* (Dublin 1968) and Ifor Williams, *Canu Taliesin* (Cardiff 1960).
16. *Anglo-Saxon Chronicle*, pp. 18, 19.
17. M. Miller, 'The Dates of Deira', at pp. 46–7.
18. *Anglo-Saxon Chronicle*, p. 18.
19. *Annales Cambriae*, sub. anno. 580.
20. Bede, book 2, chapter 1; pp. 70–1.

21. Ibid, book 2, chapter 2; pp. 73–4.
22. Ibid, book 2, chapter 12, pp. 91–4.
23. Ibid, book 2, chapters 12–13; pp. 93–6.
24. Ibid, book 2, chapter 14; p. 97.
25. Ibid, book 2, chapter 20; p. 105.
26. Ibid; and book 3, chapters 1–2; pp. 105–13.
27. John Morris, *The Age of Arthur*, pp. 169–72, 181.
28. Bede, book 2, chapter 2; pp. 72–3.
29. Ibid, book 3, chapter 3; pp. 113–14.
30. Ibid, book 4, chapters 25–6; pp. 23–7.
31. Ibid, book 2, chapter 5; pp. 77–8.
32. Ibid, book 3, chaper 7; p. 120.
33. Ibid, book 3, chapters 9–14; pp. 124–31.
34. Kirby, p. 90.
35. Bede, book 3, chapters 14 and 24; pp. 132–3, 151–2.
36. Ibid, book 3, chapter 16; p. 135.
37. Ibid, book 3, chapter 21; pp. 144–5.
38. Ibid, book 3, chapter 24; pp. 150–1.
39. Ibid, book 3, chapter 24; p. 152; also pp. 126 and 292; *Anglo-Saxon Chronicle*, p. 41.
40. Bede, book 3, chapters 25–6; pp. 152–61.

Chapter Six: Known Unknowns?

1. *Anglo-Saxon Chronicle*, pp. 14, 15; also M. A. Welch, Early Anglo-Saxon Kingdoms (*British Archaeological Reports*, British Series, no. 112, 1983), pp. 255–7.
2. Bede, book 4, chapter 16; p. 198.
3. *Anglo-Saxon Chronicle*, pp. 60, 61.
4. Ibid, pp. 56, 57.
5. *Anglo-Saxon Chronicle*, p. 66.
6. R. L. S. Bruce-Mitford, *The Sutton Hoo Ship Burial* (1975); also ibid, 'The Sutton Hoo ship burial: some foreign connections' in *Settimane di studio del centro Italiano di studi sull' alto mediaevo*, vol. 32 (Spoleto 1986) pp. 143–218.; also M. Carver, 'Sutton Hoo in context' in ibid, pp. 77–123.
7. M. Carver, 'Kingship and material culture in early Anglo-Saxon East Anglia' in S. Bassett, op. cit., pp. 141–58.
8. H. W. Bohme, 'Das ende der Romerherrschaft in Britannien und die angelsaxische Besiedlung Englande' in *5 Jahrbuche des Romische-Germanischen Zentral Museum*, vol 33 (1986) pp. 466–574.
9. Bassett, op. cit., p. 125.
10. Bede, book 3, chapters 18–19, pp. 138–40; ibid book 2, chapter 15, p. 99.
11. Ibid, book 3, chapter 18, p. 138.
12. Ibid, and also pp. 120, 122, 150, 202.
13. Ibid, book 3 chapter 7, p. 120.

14. Ibid, book 2 chapter 12, p. 94.
15. Ibid, book 3, chapter 18, p. 139.
16. Ibid, book 2, chapter 15, p. 99.
17. As n. 28.
18. Ibid, book 4 chapter 17, pp. 202–3.
19. Ibid, book 3, chapter 8, pp. 122–3.
20. Ibid, book 3, chapter 24, p. 150 and chapter 22, p. 147; also Barbara Yorke, *Kings and Kingdoms in Early Saxon England* (London 1990) p. 63.
21. Bede, book 3, chapter 22, p. 147.
22. Ibid, book 4, chapter 17, p. 199.
23. Ibid, book 4, chapter 21, p. 210.
24. Barbara Yorke, *Kings and Kingdoms of Early Anglo-Saxon England* (Routledge 2003), p. 63.
25. D. P. Kirby, *The Earliest English Kings*, pp. 131–2.
26. Ibid, p. 134.
27. Ibid; also *Symeonis Monachi Opera Omnia*, vol 2 p. 39.
28. M. R. Jones, 'Two Lives of St Ethelbert, King and Martyr' in *E H R*, vol 32 (1917) pp. 214–44, at p. 241.
29. Kirby, pp. 178, 179.
30. Ibid, pp. 192, 193; also H. R. Pagan, ' The coinage of the East Anglian kingdom' in *British Numismatic Journal*, vol 52 (1982) pp. 41–83.
31. Kirby, pp. 193–4.
32. Ibid, p. 194.
33. Bede, book 4, chapter 19, p. 207; book 5, chapter 24, p. 292.
34. Ibid, book 2, chapter 5, p. 79.
35. Ibid, book 3, chapter 30, pp. 166–7; book 4, chapter 11, p. 189.
36. Kirby, pp. 122–3.
37. Ibid, p. 118.
38. Bede, book 4, chapters 5 and 26, pp. 183 and 222.
39. Kirby, pp. 120–1.
40. *Anglo-Saxon Chronicle*, pp. 38, 39; Bede, book 5, chapter 7, pp. 244–5.
41. *Anglo-Saxon Chronicle*, pp. 18, 19.
42. Ibid, pp. 20, 21.
43. Ibid, p. 21.
44. Ibid, pp. 18, 19.
45. Ibid, p. 19.
46. Bede, book 4, chapter 12, pp. 190–1.
47. Kirby, p. 52.
48. Yorke, op. cit., pp. 145–6.
49. *Anglo-Saxon Chronicle*, p. 25.

Chapter Seven: The Picts

1. Bede, book 1, chapter 1; pp. 10–11.
2. Alfred Smyth, *Warlords and Holy Men: Scotland AD 80–1000* (Edward Arnold 1984) pp. 60–1.

3. I. M. Henderson, 'The meaning of the Pictish symbol stones' in *The Dark Ages in the Highlands* (Inverness Field Club 1971) pp. 53–67; A. Jackson, 'Pictish Social Structure and Symbol-Stones' in *Scottish Studies*, vol. 15 (1971) pp. 121–40; A. C. Thomas, 'The Animal Art of the Scottish Iron Age and its Origins' in *Archaeological Journal*, vol. 28 (1961) pp. 14–64 and ibid, 'The Interpretation of the Pictish Symbol Stones' in *Archaeological Journal*, vol. 30 (1963) pp. 31–97.

4. Smyth, ibid, especially pp. 59–84; Alex Woolf, 'Pictish Matriliny Reconsidered' in *Innes Review*, vol 49 (1998) pp. 147–67; Alasdair Ross, 'Pictish Matriliny?' in *Northern Studies*, vol 34 (1999) pp. 11–22.

5. *Geoffrey of Monmouth*, trans Thorpe, p. 75.

6. Alexander Boyel, 'Matrilineal Succession in the Pictish Monarchy' in *Scottish Historical Review*, vol. 56 no. 161 (April 1977), pp. 1–10; N Evans, 'Royal Succession and kingship among the Picts' in *Innes Review*, vol 59, no 1, pp. 1–48; Marjorie Anderson, *Kings and Kingship in Early Scotland* (Edinburgh 1973) pp. 245–9 and 261–89.

7. Anderson, ibid, especially pp. 77–8 and 82; Thomas Owen Clancy, 'Scotland and the "Nennian" Recension of the "Historia Brittonum" and the "Lebor Bretnach"' in Kings and Chronicles in Scotland 500–1297: *Essays in Honour of Marjorie Ogilvie Anderson on the Occasion of her Ninetieth Birthday*, ed. Simon Taylor (Dublin 2000) pp. 87–107.

8. Smyth, pp. 46–7.

9. Ibid, pp. 52–7.

10. Ammianus Marcellinus, *The Later Roman Empire* (Penguin edition 1986), book 27, chapter 8.

11. A. Woolf, 'Dun Nechtain, Fortriu and the geography of the Picts' in *Scottish Historical Review*, vol. 85 (2006) pp. 182–201.

12. Smyth, p. 63.

13. M Miller, 'The last century of Pictish succession' in *Scottish Studies*, vol 23 (1979) pp. 39–67.

14. Miller, p. 51.

15. John Morris, *The Age of Arthur*, p. 181, 206.

16. Isabel Anderson, *The Picts*, p. 32.

17. Dauvit Broun, 'Pictish Kings 761 – 839: integration with Dal Riada or separate development?' in *The St Andrews Sarcophagus: A Pictish Masterpiece and its International Connections*, ed. Sally Forbes (Dublin 1998) pp. 71–85.

18. D. Broun, 'The seven provinces in "De Situ Albaniae": a record of Pictish geography or an imaginary map of ancient Alba?' in *Alba, Celtic Scotland in the Medieval Era*, ed. E. Cowan and R. Andrew Macdonald (Birlinn, 2000) pp. 24–43.

19. As n. 15.

20. Smyth, p. 70.

21. Ibid, p. 65.

22. Ibid, pp. 61–2.

23. Ibid, p. 70.
24. Bede, book 4, chapter 24, pp. 221–2; Smyth, pp. 62–7.
25. T. O. Clancy, 'Philosopher-king, Nechtan mac Der-Ilei' in *Scottish Historical Review*, vol 83 (2004) pp. 125–49.
26. Smyth, pp. 176–85.

Chapter Eight: Creation of the Kingdom of England

1. *Anglo-Saxon Chronicle*, pp. 70, 71.
2. Ibid, pp. 64, 65.
3. Ibid, pp. 66, 67.
4. Kirby, op. cit., p. 196; Kirby, 'Northumbria in the Ninth century' in *Coinage in Northumbria in the Ninth Century: The Tenth Oxford Symposium on Coinage and Monetary History*, ed. D. M. Metcalf (*British Archaeological Reports*: British Series no. 180, Oxford 1987) pp. 11–25; Alfred Smyth, *Scandinavian Kings in the British Isles*, p. 190.
5. *Anglo-Saxon Chronicle*, pp. 66–69.
6. Ibid pp. 69–71; Smyth, *King Alfred the Great*, pp. 77–81; P. H. Sawyer, *Kings and Vikings*, pp. 27–8; Richard Abels, *Alfred the Great* (Longman 1998) pp. 112–24.
7. *Asser*, chapters 35–42, trans S. Keynes and M. Lapidge, pp. 78–81; Abels, op. cit., pp. 124–42; *Anglo-Saxon Chronicle*, pp. 70–3.
8. Ibid, pp. 72–3.
9. Ibid, pp. 74–5; Abels, pp. 148–51; *Asser*, chapter 49, trans Keynes and Lapidge, p. 83; R. Abels, 'King Alfred's peace-making strategies with the Danes' in *Haskins Society Journal*, vol 3 (1992) pp. 23–4.
10. *Asser*, chapter 40; *Anglo-Saxon Chronicle*, pp. 74–5; Abels, pp. 152–3.
11. 'Vita Prima Sancti Neoti et Translatio', ed M. Lapidge, in *The Anglo-Saxon Chronicle: A Collaborative Edition*, vol 17 (Cambridge 1985), chapter 12; analysis of the legend in *Asser*, ed. Keynes and Lapidge, pp. 197–202.
12. Wiliam of Malmesbury, *Gesta Rgeum*, ed. W. Stubbs (2 vols, Rolls Series, 1887–9) vol 1 p. 126.
13. *Anglo-Saxon Chronicle*, pp. 75–77; *Asser*, chapter 54, p. 84; *Aethelweard*, *Chronicon*, ed. Campbell, pp. 42–3.
14. *Anglo-Saxon Chronicle*, pp. 76–7; J. Peddie, *Alfred the Good Soldier*, pp. 120–34.
15. Abels, *Alfred the Great*, pp. 194–209; D. Hill and A. Rumble, eds, *The Defence of Wessex: The Burghal Hidage and Alfred's Fortifications* (Manchester 1996).
16. *Anglo-Saxon Chronicle*, pp 78–9.
17. *The Times*: article by David Sanderson, 11 December 2015. Also, S. Keynes, 'King Alfred and the Mercians' in *Kings, Currency and Alliances: History and Coinage of Southern England in the Ninth Century*, eds M. Blackburn and D. Dumville (1998) pp. 1–45.
18. *Anglo-Saxon Chronicle*: pp. 64–5 (851) and 78–9 (884).

19. Ibid, pp. 80–90.
20. Abels, pp. 219–42.
21. Ibid, pp. 259–60, 293–4.
22. V. H. Galbraith, 'Who wrote Asser's Life of Alfred?' in his *Introduction to the Study of History* (London 1964) pp. 113, 127–8; Alfred Smyth, *King Alfred the Great* (Oxford UP 1991) pp. 199–216; *Asser*, chapter 74, p. 74.
23. G. Craig, 'Alfred the Great: a diagnosis' in *Journal of the Royal Society of Medicine*, vol 84 (1991) pp. 303–5.
24. *Anglo-Saxon Chronicle*, pp. 84–5; Abels, pp. 294–5.
25. *Anglo-Saxon Chronicle*, pp. 92–3.
26. Ibid, pp. 94–5.
27. Ibid, pp. 96–105.
28. Ibid, pp. 103–5; Sarah Foot, *Athelstan: The First King of England* (Yale UP 2012) pp. 14–15, 32–3; *Henry of Huntingdon* (Llanerch Press reprint, 1991), book 5, chapter 17; F. T. Wainwright, 'Aethelfleda, Lady of the Mercians' in *Scandinavian England*, ed. H. Finberg (Phillimore 1975) pp. 305–24; Paul Hill, *The Age of Athelstan* (Stroud 2004) pp. 198–9; Pauline Stafford, 'Succession and Inheritance: a Gendered Perspective on Alfred's Family History' in *Alfred the Great: Papers from the Eleventh Centenary Conference* (Ashgate 2003) pp. 255–7.
29. Michael Davidson, 'The Nonsubmission of the Northern Kings in 920' in, Higham and Hill p. 203.
30. *Anglo-Saxon Chronicle*, pp. 104–5; Foot, p. 17.
31. Ibid, pp. 11–12 and 32–3; *William of Malmesbury*, book 2, chapter 131 and book 2, chapters 136–7 and 139.
32. Ibid, book 2, chapter 133; Foot, p. 32.
33. Foot, p. 17; R. Abels, 'Royal succession and the growth of political stability in ninth-century Wessex' in *Haskins Society Journal*, vol 12 (2002) pp. 96–7.
34. Foot, pp. 38–9; D. Dumville, 'The West Saxon Genealogical Regnal List and Texts' in *Anglia*, vol 114 (196) p. 29.
35. Foot, pp. 40–1; *William of Malmesbury*, book 2, chapter 131 and book 2, chapter 139.
36. Ibid, book 2, chapter 140; *Henry of Huntingdon*, book 5, chapter 118, p. 109; *Simeon of Durham*, chapter 107; *Folcuin, Gesta Abbati Sancti Bertini Sithensium*, ed. D. Holder-Egger (MGH Scriptores, vol 13, Hanover 1881) p. 629; Foot, pp. 41–2.

Chapter Nine: Royal Murders

1. Bede, book 3, chapter 14; pp. 132–3.
2. M. R. James, 'Two lives of St Aethelbert, King and Martyr' in *E H R* vol 32 (1917), pp. 214–44.
3. *William of Malmesbury*, pp. 78–9 and. 69; *Henry of Huntingdon*, p. 138.
4. *Anglo-Saxon Chronicle*, pp. 54, 55.
5 See Barbara Yorke, *Kings and Kingdoms of the Early Anglo-Saxon England* (Routledge 2002), p. 9.

6. Ibid.

7. See BBC News article online, dated 20 May 2014.

8. *Anglo-Saxon Chronicle*, pp. 119, 121.

9. Ibid, p. 118.

10. Barbara Yorke, 'The women in Edgar's Life' in D. Scragg, ed, *Edgar, King of the English* 959–975 (Boydell 2008) p. 145; Sabine Baring-Gould, 'S. Edith of Wilton' in his *Lives of the Saints*, vol 10 (1875) pp. 269–71; Susan Ridyard, *The Royal Saints of Anglo-Saxon England: a Study of West Saxon and East Anglian Cults* (Cambridge UP 1988) p. 40; A. Wilmart, 'La legend de Ste Edith en pros et en vers par le moine Goscelin' in *Analecta Bollandiana* vol 56 (1938); Ann Williams, *Aethelred the Unready: The Ill-Counselled King* (Hambledon and London 2003) pp. 2–4.

11. *Anglo-Saxon Chronicle*, p. 121; Stenton, Anglo-Saxon England, pp. 372, 455.

12. *Anglo-Saxon Chronicle*, pp. 121–2.

13. Ibid, p. 123.

14. Ibid, p. 124.

15. Barbara Yorke, 'Edward, King and Martyr: a Saxon Murder Mystery' in Laurence Keen, ed, *Studies in the Early History of Shaftesbury Abbey* (Dorchester Couny Council 1999); C. Fell, *Edward, King and Martyr* (Leeds Texts and Monographs 1971).

16. *William of Malmesbury*, pp. 143–4; M. Lappidge, ed., *Byrtferth of Ramsey: Lives of St Oswald and St Ecgwine* (Clarendon Press 2009).

17. *Henry of Huntingdon*, p. 177.

18. *Anglo-Saxon Chronicle*, p. 126.

19. Ibid, pp. 125–34.

20. Richard Cavendish, 'The St Brice's Day Massacre', in *History Today*, vol 52, no. 11 (November 2002) pp. 62–3.

21. *Anglo-Saxon Chronicle*, p. 138.

22. Ibid, p. 139.

23. Ibid, pp. 140–1.

24. Ibid, p. 140.

25. Ibid, pp. 142–4.

26. Frank Barlow, *Edward the Confessor* (Methuen 1970) pp. 28–9.

27. *Anglo-Saxon Chronicle*, p. 145.

28. Ibid, pp. 145–50.

29. Ibid, p. 151.

30. Ibid, pp. 152–3.

31. *William of Malmesbury*, p. 167; *Henry of Huntingdon*, p. 195.

32. *Anglo-Saxon Chronicle*, p. 153.

33. *Henry of Huntingdon*, p. 196.

34. *William of Malmesbury*, p. 168.

Chapter Ten: The Succession In 1066

1. *Anglo-Saxon Chronicle*, pp. 158–161; *Florence of Worcester, Chronicon ex Chronicis*, ed. B Thorpe (English Historical Society 1848–9), vol I. p. 192;

William of Poitiers, Gesta Guillelmi, ed. and trans R. Foreville (Paris 1952), pp. 6–13; *William of Jumieges, Gesta Normannorum Ducorum*, ed. J. Marx (Rouen and Paris 1914) pp. 121–2.

2. Ian Walker, *Harold, the Last Anglo-Saxon King*, pp. 10, 22, 209; E. A. Freeman, History of the Norman Conquest of England: Its Causes and Results (1867) vol I pp. 555–60.

3. *Anglo-Saxon Chronicle*, pp. 164–5.

4. *Vita Aedwardi Regis*, ed. Frank Barlow (Nelson's Medieval Texts 1962) pp. 13–14.

5. *William of Poitiers*, p. 6.

6. *Anglo-Saxon Chronicle*, pp. 138–9.

7. Ibid, pp. 165, 166, 167, 169, 171.

8. Ibid p.176; *Florence of Worcester*, vol I p. 207.

9. *Vitae Aedwardi Regis*, p. 23.

10. *Anglo-Saxon Chronicle*, pp. 152–3.

11. Ibid, pp. 181–3.

12. *William of Poitiers*, pp. 3–12, 100, 174–6; *William of Jumieges*, p. 132; *Anglo-Saxon Chronicle*, pp. 181–3. David Douglas, 'Edward the Confessor, Duke William of Normandy and the English Succession' in *E H R* vol 68 (1983) pp. 535–8; Stephen Baxter, 'Edward the Confessor and the Succession Question' in Richard Mortimer, ed, *Edward the Confessor: The Man and the Legend* (Boydell 2009) pp. 86–95.

13. Ibid, pp. 182–3; *Florence of Worcester* vol 1 p. 211.

14. Ibid vol I p. 217; *Anglo-Saxon Chronicle* pp. 184–5, 186–7; *Vita Aedwardi Regis*, pp. 33, 50–1.

15. *Anglo-Saxon Chronicle* pp. 190–3.

16. See Ian Walker, *Harold, the Last Anglo-Saxon King* pp. 111–12.

17. *Anglo-Saxon Chronicle* p. 176 ('Worcester' version only).

18. Eadmer, p. 6.

19. See Gabriel Ronay, *The Lost King of England: the East European Adventures of Edward the Exile* (Boydell 1989).

20. *Anglo-Saxon Chronicle*, pp. 184–5.

21. Ibid p. 188 ('Worcester' version only); Frank Barlow, *Edward the Confessor* (Methuen 1970), p.217.

22. *Anglo-Saxon Chronicle* ('E' version) p. 197; *Vita Aedwardi Regis* pp. 74–81, especially pp. 79–80.

23. *Anglo-Saxon Chronicle* pp. 199–200.

24. Barlow, pp. 237–8.

25. See David Bates, *William I* (Yale UP 2018) pp. 219–22.

26. See *William of Jumieges, Gesta Normannorum Ducorum*, book ii p. 158–61; *William of Poitiers, Gesta Gullielmi*, pp. 68–77.

27. *Carmen de Hastingae Proelio*, vol ii pp. 291–6; *William of Poitiers*, pp. 110–12 and 176; *William of Jumieges* p. 132.

28. *William of Malmesbury*, vol iv pp. 416–19.

29. See Andrew Bridgeman, *1066: The Hidden History of the Bayeux Tapestry*.
30. See Eadmer, Historia Novorum in Anglia, trans G Bosanquet (London 1964), pp. 6–7; *Henry of Huntingdon, History*, trans Thomas Forester (1853, reprint Llanerch Press 1991), p. 206; also Ian Walker, p. 94.
31. *Eadmer*, trans Bosanquet, ibid.
32. Reference to Agatha in *Orderic Vitalis*, book 3 pp. 115–16; also Bates, *William I*, p. 331. Walker, p. 94.
33. *Eadmer*, p. 7.
34. *William of Poitiers*, p. 118; *Orderic Vitalis*, book 2, chs. 134–9.
35. See D. T. Bernstein, *The Mystery of the Bayeux Tapestry* (London 1986), pp. 116–23; *The Bayeux Tapestry*, ed. David Wilson (1981) p. 201–2.
36. *Vita Aedwardi Regis*, pp. 79–80.
37. *Orderic Vitalis*, book 4, chapters 94–5.
38. Ibid, p. 236.

Bibliography

Abbo of Fleury, Passio Sancti Edmundi: Three Lives of English Saints, ed. M. Winterbottom (1972).

Richard Abels, 'King Alfred's peace-making strategies with the Danes' in *Haskins Society Journal*, vol 3 (1992) pp. 23–4.

——, *Alfred the Great; War, Kingship and Culture in Anglo-Saxon England* (Longman 1998).

——, 'Royal succession and the growth of political stability in ninth-century Wessex' in *Haskins Society Journal*, vol 12 (2002) pp. 96–7.

Adomnan of Iona, Life of St Columba, trans Richard Sharpe (Penguinh 1995).

The Chronicle of Aethelweard, ed A Campbell (1962).

F. Aldsworth, 'Droxford Anglo-Saxon Cemetery, Soberton, Hampshire' in *Proceedings of the Hants Field Club and Archaeological Society*, vol 35 (1979) pp.93–182.

Marjorie Anderson, *Kings and Kingship in Early Scotland* (Edinburgh 1973)

T. M. Anderson, 'The Viking Policy of Ethelred the Unready' in *Scandinavian Studies*, vol 59 (1987) pp. 287–97.

The Anglo-Saxon Chronicle, trans and ed Micahel Swanton (Dent 1996).

The Annales Cambriae and Other Welsh Chronicles, ed. K. Hughes (Oxford UP 1974).

Annales de St Bertin, ed. F. Grat, J. Viellard, and S. Clemencet (Paris 1964).

The Annals of Tigernach, ed. W. Stoles, in Revue Celtique, vol 27 (1986).

The Annals of Ulster, ed. S. MacAirt and G. Mac Niocaill (Dublin Institute for Advances Studies 1983).

Mike Ashley, *The Mammoth Book of King Arthur* (Robinson 2005)

Asser, Life of King Alfred, ed. S. Keynes and M. Lapidge.

B. Bachrach, 'Gildas, Vortigern and Constitutionalism in Sub-Roman Britain' in *Nottingham Medieval Studies*, vol 32 (1988) pp. 132–40.

J. Bannerman, *Studies in the History of Dalriada* (Scottish Academy Press, Edinburgh 1984).

C. Barber and D. Pykitt, *Journey to Avalon: the Final Discovery of King Arthur* (Blorenge Books 1993).

Sabine Baring-Gould, 'S. Edith of Wilton' in his *Lives of the Saints*, vol 10 (1875) pp. 269–71.

Frank Barlow, 'Edward the Confessor's Early Life, Character and Attitudes' in *E H R* vol 80 (1965) pp. 225–51.

——, *Edward the Confessor* (Methuen 1970).

P. Bartrum, *EarlyWelsh Genealogical Tracts* (Cardiff 1966).

Stephen Bassett, ed, *The Origins of Anglo-Saxon Kingdoms* (Leicester UP 1989).

Janet Bateley, 'The Compilation of the Anglo-Saxon Chronicle, 60bc to ad 890: Vocabulary as Evidence' in *Proceedings of the British Academy*, vol 64 (1978) pp. 93–129.

David Bates, *William I* (Yale UP 2018).

Stephen Baxter, 'Edward the Confessor and the Succession Question' in Richard Mortimer, ed, *Edward the Confessor: The Man and the Legend* (Boydell 2009) pp. 86–95.

M. L. Beavan, 'The Regnal Dates of Alfred, Edward the Elder and Athelstan' in *E H R* vol 32 (1917) pp. 517–31.

Bede, *Ecclesiastical History of the English People*, ed. Judith McClure and Roger Collins (Penguin Classics 1994).

Baram Blackett and Alan Wilson, *Artorius Rex Discovered* (1985).

S. Blake and S. Lloyd, *The Keys to Avalon* (Rider 2000).

Roger Bland and Catherine Nixon, 'The Hoxne Late Roman Treasure' in *Britannia*, vol 25, 1994

——, *The Hoxne Treasure – The Illustrated Handbook* (British Museum 2005).

——, and Kevin Leahy, The Staffordshire Hoard (British Museum Publications, 2005).

John Blair, *Building Anglo-Saxon England*.

H. W. Bohme, 'Das ende der Romerherrschaft in Britannien und die angelsaxische Besiedlung Englande' in *5 Jahrbuche des Romische-Germanischen Zentral Museum*, vol 33 (1986) pp. 466–574.

Alexander Boyel, 'Matrilineal Succession in the Pictish Monarchy' in *Scottish Historical Review*, vol 56 no. 161 (April 1977), pp. 1–10.

P. Brandon, *The South Saxons* (Phillimore, Chichester 1998).

Andrew Bridgeman, *1066: The Hidden History of the Bayeux Tapestry*.

D. N. Brooks, 'Gildas' De Excidio: Its Revolutionary Meaning and Purpose' in *Studia Celtica*, vol 18 (1983) pp. 1–10.

—— 'A Review of the Evidence for Continuity in British Towns in the Fifth and Sixth Centuries' in *Oxford Journal of Archaeology*, no. 5, part 1, 1986, pp. 77–102.

N. Brooks, 'England in the Ninth Century: The Crucible of Defeat' in *Transactions of the Royal Historical Society*, vol 29 (1979) pp. 1–20.

Dauvit Broun, 'Pictish Kings 761–839: integration with Dal Riada or separate development?' in *The St Andrews Sarcophagus: A Pictish Masterpiece and its International Connections*, ed Sally Forbes (Dublin 1998) pp. 71–85.

——, 'The seven provinces in "De Situ Albaniae": a record of Pictish geography or an imaginary map of ancient Alba? 'in *Alba, Celtic Scotland in the Medieval Era*, ed. E. Cowan and R. Andrew Macdonald (Birlinn, 2000) pp. 24–43.

J. Brownbill, 'The Tribal Hidage' in *English Historical Review*, vol 40 (1925) pp. 49–103.

R. L. S. Bruce-Mitford, *The Sutton Hoo Ship Burial* (1975); also ibid, 'The Sutton Hoo ship burial: some foreign connections' in *Settimane di studio del centro Italiano di studi sull' alto mediaevo*, vol 32 (Spoleto 1986) pp. 143–218.; M Carver, 'Sutton Hoo in context' in ibid, pp. 77–123.

Brut y Tywysogion or the *Chronicle of the Princes*, ed. and trans T. Jones (University of Wales, Cardiff Press 1993).

F. J. Byrne, *Irish Kings and High Kings* (Batsford, London 1973).

A. Campbell, 'The End of the Kingdom of Northumbria' in E. H. R. vol 57 (1942) pp. 91–7.

J. Campbell, 'Bede's Reges and Principes' (Jarrow Lecture for 1979), reprinted in Campbell, *Essays in Anglo-Saxon History* (1986) p. 85–98.

——, 'The First Century of Christianity in England' in ibid, pp. 69–84.

Canu Aneirin, ed. Ifor Williams (University of Wales Press, Cardiff 1938).

M. Carver, *The Age of Sutton Hoo: The Seventh Century in NW Europe* (Boydell 1992).

——, *Sutton Hoo: A Seventh Century Princely Burial Ground and Its Context* (London 2005).

H. M. Chadwick, *The Origins of the English Nation* (1907).

N. K. Chadwick, ed, *Studies in Early British History* (1954).

—— ed, *Celt and Saxon: A Study of the Early British Border* (1963).

T. Charles-Edwards, 'The origins of Northumbria' in *Archaeologia Aeliana*, 4th series, vol xxv (1947) pp. 1–51;

——, ' The authenticity of the Gododdin: a historical view' in *Artudiaethau ar yr Hengerdd*, ed R Bromwich and R B Jones (1974) pp. 44–7.

R. W. Chambers, *Beowulf*, 3rd edition (Cambridge 1959).

S. B. Church, 'Paganism in Conversion Age Anglo-Saxon England: The Evidence of Bede's Ecclesiastical History Reconsidered' in *History*, vol 93 (2008) pp. 162–80.

Thomas Owen Clancy, 'Scotland and the "Nennian" Recension of the "Historia Brittonum" and the "Lebor Bretnach" 'in *Kings and Chronicles in Scotland 500 – 1297: Essays in Honour of Marjorie Ogilvie Anderson on the Occasion of her Ninetieth Birthday*, ed. Simon Taylor (Dublin 2000) pp. 87–107.

——, 'Philosopher-king, Nechtan mac Der-Ilei' in *Scottish Historical Review*, vol 83 (2004) pp. 125–49.

R. Coates, 'On Some Controversy surrounding Gewissae/Gewissi, Cerdic and Ceawlin' in *Nomina*, vol 13 (1989–90) pp. 1–11.

R. G. Collingwood and N. L. Myres, *Roman Britain and the English Settlements* (1937).

E. Conybeare, *Alfred in the Chroniclers* (1900).

G. Craig, 'Alfred the Great: a diagnosis' in *Journal of the Royal Society of Medicine*, vol 84 (1991) pp. 303–5.

W. Cummins, *The Age of the Picts* (Sutton, 1995).

R. E. Cutler, 'The Godwinist Hostages: The Case for 1051' in *Annuale Medievale*, vol 12 (1972) pp. 70–77.

Kenneth Dark, 'A Sub-Roman Defence of Hadrian's Wall?' in *Britannia*, vol 23 (1992) pp. 111–20.

Petra Dark, *From Civitas to Kingdom: AD 300–800* (Leicester UP 1994).

——, *Britain and the end of the Roman Empire* (Tempus 2000).

W. Davies, 'Annals and the Origin of Mercia' in *Mercian Studies*, ed. A. Dornier (1977) pp. 17–29.

——, ed, *The Llandaff Charters* (Cardiff 1979).

Michael Davidson, 'The (Non-) Submission of the Northern Kings in 920' in N. Higham and D. Hill, eds, *Edward the Elder*, p. 200–11.

P. H. Dixon, 'The Anglo-Saxon Settlement at Mucking: An Interpretation' in Anglo-Saxon Studies in *History and Archaeology*, vol 6 (1993) pp. 125–47.

David Douglas, 'Edward the Confessor, Duke William of Normandy and the English Succession' in *E H R* vol 68 (1983) pp. 535–8.

David Dumville, 'Nennius and the Historia Brittonum' in *Studia Celtica*, vol 10–11 (1975–6), pp. 78–95.

——, 'On the North British section of the Historia Brittonum' in *Welsh History Review*, vol 8 (1976–7) pp. 345–54.

——, 'Sub-Roman Britain: History and Legend' in *History*, new series, vol 42 (1977) pp. 173–92.

—— 'Kingship, genealogies and regnal lists' in P. Sawyer and L. Wood, eds, *Early Medieval Kingship* (1977) pp. 72–104.

—— 'The Atheling: a Study in Anglo-Saxon Constitutional History' in *Anglo-Saxon England*, vol 8 (1979), pp. 1–33.

——, 'The West Saxon Genelaogical Regnal List and the Chronology of Early Wessex' in *Peritia*, vol 4 (1985) pp. 21–66.

——, 'The Historical Value of the Historia Brittonum' in *Arthurian Literature*, vol 6 (1986) pp. 1–26.

——, 'Early Welsh poetry: problmes of historicity' in *Early Welsh Poetry: studies in the Book of Aneirin*, ed. B. F. Roberts (1988).

Memorials of St Dunstan, Archbishop of Canterbury, ed. William Stubbs (London 1874).

Eadmer, Historia Novorum in Anglia, trans G. Bosanquet (London 1964).

Eddi Stephanus, *The Life of Bishop Wilfrid*.

The Life of King Edward Who Rests At Westminster, ed. and trans. Frank Barlow (Oxford UP 1992).

Encomium Emmae Reginae, ed. A. Campbell (*London Historical Society*, 1949).

N. Evans, 'Royal Succession and kingship among the Picts' in *Innes Review*, vol 59, no 1, pp. 1–48.

A. Everitt, *Continuity and Colonization: the Evolution of Kentish Settlements* (1986) pp. 93–117.

——, *Felix's Life of St Guthlac*, ed. B. Colgrave (1956).

C. Fell, *Edward, King and Martyr* (Leeds Texts and Monographs 1971).

H. P. R. Finberg, 'The princes of the Hwicce' in *Early Charters of the West Midlands* (1961) pp. 167–80;

——, 'St Mildburg's Testament' in ibid, pp. 197–217.

——, 'The princes of the Magonsaete' in ibid, pp. 217–25.

D. V. Fisher, 'The anti-monastic reaction in the reign of Edward the Martyr' in *Cambridge Historical Journal*, vol 10 (1950–2) pp. 254–70.

Florence of Worcester, Chronicon ex Chronicis, ed. B. Thorpe (*English Historical Society* 1848–9), vol I.

Sarah Foot, Athelstan: The First King of England (Yale UP 2012).

M. Fowler', Anglian settlement of the Derbyshire – Staffordshire Peak District' in *Derbyshire Archaeological Journal*, vol 74 (1954) pp. 134–51.

E. A. Freeman, *History of the Norman Conquest of England: Its Causes and Results* (1867) vol I.

V. H. Galbraith, 'Who wrote Asser's Life of Alfred?' in his *Introduction to the Study of History* (London 1964) pp. 113, 127–8

Margaret Gelling, *The West Midlands in the Early Middle Ages* (1992).

Geoffrey of Monmouth, *A History of the Kings of Britain*, ed and trans. Lewis Thorpe (1966).

Edward Gibbon, *Decline and Fall of the Roman Empire* (Dent Everyman edition, 6 vols), vol 4 (1969).

Gildas, The Ruin of Britain and Other Works, ed. and trans. M. Winterbottom (1978).

P. Graves-Brown, S. Jones and C. Gamble, eds, *Cultural Identity and Archaeology: The Construction of European Communities* (Routledge 1996), especially: S. Jones, 'Discourses of Identity in the Interpretation of the Past', pp. 62–80; J. Hines, 'Britain After Rome: Between Multiculturalism and Monoculuralism', pp. 266–70.

Thomas/Caitlyn Green, *Concepts of Arthur* (Tempus 2007).

Scott Gwara, *Heroic Identity in the World of Beowulf* (Brill 2008).

D. Hadley, *The Vikings in England: Settlement, Society and Culture* (Manchester UP 2006).

R. Hanning, *The Vision of History in Early Britain: From Gildas to Geoffrey of Monmouth* (Columbia UP, New York 1996).

C. Hart, 'Athelstan Half-King and his Family' in *Anglo-Saxon England*, vol 2 (1973) pp. 115–44.

S. .C Hawkes, 'The Early Saxon period' in T. Rowley et al, ed, *The Archaeology of the Oxford Region* (1986) pp. 64–108.

I. M. Henderson, 'The meaning of the Pictish symbol stones' in *The Dark Ages in the Highlands* (Inverness Field Club 1971) pp. 53–67.

Henry of Huntingdon, Chronicle (Llanerch Press reprint 1989).

Nicholas Higham, *The Kingdom of Northumbria AD 350–1100* (Sutton 1993).

——, *King Arthur: Myth-Making and History* (Routledge 2002).

—— and D. Hill, eds, *Edward the Elder 899–924* (Routledge 2001): articles include: J. Campbell, 'What is not known about Edward the Elder'(pp.20–46); S Keynes, 'Edward, King of the Anglo-Saxons' (pp. 40–66).

—— and M. Ryan, eds, *The Northern World* (Yale UP 2013).

D. Hill, *Ethelred the Unready: Papers From the Millenary Conference* (1978).

D. Hill and A. Rumble, eds, *The Defence of Wessex: The Burghal Hidage and Alfred's Fortifications* (Manchester 1996).

J. Hines, *The Scandinavian Character of Anglian England in the Pre-Viking Period* (British Archaeological Reports: British Series, no. 124, Oxford 1984).

——, 'The becoming of the English: identity, material culture and language in early Anglo-Saxon England' in *Anglo-Saxon Studies*, vol 7 (1994) pp. 49–59.

R. H. Hodgkin, *A History of the Anglo-Saxons*, 3rd edition (2 vols, 1952) vol 2 p. 389.

S. Hollis, ed, *Writing The Wilton Women* (Turnhout, 2004).

D. Hooke, *Anglo-Saxon Landscape: The Kingdom of the Hwicce* (Manchester 1985).

K. Hughes, *Celtic Britain in the Early Middle Ages: Studies in Scottish and Welsh Sources* (1980).

P. Hunter Blair, 'The Northumbrians and their southern frontier' in *Archaeologia*
——, *Aeliana*, 4th series, vol 26 (1948) pp. 98–126.

——, 'The Moore Memorandum on Northumbrian History; in C. Fox and B. Dickens, eds, *The Early Culture of North-West Europe* (1950).

C. Hurt, 'The Tribal Hidage' in *Transactions of the Royal Historical Society*, 5th series, vol 21 (1977), pp. 133–57.

A. Jackson, 'Pictish Social Structure and Symbol-Stones' in *Scottish Studies*, vol 15 (1971) pp. 121–40.

Kenneth Jackson, *The Gododdin: the oldest Scottish poem* (1969) pp. 69–75.

The Chronicles of John of Worcester, vol 2, eds R. Darlington and P. McGurk (Oxford UP 1995).

Stephen Johnson, *The Roman Forts of the Saxon Shore* (London 1976).

M. Jones, 'The Appeal to Aetius in Gildas' in *Nottinghamshire Medieval Studies*, vol 32 (1988) pp. 141–55.

——, 'The Gallic Chronicle Exploded?' in *Britannia*, vol 22, 1991, pp. 211–16.

——, *The End of Roman Britain* (Cornell UP, New York 1996).

M. K. Jones, 'Two Lives of St Ethelbert, King and Martyr' in *E H R*, vol 32 (1917) pp. 214–44

J. P. C. Kent, 'The end of Roman Britain: the literary and numismatic evidence reviewed' in *The End of Roman Britain*, ed. P. Casey (*British Archaeological Reports: British Series no. 71*, Oxford 1979) pp. 15–27.)

S. Keynes, 'Raedwald the Bretwalda' in C.B. Kendall and P.S. Wells, *Voyage to the Other World: the Legacy of Sutton Hoo* (Minneapolis 1992).

——, 'The Control of Kent in the Ninth Century' in *Medieval Europe*, vol 2 (1993) pp. 111–32.

——, 'On the Authenticity of Asser's Life of King Alfred' in *Journal of Ecclesiastical History*, vol 47 (1996) pp 526–51.

——, 'King Alfred and the Mercians' in *Kings, Currency and Alliances: History and Coinage of Southern England in the Ninth Century*, eds M. Blackburn and D. Dumville (1998) pp. 1–45.

——, 'The declining reputation of King Aethelred the Unready' in *Anglo-Saxon History: Basic Readings*, ed D.A. Pelteret (2000), pp. 157–90.

D. P. Kirby, 'Problems of early West Saxon history' in *English Historical Review*, vol 80 (1961) pp. 10–29.

——, 'Asser and his Life of King Alfred' in *Studia Celtica*, vol 6 (1971) pp. 11–35.

——, 'Northumbria in the Ninth century' in *Coinage in Northumbria in the Ninth Century: The Tenth Oxford Symposium on Coinage and Monetary History*, ed. D. M. Metcalf (*British Archaeological Reports: British Series* no. 180, Oxford 1987) pp. 11–25.

——, *The Earliest English Kings* (Routledge 1991).

Vita Prima Sancti Neoti et Translatio', ed. M. Lapidge, in *The Anglo-Saxon Chronicle: A Collaborative Edition*, vol 17 (Cambridge 1985).

M. Lapidge and D. Dumville, *Gildas: New Approaches* (Boydell, Woodbridge 1994).

Ryan Lavelle, *Aethelred II, King of the English 978–1016* (2001).

M. K. Lawson, 'Danegeld and Heregeld Once More' in *E H R* vol 105 (1990) pp. 951–61.

——, *Cnut: The Danes in England in the Early Eleventh Century* (Longman 1993).

E. T. Leeds, 'The West Saxon Invasion and the Icknield Way' in *History*, vol 10 (1926) pp. 97–109.

Jack Lindsay, *Arthur And His Times* (Frederick Muller, 1958).

S. Losco-Bradley and H. M. Wheeler, 'Anglo-Saxon settlement in the Trent valley: some aspects' in *Anglo-Saxon Settlement*, ed. M. L. Faull (1984) pp.101–14

M. R. Loyn, *The Vikings in Britain* (1994).

Marwynad Cyndylan, in *Canu Llywarch Hen*, ed. Ifor Wiliams (1935)

T. H. McClough, A. Dornier and R. A. Rutland, *Anglo-Saxon and Viking Leicestershire* (1975).

M. Miller, 'Forms and uses of pedigrees' in *Transactions of the Honourable Society of Cymmrodorion* (1978) pp. 195–206.

——, 'Royal pedigrees of the insular Dark Ages: a progress report' in *History in Africa*, vol 7 (1980) pp. 201–24.

——, 'The dates of Deira' in *Anglo-Saxon England*, vol 8 (1979) pp. 35–61.

——, 'The last century of Pictish succession' in *Scottish Studies*, vol 23 (1979) pp. 39–67.

H. Moisl, 'Anglo-Saxon genealogies and Germanic oral tradition' in *Journal of Medieval History*, vol 7 (1981) pp. 219–23 and 235–6.

S. Morillo, ed, *The Battle of Hastings* (Boydell, 1996).

John Morris, *The Age of Arthur* (Weidenfeld and Nicolson 1973)

V. E. Nash-Williams, *Early Christian Monuments in Wales* (1950) .

Janet Nelson, 'Reconstructing a Royal Family: reflections on Alfred from Asser' in *People and Places in Northern Europe from 500 to 1600: Essays in Honour of P. H. Sawyer*, ed. Ian Wood and N. Lund (19910 pp. 47–66.

Nennius, British History and the Welsh Annals, trans John Morris (1980).

Elizabeth Norton, *Elfrida: The First Crowned Queen of England* (Amberley 2013).

Vita Sancti Oswaldi autore anonymo in The History of the Church of York and its Archbishops (Rolls Series vol 72, 1879) p. 399–475.

A. Ozanne, 'The Peak dwellers' in *Medieval Archaeology*, vol 6–7 (1962–3) pp. 15–52.

Oliver Padel, 'The name of Arthur' in *Cambrian Medieval Celtic Studies*, vol 27, pp. 1–31.

H. R. Pagan, 'The coinage of the East Anglian kingdom' in *British Numismatic Journal*, vol 52 (1982) pp. 41–83.

Andrew Pearson, *The Roman Saxon Shore Fortresses: Coastal Defence of Southern Britain* (Tempus 2002).

John Peddie, *Alfred the Good Soldier: A History of His Campaigns* (1991).

Ptolemy, *Geography*, ed. C. Muller (2 vols, Paris 1883–1901)

Francis Pryor, *Britain* AD (Harper Perennial, 2004).

Oliver Rackham, *History of the Countryside* (Phoenix 1986)

Richard Reece, 'Town and Country: the End of Roman Britain' in *World Archaeology*, vol 12, 1980, pp. 77–92.

Susan Ridyard, *The Royal Saints of Anglo-Saxon England: a Study of West Saxon and East Anglian Cults* (Cambridge UP 1988).

Roger of Hoveden, *Annals of English History*, trans H. Riley, part 1 (Llanerch reprint 1994).

Roger of Wendover's Flowers of History, trans J. A. Giles, vol 1 (Llanerch reprint 1993).

Alasdair Ross, 'Pictish Matriliny?' in *Northern Studies*, vol 34 (1999) pp. 11–22.

Donald Scragg, *The Battle of Maldon* AD 991 (1991).

——, ed, *Edgar, King of the English 959–975* (Boydell, Woodbridge 2008).

Patrick Sims-Williams, 'The settlement of England in Bede and the Chronicle' in *Anglo-Saxon England*, vol 12 (1983) pp. 1–41.

K. Sisam, 'Anglo-Saxon Royal Genealogies' in *Proceedings of the British Academy*, vol. 39 (1953) pp. 289–356.

Alfred Smyth, *Warlords and Holy Men: Scotland* AD 80–1000 (Edward Arnold 1984).

——, *King Alfred the Great* (1991).

C. Snyder, *An Age of Tyrants: Britain and the Britons* AD 400–600 (Sutton 1998).

Pauline Stafford, 'The King's Wife in Wessex, 800–1066' in *Past and Present*, vol 91 (1981) pp. 7–27.

——, 'Succession and Inheritance: a Gendered Perspective on Alfred's Family History' in *Alfred the Great: Papers from the Eleventh Centenary Conference* (Ashgate 2003) pp. 255–7.

Strabo, *Geography*, ed. G. Augac (Paris 1990).

Snorri Sturlason, *Heimskringla: The Olaf Sagas*, trans. S. Laing (1964).

Diodorus Siculus, History, ed. C. H. Oldfather (1939)

Sir Frank Stenton, *Anglo-Saxon England* (1989 edition).

—— and A. Mawer, eds, *The Place-Names of Worcestershire* (English Place-Name Society, vol 4, 1927) p. xxii.

Symeon of Durham, Opera Omnia, ed. T. Arnold (Rolls Series, 1982).

A. C. Thomas, 'The Animal Art of the Scottish Iron Age and its Origins' in *Archaeological Journal,* vol 28 (1961) pp. 14–64.

——, 'The Interpretation of the Pictish Symbol Stones' in *Archaeological Journal,* vol 30 (1963) pp. 31–97.

J. R. R. Tolkien, *Finn and Hengest* (Harper Collins 2006).

Sharon Turner, *History of the Anglo-Saxons* (1799–1805), vol 1.

J. E. Turville-Petre, 'Hengest and Horsa' in *Saga-Book of the Viking Society,* vol 14 (1957) pp. 273–90.

T. M. Venning, *Anglo-Saxon Kings and Queens* (Amberley 2011).

——, *A Chronology of Early Medieval Western Europe* 450–1066 (Routledge 2018).

Sheila Waddington, 'The origins of Anglo-Saxon Herefordshire: a study in land-unit antiquity', University of Birmingham thesis 2013.

F. T. Wainwright, 'Aethelfleda, Lady of the Mercians' in *Scandinavian England,* ed. H. Finberg (Phillimore 1975) pp. 305–24.

H. E. Walker, 'Bede and the Gewissae: the Political Evolution of the Heptarchy and its Nomenclature' in *Cambridge Historical Review,* vol 12 (1956), pp.1 174–86.

Ian Walker, *Harold: The Last Anglo-Saxon King* (Sutton 1997).

J. M. Wallace-Hadrill, *Early Germanic Kingship in England and on the Continent* (Oxford UP 1971).

M. A. Welch, *Early Anglo-Saxon Kingdoms* (British Archaeological Reports, British Series, no. 112, 1983).

William of Jumieges, Gesta Normannorum Ducorum, ed. J. Marx (Rouen and Paris 1914) pp. 121–2.

William of Malmesbury, The Kings Before the Norman Conquest, ed. Joseph Stevenson (Llanerch Press reprint, 1989) p. 37.

——, *Gesta Regum,* ed. W. Stubbs (2 vols, Rolls Series, 1887–9) vol 1.

William of Poitiers, Gesta Guillelmi, ed. and trans. R. Foreville (Paris 1952).

Ann Williams, *Aethelred the Unready: The Ill-Counselled King* (Hambledon and London 2003) pp. 2–4.

J. E. Carwyn Williams, ed., *The Poems of Taliesin* (Dublin 1968).

Ifor Williams, *Canu Taliesin* (Cardiff 1960).

——, *The beginnings of Welsh Poetry* (1972).

Taliesin Williams, ed, *The Iolo Manuscripts* (Liverpool 1888 edition).

Tony Wilmott and P. Wilson, eds, *The Late Roman Transition in the North* (British Archaeological Reports: British Series, no. 299, Oxford 2000).

Tony Wilmott, *Birdoswald Roman Fort: 1800 Years on Hadrian's Wall* (Tempus 2002).

Michael Wood, 'The Making of Athelstan's Empire: An English Charlemagne' in *Ideal and Reality in Frankish and Anglo-Saxon Society,* ed P. Wormald, D. Bullough and R. Collins (1983) pp. 250–72.

Alex Woolf, 'Pictish Matriliny Reconsidered' in *Innes Review,* vol 49 (1998) pp. 147–67.

——, 'Dun Nechtain, Fortriu and the geography of the Picts' in *Scottish Historical Review*, vol 85 (2006) pp. 182–201.

P. Wormald, 'Bede, Bretwaldas and the origin of the Gens Anglorum' in S. Bassett, ed, *The Origins of Anglo-Saxon Kingdoms* (Leicester UP 1989) pp. 53–74, at p. 59.

T. Wright, 'Some Historical Doubts Relating to the Biographer Asser' in *Archaeologica*, vol 29 (1841) pp. 192–201.

Barbara Yorke, 'The Jutes of Hampshire and Wight and the origins of early Wessex' in Steven Bassett, ed, *The Origins of Anglo-Saxon Kingdoms* (Leicester UP 1989) pp. 84–96.

——, *Kings and Kingdoms in Early Saxon England* (London 1990).

——, *Wessex in the Early Middle Ages* (1995).

——, 'Edward, King and Martyr: a Saxon Murder Mystery' in Laurence Keen, ed, *Studies in the Early History of Shaftesbury Abbey* (Dorchester Couny Council 1999).

——, 'The women in Edgar's Life' in D. Scragg, ed, *Edgar, King of the English 959–975* (Boydell 2008).

G. M. Young, *Origins of the West Saxon Kingdom* (1954).

Index